THE NATURE
OF LAW

ào

READINGS IN
LEGAL PHILOSOPHY

CONSULTING EDITOR

V. C. Chappell

UNIVERSITY OF CHICAGO

THE NATURE

OF LAW

READINGS IN
LEGAL PHILOSOPHY

EDITED BY

M. P. GOLDING

Columbia University

RANDOM HOUSE   *New York*

FIRST PRINTING

© *Copyright, 1966, by Random House, Inc.*

All rights reserved under International and Pan-
American Copyright Conventions. Published in New
York by Random House, Inc. and simultaneously in
Toronto, Canada, by Random House of Canada
Limited.
Library of Congress Catalog Card Number: 66-15807
*Manufactured in the United States of America by
The Haddon Craftsmen, Inc.,
Scranton, Penna.*

DESIGN BY VINCENT TORRE

Preface

This book is designed to provide the student of legal philosophy and political theory a handy access to some of the most important attempts to answer the question "What is law?" It does not aim at comprehensiveness. In the opinion of the editor one of the major faults of most existing collections of readings in this field is that they supply a mere catalog of opinions held by famous men. But such a catalog, while important for achieving an historical over-view, is of little use to the student who wishes to enter into the arguments that are meant to buttress the positions that have been maintained. Indeed, to have included extracts of adequate length from all, or even a large number, of the important writers on this question would have meant producing a reader of greater scope than could be covered usefully in most courses in the philosophy of law or jurisprudence. Such courses also include materials on other problems in this field: the nature of legal reasoning, property, and punishment, for example. Therefore, I was strongly inclined to limit my selections in attempting to supply a collection that has coverage but avoids snippets. Although legal thought has its origins in antiquity, I have chosen to focus on recent writers in order to emphasize the topicality of the problems. The outstanding exception is the selection from Thomas Aquinas; but although his views find vigorous support in our day, hardly any of their exponents improve on the original statement.

In teaching courses with these materials I have not always followed the order presented herein. Most students at Columbia College already have some familiarity with the broader

aspects of the natural law and legal positivist traditions, and
I have frequently found it stimulating to begin with a writer
such as Oliver Wendell Holmes, who attempts to look at law
as the "bad man" views it. I suggest that other instructors try
this too. Many who read this book will find the three organiza-
tional rubrics highly misleading. What is important about
these writers is not the tradition into which they are placed
but how they argue for their respective solutions to the problem of the nature of law. (The instructor might therefore
consider juxtaposing items from different sections: for example, the discussion by H. L. A. Hart of a "régime of
primary rules" and Eugen Ehrlich's treatment of the "inner
order" of associations.) It may be further misleading to suggest, as does the title of this book, that all these writers are
always attempting to answer the same question, or set of
questions. But it is, after all, the task of the careful reader to
decide this. One of the most important aspects of one's philosophical education is to learn how to distinguish the various
issues involved in a problem.

Underlying the guiding principle in organizing the materials
into the three main sections has been the thought that some
writers are closer in outlook than others. Yet I hope that each
author selected may be said to hold some distinctive position
regarding the nature of law, or on one of the issues related to
dealing with the question "What is law?," so that no exact
duplication has resulted. Again, the careful student will want
to point out similarities between writers who apparently fall
into different traditions, as well as to note contrasts between
writers who fall into the same tradition, when broadly conceived.

I should add here that most of the selections are designated
as having been "abridged by the editor." This means that
certain paragraphs or sentences at the beginning and end of
a paragraph have been omitted. Except for a few isolated cases
nothing has been deleted from the middle of a paragraph that
is included in the text. Editor's footnotes are indicated by
asterisks.

I close this preface by thanking my wife, who has helped me to prepare this collection.

M. P. G.

New York City
June, 1965

Contents

x) CONTENTS

THE NATURE
OF LAW

✒

READINGS IN

LEGAL PHILOSOPHY

Introduction

Hardly anyone living in a civilized society has not at some time been told to do something, or to refrain from doing something, because there is a law requiring it, or because it is against the law. What do we mean when we say such things? More generally, how are we to understand statements of the form "x is a law"? This is an ancient question. In his *Memorabilia* (I,ii), Xenophon reports a statement of the young Alcibiades, companion of Socrates, who in conversation with the great Pericles remarked that "no one can really deserve praise unless he knows what a law is." At the end of the 18th century, Immanuel Kant wrote of the question "What is law (*Recht*)?" that it "may be said to be about as embarrassing to the jurist as the well-known question 'What is truth?' is to the logician." In our own day, H. L. A. Hart, referring to legal thought in the last 150 years, points out that we "find a situation not paralleled in any other subject systematically studied as a separate academic discipline. No vast literature is dedicated to answering the questions 'What is chemistry?' or 'What is medicine?', as it is to the question 'What is law?'."[1]

Various explanations of the persistence of this question may be offered. One relates to what may be a general trait of the history of human thought. No age is completely satisfied with the solutions handed over to it from a prior age. Legal theory drifts, at least to some extent, with the changing tides of philosophical thought. It is always interesting to take a turn at applying new methods to old problems. Few philosophers of law have considered issues in legal theory in total separation

[1] I doubt that the situation is entirely unparalleled. Compare discussions of "What is art?," "What is history?," "What is philosophy?."

from their broader philosophic perspectives. A non-meta-physical (or even anti-metaphysical) age—if such there be—can hardly be expected to treat the problems of legal philosophy in the same manner as a more metaphysically minded era. And if legal philosophy is subject to the influence of general changes in philosophic orientation, it is moreover influenced by social change. The development of new forms of political and social organization is the most powerful stimulant to fresh thinking in this field. It is no accident that the view that law is the sovereign's command finds such strong support in the period of the consolidation of the nation-state; similarly, in our own bureaucratic times law is conceived by many as "official behavior of any kind."

A second explanation of the persistence of the question of the nature of law and, particularly, of the variety of answers to it resides in the complexity of the question itself. Law seems to serve many of the same ends as religion, morals, and various types of informal social arrangement. Rules and regulations of some kind are present in all of these. We speak of "oughts" and "ought nots" in bridge-playing as well as in filling out tax returns. And we speak of legal, religious, and familial "duties." This list is easily extended; as regards terminology, purpose, and achievement the law frequently overlaps other areas. The chief point is that any understanding of the nature of law requires the showing of both the contrasts and similarities between these various items and their counterparts in law. The complexity of this task, answering the question "What is law?," gives rise to the proliferation of legal theories. It is too short a way of dealing with this diversity to say that it results from verbal confusion and that each writer finally stipulates some definition of "law" in an arbitrary fashion. For in the last analysis, what may partially account for disagreement among legal philosophers, aside from what is occasioned by differences in their general philosophic outlook, are the different ways in which they interpret the social situations in which religion, law, morals, and Hoyle's "Rules of Games," etc. are made manifest in everyday living.

Finally, one reason for the persistence of the question "What is law?" is the connection that answers to it have had to burning issues of moral action and social policy. Thus, many writers have embedded their treatment of this question in theories of why and when political authority ought to be obeyed. For in the case of the law we have a phenomenon intimately bound up with our views of what constitutes proper social conduct; moreover we are often prone to restrict our activity because "it's against the law" even when we believe the law to be ill-advised or downright wrong. This situation is a source of great perplexity. Mankind's perennial interest in such theories about political obligation and the constant need to re-think them have thus helped to sustain our original question. In this large area of thought, theory has had a great influence on practice. It is hardly surprising, therefore, to find that some writers will reject some answer to the question "What is law?" partially because of its alleged dangerous consequences. Thus, John Austin believed that natural law doctrines, which maintain a special connection between law and morals, open the door to anarchy. And the late Hermann Kantorowicz argued that Austin's own theory (that a law "strictly so called" is a general command of the sovereign) had the bad result of impeding the growth and authority of international law. When a theory is believed to have pernicious tendencies it is only natural to re-open discussion on the question that the theory purports to answer.

We shall not here survey the answers that have been given to our initial question. For that the reader must turn to the selections themselves. We shall confine ourselves to a brief characterization of each of the three rubrics under which the selections have been organized: natural law, legal positivism, and legal realism and sociological jurisprudence. It is worth pointing out, as has already been noted in the Preface, that differences do exist even among the writers who have been grouped together under the same heading, let alone among writers grouped separately.

Writers who describe themselves as falling within the broad

tradition of natural law reject the ancient statement that
"what pleases the prince has the force of law." They view law-
creating as a purposive activity that under certain conditions
gives rise to obligations. We cannot in general truly say that
someone has such an obligation *merely* because some officially
designated person has issued a pronouncement to that effect.
There must, in addition, be some "rational" basis or ground
for his pronouncement. Otherwise, we may simply have an
expression of the official's desires, but nothing that could impose upon us an *obligation* to do or refrain from doing anything. The crucial issue here concerns the nature of this
"rational" ground. Natural lawyers usually link this to a conception of the public good, and this in turn is ultimately interpreted in accordance with some conception of morality, human
nature, or social organization. There is, of course, ample room
for diversity of opinion as to how these conceptions are to be
worked out and how the precise relation between them and
human law-making is to be formulated.

While many legal positivists would agree that human law-
creating ought to seek the public good, they deny that we can
in general truly say that law has been made only when our
official's pronouncement has a "rational" basis, however we
wish to interpret this. They maintain that many laws have been
made which demonstrably do not have the sort of relation to
morality, human nature, or social organization that natural
lawyers have indicated. To be sure, laws are made and obligations are created only under special social conditions; but it is
crucial to the positivist position that these conditions can be
described *without* reference to moral notions in particular.
Laws may be said to exist and be made, according to most
positivists, when a certain form of social control exists in a
society. In its classic formulation, laws may be created only
when all, or most, of the members of a society are obedient to
some individual or set of individuals who are in a position to
back up their commands by the use of force. These commands
constitute the law. Later positivists have found this formulation to be inadequate for a variety of reasons, and it is plain

that there is room for disagreement among them as to what conditions must be fulfilled before one can say that a law exists or has been created.

It is very difficult to characterize briefly the views of the legal realists and sociological jurists. Many writers who describe themselves as such deny that they constitute a "school." Legal realism (which has nothing whatever to do with platonic realism) and sociological jurisprudence are relatively recent comers onto the philosophic scene. Many of the leading exponents claim that they merely do descriptive sociology of law, having no theory about the nature of law. And this is frequently the case. But not always—for many of them share a general attitude or approach to the study of legal phenomena that often consciously reflects an answer to the question "What is law?" While both the natural lawyers and legal positivists would agree that it makes good sense to speak of the existence of laws or legal rules, many realists and sociological jurists would at best allow this as mere *façon de parler*. Laws are to be explained as the concurrence of certain types of social behavior. Thus, some writers with a sociological or realist bent have identified law with given social habits or customary practices. To say that a law exists or is made is merely to say (or to predict) that certain people (ordinary citizens or public officials, or both) are behaving (or will behave) in certain ways. Other writers, holding that an analysis of law solely in terms of overt behavior is too narrow, also include reference to psychological states or attitudes in their definitions of "law." Needless to say, there is much room for disagreement as to what types of behavior, states, or attitudes constitute the very being of law and legal institutions.

One must add here that sociological jurists and realists are not necessarily committed to disregarding ethical issues. Roscoe Pound, one of the leading American practitioners of sociological jurisprudence, stressed the importance of the sociological study of law as a preparation for law-making. But this entailed for him not only a study of the interests that the law does in fact serve, but also the evaluation of these interests in

terms of their relative worth.[2] Karl N. Llewellyn, writing of
legal realism, insisted that the "divorce of Is and Ought" is
only temporary; for "realists believe that experience shows the
intrusion of Ought-spectacles *during the investigation of the
facts* to make it very difficult to see what is being done."[3] Our
selection by Harry W. Jones sheds further light on this point.

The reader may find the above characterizations of the three
main headings to be less than helpful. Perhaps it would be
useful to begin with the parts entitled "Comment" at the end
of each section of the book. By first focusing on criticisms of
the various positions, the student might be guided on what to
look for in the main expositions. After reading them he will
appreciate the difficulty in attempting to epitomize in a simple
formula so wide a range of answers to the question "What is
law?"

[2] See Pound's article "Jurisprudence," in H. E. Barnes (ed.), *The History
and Prospects of the Social Sciences* (New York: Alfred A. Knopf, Inc., 1925),
pp. 444-79.
[3] See Llewellyn's article "Some Realism about Realism," in *Harvard Law
Review*, vol. 44 (1931).

PART I
NATURAL LAW

The Thomistic Statement

THOMAS AQUINAS

Law as an Ordinance of Reason

*The natural law doctrine that came to fruition in the writings
of Thomas Aquinas (1225–74) was a grand synthesis of many
elements, Stoic, Aristotelian, and Christian. This selection,
from the part of the* Summa Theologica *entitled "Treatise
on Law," has been abridged by the editor in the form of a connected essay, since the objection and response method employed by Aquinas often proves to be a stumbling-block for
the modern reader.*

Question XC: On the Essence of Law

Concerning law, we must consider (I) law itself in general; (II)
its parts. Concerning law in general three points offer themselves
for our consideration: (i) its essence; (ii) the different kinds of
law; (iii) the effects of law.

Under the first head there are four points of inquiry: (1)
Whether law is something pertaining to reason? (2) Concerning
the end of law. (3) Its cause. (4) The promulgation of law.

(1) According to the words of the Jurist:[1] *Whatsoever pleaseth
the sovereign has the force of law.*

Reprinted with permission from *Basic Writings of St. Thomas Aquinas* (ed.
A. C. Pegis), vol. II; Random House, New York, and Burns and Oates,
London, 1945. Copyright 1945 by Random House, Inc. Abridged by the
editor.
[1] *Digest*, I, iv, 1.

On the contrary, It belongs to the law to command and to forbid. But it belongs to reason to command, as was stated above.[2] Therefore law is something pertaining to reason.

Law is a rule and measure of acts, whereby man is induced to act or is restrained from acting; for *lex* [*law*] is derived from *ligare* [*to bind*], because it binds one to act. Now the rule and measure of human acts is the reason, which is the first principle of human acts. For it belongs to the reason to direct to the end, which is the first principle in all matters of action, according to the Philosopher.[3]

Since law is a kind of rule and measure, it may be in something in two ways. First, as in that which measures and rules; and since this is proper to reason, it follows that, in this way, law is in the reason alone.—Secondly, as in that which is measured and ruled. In this way, law is in all those things that are inclined to something because of some law; so that any inclination arising from a law may be called a law, not essentially, but by participation as it were. And thus the inclination of the members to concupiscence is called *the law of the members* [*of the body*].

Reason has its power of moving from the will, for it is due to the fact that one wills the end, that the reason issues its commands as regards things ordained to the end. But in order that the volition of what is commanded may have the nature of law, it needs to be in accord with some rule of reason. And in this sense is to be understood the saying that will of the sovereign has the force of law; or otherwise the sovereign's will would savor of lawlessness rather than of law.

(2) Isidore* says that *laws are enacted for no private profit, but for the common benefit of the citizens.*

As we have stated above, law belongs to that which is a principle of human acts, because it is their rule and measure. Now as reason is a principle of human acts, so in reason itself there is something which is the principle in respect of all the rest. Hence to this principle chiefly and mainly law must needs be referred. Now the first principle in practical matters, which are the object of

[2] Q. 17, a. 1.
[3] *Phys.*, II, 9 (200a 22); *Eth.*, VII, 8 (1151a 16).
* [Spanish encyclopaedist (c. 560–636).]

the practical reason, is the last end: and the last end of human life is happiness or beatitude. Consequently, law must needs concern itself mainly with the order that is in beatitude. Moreover, since every part is ordained to the whole as the imperfect to the perfect, and since one man is a part of the perfect community, law must needs concern itself properly with the order directed to universal happiness [of the community].

Consequently, since law is chiefly ordained to the common good, any other precept in regard to some individual work must needs be devoid of the nature of a law, save in so far as it regards the common good. Therefore every law is ordained to the common good.

A command denotes the application of a law to matters regulated by law. Now the order to the common good, at which law aims, is applicable to particular ends. And in this way commands are given even concerning particular matters.

Actions are indeed concerned with particular matters, but those particular matters are referable to the common good, not as to a common genus or species, but as to a common final cause, according as the common good is said to be the common end.

Just as nothing stands firm with regard to the speculative reason except that which is traced back to the first indemonstrable principles, so nothing stands firm with regard to the practical reason, unless it be directed to the last end which is the common good. Now whatever stands to reason in this sense has the nature of a law.

(3) A law, properly speaking, regards first and foremost the order to the common good. Now to order anything to the common good belongs either to the whole people, or to someone who is the vicegerent of the whole people. Hence the making of a law belongs either to the whole people or to a public personage who has care of the whole people; for in all other matters the directing of anything to the end concerns him to whom the end belongs.

A private person cannot lead another to virtue efficaciously; for he can only advise, and if his advice be not taken, it has no coercive power, such as the law should have, in order to prove an efficacious inducement to virtue. But this coercive power is vested in the whole people or in some public personage, to whom it belongs to inflict penalties, as we shall state further on.⁴ Therefore the framing of laws belongs to him alone.

(4) It is laid down in the *Decretals* that *laws are established when they are promulgated.*

As was stated above, a law is imposed on others as a rule and measure. Now a rule or measure is imposed by being applied to those who are to be ruled and measured by it. Therefore, in order that a law obtain the binding force which is proper to a law, it must needs be applied to the men who have to be ruled by it. But such application is made by its being made known to them by promulgation. Therefore promulgation is necessary for law to obtain its force.

Thus, from the four preceding articles, the definition of law may be gathered. Law is nothing else than an ordinance of reason for the common good, promulgated by him who has the care of the community.

The natural law is promulgated by the very fact that God instilled it into man's mind so as to be known by him naturally.

Those who are not present when a law is promulgated are bound to observe the law, in so far as it is made known or can be made known to them by others, after it has been promulgated.

The promulgation that takes place in the present extends to future time by reason of the durability of written characters, by which means it is continually promulgated. Hence Isidore says that *lex [law] is derived from legere [to read] because it is written.*

Question XCI: On the Various Kinds of Law

We must now consider the various kinds of law, under which head there are six points of inquiry: (1) Whether there is an eternal law? (2) Whether there is a natural law? (3) Whether there is a human law? (4) Whether there is a divine law? (5) Whether there is one divine law, or several? (6) Whether there is a law of sin?*

(1) As we have stated above, law is nothing else but a dictate

---

⁴ Q. 92, a. 2, ad 3; II-II, q. 64, a. 3.
* [The discussion of (5) is omitted here.]

of practical reason emanating from the ruler who governs a perfect community. Now it is evident, granted that the world is ruled by divine providence, as was stated in the First Part,[5] that the whole community of the universe is governed by the divine reason. Therefore the very notion of the government of things in God, the ruler of the universe, has the nature of a law. And since the divine reason's conception of things is not subject to time, but is eternal, according to *Prov.* viii. 23, therefore it is that this kind of law must be called eternal.

(2) As we have stated above, law, being a rule and measure, can be in a person in two ways: in one way, as in him that rules and measures; in another way, as in that which is ruled and measured, since a thing is ruled and measured in so far as it partakes of the rule or measure. Therefore, since all things subject to divine providence are ruled and measured by the eternal law, as was stated above, it is evident that all things partake in some way in the eternal law, in so far as, namely, from its being imprinted on them, they derive their respective inclinations to their proper acts and ends. Now among all others, the rational creature is subject to divine providence in a more excellent way, in so far as it itself partakes of a share of providence, by being provident both for itself and for others. Therefore it has a share of the eternal reason, whereby it has a natural inclination to its proper act and end; and this participation of the eternal law in the rational creature is called the natural law. Hence the Psalmist, after saying (*Ps.* iv. 6): *Offer up the sacrifice of justice,* as though someone asked what the works of justice are, adds: *Many say, Who showeth us good things?* in answer to which question he says: *The light of Thy countenance, O Lord, is signed upon us.* He thus implies that the light of natural reason, whereby we discern what is good and what is evil, which is the function of the natural law, is nothing else than an imprint on us of the divine light. It is therefore evident that the natural law is nothing else than the rational creature's participation of the eternal law.

(3) Augustine distinguishes two kinds of law, the one eternal, the other temporal, which he calls human.

As we have stated above, a law is a dictate of the practical rea-

5 *S. T.,* I, q. 22, a. 1, ad 2.

son. Now it is to be observed that the same procedure takes place in the practical and in the speculative reason, for each proceeds from principles to conclusions. Accordingly, we conclude that, just as in the speculative reason, from naturally known indemonstrable principles we draw the conclusions of the various sciences, the knowledge of which is not imparted to us by nature, but acquired by the efforts of reason, so too it is that from the precepts of the natural law, as from common and indemonstrable principles, the human reason needs to proceed to the more particular determination of certain matters. These particular determinations, devised by human reason, are called human laws, provided that the other essential conditions of law be observed.

The human reason cannot have a full participation of the dictate of the divine reason, but according to its own mode, and imperfectly. Consequently, just as on the part of the speculative reason, by a natural participation of divine wisdom, there is in us the knowledge of certain common principles, but not a proper knowledge of each single truth, such as that contained in the divine wisdom, so, too, on the part of the practical reason, man has a natural participation of the eternal law, according to certain common principles, but not as regards the particular determinations of individual cases, which are, however, contained in the eternal law. Hence the need for human reason to proceed further to sanction them by law.

Human reason is not, of itself, the rule of things. But the principles impressed on it by nature are the general rules and measures of all things relating to human conduct, of which the natural reason is the rule and measure, although it is not the measure of things that are from nature.

The practical reason is concerned with operable matters, which are singular and contingent, but not with necessary things, with which the speculative reason is concerned. Therefore human laws cannot have that inerrancy that belongs to the demonstrated conclusions of the sciences. Nor is it necessary for every measure to be altogether unerring and certain, but according as it is possible in its own particular genus.

(4) Besides the natural and the human law it was necessary for the directing of human conduct to have a divine law. Now if man

were ordained to no other end than that which is proportionate to his natural ability, there would be no need for man to have any further direction, on the part of his reason, in addition to the natural law and humanly devised law which is derived from it. But since man is ordained to an end of eternal happiness which exceeds man's natural ability, therefore it was necessary that, in addition to the natural and the human law, man should be directed to his end by a law given by God.

Secondly, because, by reason of the uncertainty of human judgment, especially on contingent and particular matters, different people form different judgments on human acts; whence also different and contrary laws result. In order, therefore, that man may know without any doubt what he ought to do and what he ought to avoid, it was necessary for man to be directed in his proper acts by a law given by God, for it is certain that such a law cannot err.

(6) Under the divine Lawgiver, various creatures have various natural inclinations, so that what is, as it were, a law for one, is against the law for another. Thus, I might say that fierceness is, in a way, the law of a dog, but against the law of a sheep or another meek animal. And so the law of man, which, by the divine ordinance, is allotted to him according to his proper natural condition, is that he should act in accordance with reason; and this law was so effective in man's first state, that nothing either outside or against reason could take man unawares. But when man turned his back on God, he fell under the influence of his sensual impulses. In fact, this happens to each one individually, according as he has the more departed from the path of reason; so that, after a fashion, he is likened to the beasts that are led by the impulse of sensuality, according to Ps. xlviii. 21: *Man, when he was in honor, did not understand: he hath been compared to senseless beasts, and made like to them.*

Accordingly, then, this very inclination of sensuality, which is called the "fomes," in other animals has absolutely the nature of law, yet only in so far as we may consider as law what is an inclination subject to law. But in man, it has not the nature of law in this way; rather is it a deviation from the law of reason. But since, by the just sentence of God, man is deprived of original justice, and his reason bereft of its vigor, this impulse of sensuality, whereby he is led, has the nature of a law in so far as it is a penalty following from the divine law depriving man of his proper dignity.

Question XCIII: The Eternal Law [and Its Relation to Human Law]

Just as in every artificer there pre-exists an exemplar of the things that are made by his art, so too in every governor there must pre-exist the exemplar of the order of those things that are to be done by those who are subject to his government. And just as the exemplar of the things yet to be made by an art is called the art or model of the products of that art, so, too, the exemplar in him who governs the acts of his subjects bears the character of a law, provided the other conditions be present which we have mentioned above as belonging to the nature of law. Now God, by His wisdom, is the Creator of all things, in relation to which He stands as the artificer to the products of his art. Moreover, He governs all the acts and movements that are to be found in each single creature. Therefore, just as the exemplar of the divine wisdom, inasmuch as all things are created by it, has the character of an art, a model or an idea, so the exemplar of divine wisdom, as moving all things to their due end, bears the character of law. Accordingly, the eternal law is nothing else than the exemplar of divine wisdom, as directing all actions and movements.

Human law has the nature of law in so far as it partakes of right reason; and it is clear that, in this respect, it is derived from the eternal law. But in so far as it deviates from reason, it is called an unjust law, and has the nature, not of law, but of violence. Nevertheless, even an unjust law, in so far as it retains some appearance of law, through being framed by one who is in power, is derived from the eternal law; for all power is from the Lord God, according to *Rom.* xiii. i.

Human law is said to permit certain things, not as approving of them, but as being unable to direct them. And many things are directed by the divine law, which human law is unable to direct, because more things are subject to a higher than to a lower cause. Hence the very fact that human law does not concern itself with matters it cannot direct comes under the ordination of the eternal law. It would be different, were human law to sanction what the eternal law condemns. Consequently, it does not follow that human law is not derived from the eternal law; what follows is rather that it is not on a perfect equality with it.

Question XCIV: The Natural Law

We must now consider the natural law, concerning which there are six points of inquiry: (1) What is the natural law? (2) What are the precepts of the natural law? (3) Whether all the acts of the virtues are prescribed by the natural law? (4) Whether the natural law is the same in all? (5) Whether it is changeable? (6) Whether it can be abolished from the mind of man?*

(2) The precepts of the natural law in man stand in relation to operable matters as first principles do to matters of demonstration. But there are several first indemonstrable principles. Therefore there are also several precepts of the natural law.

As was stated above, the precepts of the natural law are to the practical reason what the first principles of demonstrations are to the speculative reason, because both are self-evident principles. Now a thing is said to be self-evident in two ways: first, in itself; secondly, in relation to us. Any proposition is said to be self-evident in itself, if its predicate is contained in the notion of the subject; even though it may happen that to one who does not know the definition of the subject, such a proposition is not self-evident. For instance, this proposition, *Man is a rational being,* is, in its very nature, self-evident, since he who says *man,* says *a rational being;* and yet to one who does not know what a man is, this proposition is not self-evident. Hence it is that, as Boethius says, certain axioms or propositions are universally self-evident to all; and such are the propositions whose terms are known to all, as, *Every whole is greater than its part,* and, *Things equal to one and the same are equal to one another.* But some propositions are self-evident only to the wise, who understand the meaning of the terms of such propositions. Thus to one who understands that an

* [(1), (3) and (6) are omitted here. In (1) Aquinas argues that the natural law is not a habit.]

angel is not a body, it is self-evident that an angel is not circum-scriptively in a place. But this is not evident to the unlearned, for they cannot grasp it.

Now a certain order is to be found in those things that are appre-hended by men. For that which first falls under apprehension is *being*, the understanding of which is included in all things what-soever a man apprehends. Therefore the first indemonstrable prin-ciple is that *the same thing cannot be affirmed and denied at the same time*, which is based on the notion of *being* and *not-being*: and on this principle all others are based, as is stated in *Metaph.* iv.[6] Now as *being* is the first thing that falls under the apprehen-sion absolutely, so *good* is the first thing that falls under the ap-prehension of the practical reason, which is directed to action (since every agent acts for an end, which has the nature of good). Consequently, the first principle in the practical reason is one founded on the nature of good, viz., that *good is that which all things seek after*. Hence this is the first precept of law, that *good is to be done and promoted, and evil is to be avoided*. All other precepts of the natural law are based upon this; so that all the things which the practical reason naturally apprehends as man's good belong to the precepts of the natural law under the form of things to be done or avoided.

Since, however, good has the nature of an end, and evil, the na-ture of the contrary, hence it is that all those things to which man has a natural inclination are naturally apprehended by reason as being good, and consequently as objects of pursuit, and their con-traries as evil, and objects of avoidance. Therefore, the order of the precepts of the natural law is according to the order of natural inclinations. For there is in man, first of all, an inclination to good in accordance with the nature which he has in common with all substances, inasmuch, namely, as every substance seeks the preservation of its own being, according to its nature; and by rea-son of this inclination, whatever is a means of preserving human life, and of warding off its obstacles, belongs to the natural law. Secondly, there is in man an inclination to things that pertain to him more specially, according to that nature which he has in common with other animals; and in virtue of this inclination,

---

[6] Aristotle, *Metaph*, III, 3 (1005b 29).

those things are said to belong to the natural law *which nature has taught to all animals,*[7] such as sexual intercourse, the education of offspring and so forth. Thirdly, there is in man an inclination to good according to the nature of his reason, which nature is proper to him. Thus man has a natural inclination to know the truth about God, and to live in society; and in this respect, whatever pertains to this inclination belongs to the natural law: *e.g.,* to shun ignorance, to avoid offending those among whom one has to live, and other such things regarding the above inclination.

All these precepts of the law of nature have the character of one natural law, inasmuch as they flow from one first precept.

All the inclinations of any parts whatsoever of human nature, *e.g.,* of the concupiscible and irascible parts, in so far as they are ruled by reason, belong to the natural law, and are reduced to one first precept, as was stated above. And thus the precepts of the of the natural law are many in themselves, but they are based on one common foundation.

(4) Isidore says: *The natural law is common to all nations.*

As we have stated above, to the natural law belong those things to which a man is inclined naturally; and among these it is proper to man to be inclined to act according to reason. Now it belongs to the reason to proceed from what is common to what is proper, as is stated in *Physics* i.[8] The speculative reason, however, is differently situated, in this matter, from the practical reason. For, since the speculative reason is concerned chiefly with necessary things, which cannot be otherwise than they are, its proper conclusions, like the universal principles, contain the truth without fail. The practical reason, on the other hand, is concerned with contingent matters, which is the domain of human actions; and, consequently, although there is necessity in the common principles, the more we descend towards the particular, the more frequently we encounter defects. Accordingly, then, in speculative matters truth is the same in all men, both as to principles and as to conclusions; although the truth is not known to all as regards the conclusions, but only as regards the principles which are called *common notions*. But in matters of action, truth or practical rectitude is not

[7] *Digest,* I, i, 1.
[8] Aristotle, *Phys.,* I, 1 (184a 16).

the same for all as to what is particular, but only as to the common principles; and where there is the same rectitude in relation to particulars, it is not equally known to all.

It is therefore evident that, as regards the common principles whether of speculative or of practical reason, truth or rectitude is the same for all, and is equally known by all. But as to the proper conclusions of the speculative reason, the truth is the same for all, but it is not equally known to all. Thus, it is true for all that the three angles of a triangle are together equal to two right angles, although it is not known to all. But as to the proper conclusions of the practical reason, neither is the truth or rectitude the same for all, nor, where it is the same, is it equally known by all. Thus, it is right and true for all to act according to reason, and from this principle it follows, as a proper conclusion, that goods entrusted to another should be restored to their owner. Now this is true for the majority of cases. But it may happen in a particular case that it would be injurious, and therefore unreasonable, to restore goods held in trust; for instance, if they are claimed for the purpose of fighting against one's country. And this principle will be found to fail the more, according as we descend further towards the particular, e.g., if one were to say that goods held in trust should be restored with such and such a guarantee, or in such and such a way; because the greater the number of conditions added, the greater the number of ways in which the principle may fail, so that it be not right to restore or not to restore.

Consequently, we must say that the natural law, as to the first common principles, is the same for all, both as to rectitude and as to knowledge. But as to certain more particular aspects, which are conclusions, as it were, of those common principles, it is the same for all in the majority of cases, both as to rectitude and as to knowledge; and yet in some few cases it may fail, both as to rectitude, by reason of certain obstacles (just as natures subject to generation and corruption fail in some few cases because of some obstacle), and as to knowledge, since in some the reason is perverted by passion, or evil habit, or an evil disposition of nature. Thus at one time theft, although it is expressly contrary to the natural law, was not considered wrong among the Germans, as Julius Caesar relates.

(5) It is said in the *Decretals: The natural law dates from the creation of the rational creature. It does not vary according to time, but remains unchangeable.*

A change in the natural law may be understood in two ways. First, by way of addition. In this sense, nothing hinders the natural law from being changed, since many things for the benefit of human life have been added over and above the natural law, both by the divine law and by human laws.

Secondly, a change in the natural law may be understood by way of subtraction, so that what previously was according to the natural law, ceases to be so. In this sense, the natural law is altogether unchangeable in its first principles. But in its secondary principles, which, as we have said, are certain detailed proximate conclusions drawn from the first principles, the natural law is not changed so that what it prescribes be not right in most cases. But it may be changed in some particular cases of rare occurrence, through some special causes hindering the observance of such precepts, as was stated above.

Question XCV: Human Law

As we have stated above, man has a natural aptitude for virtue; but the perfection of virtue must be acquired by man by means of some kind of training.[9] Since some are found to be dissolute and prone to vice, and not easily amenable to words, it was necessary for such to be restrained from evil by force and fear, in order that, at least, they might desist from evil-doing, and leave others in peace, and that they themselves, by being habituated in this way, might be brought to do willingly what hitherto they did from fear, and thus become virtuous. Now this kind of training, which compels through fear of punishment, is the discipline of laws. Therefore, in order that man might have peace and virtue, it was necessary for laws to be framed; for, as the Philosopher says, *as man is the most noble of animals if he be perfect in virtue, so he is the lowest of all, if he be severed from law and justice.*[10] For man can

[9] Q. 63, a. 1; q. 94, a. 3.
[10] *Polit.*, I, 1 (1253a 31).

use his reason to devise means of satisfying his lusts and evil passions, which other animals are unable to do.

Moreover, the Philosopher says, *it is better that all things be regulated by law, than left to be decided by judges.*[11] And this for three reasons. First, because it is easier to find a few wise men competent to frame right laws, than to find the many who would be necessary to judge rightly of each single case.—Secondly, because those who make laws consider long beforehand what laws to make, whereas judgment on each single case has to be pronounced as soon as it arises; and it is easier for man to see what is right, by taking many instances into consideration, than by considering one solitary instance.—Thirdly, because lawgivers judge universally and about future events, whereas those who sit in judgment judge of things present, towards which they are affected by love, hatred, or some kind of cupidity; and thus their judgment becomes perverted.

Since, then, the animated justice of the judge is not found in every man, and since it can be bent, therefore it was necessary, whenever possible, for the law to determine how to judge, and for very few matters to be left to the decision of men.

Certain individual facts which cannot be covered by the law *have necessarily to be committed to judges,* as the Philosopher says in the same passage: *e.g., concerning something that has happened or not happened,* and the like.

WHETHER EVERY HUMAN LAW IS DERIVED FROM THE NATURAL LAW?
Augustine says, *that which is not just seems to be no law at all.* Hence the force of a law depends on the extent of its justice. Now in human affairs a thing is said to be just from being right, according to the rule of reason. But the first rule of reason is the law of nature, as is clear from what has been stated above. Consequently, every human law has just so much of the nature of law as it is derived from the law of nature. But if in any point it departs from the law of nature, it is no longer a law but a perversion of law.

But it must be noted that something may be derived from the natural law in two ways: first, as a conclusion from principles; secondly, by way of a determination of certain common notions. The first way is like to that by which, in the sciences, demonstrated

11 *Rhetor.,* I, 1 (1354a 31).

conclusions are drawn from the principles; while the second is likened to that whereby, in the arts, common forms are determined to some particular. Thus, the craftsman needs to determine the common form of a house to the shape of this or that particular house. Some things are therefore derived from the common principles of the natural law by way of conclusions: *e.g.*, that *one must not kill* may be derived as a conclusion from the principle that *one should do harm to no man*; while some are derived therefrom by way of determination: *e.g.*, the law of nature has it that the evildoer should be punished, but that he be punished in this or that way is a determination of the law of nature.

Accordingly, both modes of derivation are found in the human law. But those things which are derived in the first way are contained in human law, not as emanating therefrom exclusively, but as having some force from the natural law also. But those things which are derived in the second way have no other force than that of human law.

The common principles of the natural law cannot be applied to all men in the same way because of the great variety of human affairs; and hence arises the diversity of positive laws among various people.

WHETHER HUMAN LAW BINDS A MAN IN CONSCIENCE?* Laws framed by man are either just or unjust. If they be just, they have the power of binding in conscience from the eternal law whence they are derived, according to *Prov.* viii. 15: *By Me kings reign, and lawgivers decree just things.* Now laws are said to be just, both from the end (when, namely, they are ordained to the common good), from their author (that is to say, when the law that is made does not exceed the power of the lawgiver), and from their form (when, namely, burdens are laid on the subjects according to an equality of proportion and with a view to the common good). For, since one man is a part of the community, each man, in all that he is and has, belongs to the community; just as a part, in all that it is, belongs to the whole. So, too, nature inflicts a loss on the part in order to save the whole; so that for this reason such laws as these, which impose proportionate burdens, are just and binding in conscience, and are legal laws.

* [Q. 96. Art. 4.]

On the other hand, laws may be unjust in two ways: first, by being contrary to human good, through being opposed to the things mentioned above:—either in respect of the end, as when an authority imposes on his subjects burdensome laws, conducive, not to the common good, but rather to his own cupidity or vainglory; or in respect of the author, as when a man makes a law that goes beyond the power committed to him; or in respect of the form, as when burdens are imposed unequally on the community, although with a view to the common good. Such are acts of violence rather than laws, because, as Augustine says, *a law that is not just seems to be no law at all.* Therefore, such laws do not bind in conscience, except perhaps in order to avoid scandal or disturbance, for which cause a man should even yield his right, according to *Matt.* v. 40, 41: *If a man . . . take away thy coat, let go thy cloak also unto him; and whosoever will force thee one mile, go with him other two.*

Secondly, laws may be unjust through being opposed to the divine good. Such are the laws of tyrants inducing to idolatry, or to anything else contrary to the divine law. Laws of this kind must in no way be observed, because, as is stated in *Acts* v. 29, *we ought to obey God rather than men.*

Modern Formulations

JEAN DABIN

Is There a Juridical Natural Law?

Jean Dabin was born in Belgium in 1889 and was a professor of law at the University of Louvain, an eminent Roman Catholic center of learning. His legal philosophy takes its inspiration from Thomas Aquinas, with some qualifications and changes of emphasis. This selection is translated from Dabin's Théorie générale du droit *(1944).*

The Ambiguity of the Concept of Natural Law. [There is an] ambiguity which has not ceased to befog the concept of natural law from the day the state began to legislate: To what sort of regulation is the natural law related? To the regulation which, aiming at the moral perfection of men, obligates them before their conscience and before God to practice the good and avoid the bad, in short, the moral rule? Or to the regulation of societal origin, laid down by (domestic or international) public authority with a view to the temporal public good (of individuals or states), in short, the legal rule? Or again to both sorts of rules cumulatively, whether they are considered as distinct at least in form or taken for inseparable at least up to a certain point? In a word, is natural law the directing principle of morals or of law?

Reprinted by permission of the publishers from Kurt Wilk, trans., *Legal Philosophies of Lask, Radbruch, and Dabin* (Cambridge, Mass.: Harvard University Press), pp. 422–31. Copyright, 1950, by the President and Fellows of Harvard College. Abridged by the editor.

The question no doubt was less important practically in periods of not very complex civilization when the civil law was most often content with the rôle of servant and executor of morals. But in our times, with the threefold phenomenon of the increase of wants, above all material wants, the development of technology, and the emergence of the masses, the civil law is led to formulate many requirements which bear no more than an indirect relationship to morality. Hence the present interest of the problem as to the order of regulation to which the rule of conduct called natural law belongs.

Historically, Natural Law Provides Principles of Moral Conduct. With terminology offering no ground for argument either way, since the words "law," "right," and "rule" may refer indifferently to the moral rule and the juridical or legal rule, the answer is supplied by history: What one has always sought of "natural law" is principles of moral conduct, it being understood that man is a social and political being and that morally he has social and political duties. Natural law, the Schoolmen tell us, dictates to man what he must do to arrive at the ultimate end of human life, that is, happiness; it is the rule and measure of peculiarly human actions; its first principle and first precept is that one ought to practice the good and avoid the bad. The traditional teaching is echoed by the "law of nature and of nations" school. According to Grotius,* for instance, the law "obliges to what is good and praiseworthy and not merely to what is just, since law, according to the idea we attach to it here, is not confined to the duties of justice but also embraces what makes up the subject matter of the other virtues." Hence this definition: Natural law "consists in certain principles of right reason, which causes us to know that an action is morally honest or dishonest according to its necessary agreement or disagreement with a rational and sociable nature." The connection is clear: Natural law figures among the first notions of moral philosophy or general ethics in the chapter on laws, side by side with the theory of human acts; and the treatises of natural law, where the applications of the rule of natural law to the different

* [Dutch jurist (1583–1645), author of *De jure belli ac pacis*, a classic work on international law.]

matters are set forth and discussed, are nothing else than treatises on special ethics.

Natural Law and Special Morals. It matters little, moreover, that the morality of acts requires an element of right intention, without which there can be neither good nor virtue in the actor. Only the objective materiality of the precepts, outside of the dispositions of the soul, is here considered. Materially, then, natural law and special morals dictate the same rules, found the same institutions; or, according to the restrictive conception of the Schoolmen, natural law furnishes special morals with its first principles. Indeed, no difference has ever been established between interindividual natural law and interindividual morals, between the natural law of sexual union, generation, and education, and family morals, between political natural law and political morals, save that, in speaking in strict terms, natural law, expressing the requirements of nature, represents the source from which the solutions of morals in those various matters are derived.

Nor is there any distinction between two parts in morals: A morals of rules of action, which would be morals properly so called, and a morals of institutions, or "institutional morals," which would govern the relations dominated by a peculiarly social idea and which would be called "law." Not only would such an interpretation be novel, involving a rejection of the expressions "family morals," "political morals," and even "social morals"; not only would even the formal dissociation of law from morals run the risk of leading to their separation; but the distinction is also really factitious and, despite appearances, superficial. Morals indeed governs everything human, including the human that is social, directly and without any interpreter. And if, with regard to the social and in view of the human, morals is called upon to establish institutional structures of an objective and to a certain degree formal nature—such as the one and indissoluble marriage, marital authority, and state power—these structures, which by the way can be traced back to rules of conduct, have the same moral and natural character as the dispositions that directly command, forbid, or advise. One can thus conclude in the clearest manner that natural law is nothing else than the moral rule taken in its homogeneous totality, without exclusion of any matters, but is limited to indicating their basic nature, in anticipation of developments provided by the positive moral rule and by the scientific work of the moralists. *Relationships between the Natural Moral Rule and the Legal Rule.* To be sure, natural law in the sense just defined, i.e., as the natural moral rule (at least as to first principles), is not unrelated to law, in the sense of the rule established by the state. Under the name of "human law" St. Thomas shows us the civil law coming to the aid of natural law "in order by force and fear to compel perverted and ill-disposed men to abstain from evil, at least so that in ceasing to do evil they leave others in peace." On the other hand, the civil laws are called upon to complete natural law, either by way of conclusions derived from the first principles (as in the case of the *jus gentium*) or by way of concrete determination of the first principles (as in the case of the *jus civile* properly so called). For instance, the law of nature prescribes that he who shall commit an offense shall be punished and the civil law defines the kind of penalty. The same analysis is found in the authors of the law of nature school:* The rôle of the civil law is to sanction natural law, in particular in so far as it prescribes what is just. Is it not the first end of the state, and therefore of the law set down by the state, to guarantee "the peaceful enjoyment of one's rights"? It is natural law, moreover, which either on the ground of the necessity of political society (man is a "political animal") or on the ground of the "social contract" (the faith of promises) gives the civil laws their foundation and justifies the subjects' duty of obedience. Finally, everybody admits that civil laws contrary to natural law are bad laws and even that they do not answer to the concept of a law.

But These Relationships Entail No Confusion of the Disciplines. But what conclusions are to be drawn from these necessary ties of dependence and derivation of the civil law with natural law?

Let us note first of all that the phenomenon is not peculiar to the civil law. All positive rules, institutions, and prescriptions whatsoever, human and even divine, in some manner depend upon and derive from natural law. No doubt the civil law does so, both private and public, municipal and international law; but so too, in

* [E.g., Grotius.]

the religious and ecclesiastic domain, do the canon law (as regards, say, the worship to be rendered unto God in application of the natural virtue of religion) and above all the positive moral laws laid down by the competent authority—God and the Church— the rôle of which is to render precise and complete the "given" of the moral rule of nature.

Thus, the civil law cannot claim a monopoly in natural law as the principle of its special discipline. On the contrary, natural law is necessarily found at the base of every regulatory norm of human conduct, such a norm being conceivable only along the line of nature. But whereas the influence of natural law is direct in the case of morals, it is only indirect in the case of the civil law. And this is logical. Morals alone is placed immediately and exclusively upon the plane of human nature; its solutions alone, as to its first principles, possess the universality, immutability, and certainty which characterize the requirements of nature; the moral rule alone can be called natural in this sense. As for the other disciplines regulative of conduct, they partake of nature only through the intermediary of morals and only in their principles, not in their positive solutions.

What does it matter, after all, that the civil law borrows a number of its precepts from natural law? From this it follows neither that natural law would cease to belong to the category of morals so as to become the primary "given" or the nucleus of the civil law,—nor that the civil law would have lost its proper nature so as to become the lining or the "supplement" of natural law. Notwithstanding interpenetrations or mutual aid, their essences will remain distinct as long as the differences of their ends and functions subsist. Now, if the end and the function of natural law, rendered explicit, developed, and fecundated by moral science, are to define the good and the just in conformity with the "given" of nature, the end and the function of the civil law are to contribute to the public good, which no doubt in large part comprises the defense and safeguard of the good and the just (reserving however possibilities of environment and technique) but also many other measures besides, aiming at "things useful to human life," invested by human reason and not given by nature.[1]

---

[1] Cf. St. Thomas. Summa, Ia IIae, qu. 94, art. 5 ad resp. and ad 3, who

Extension of the Concept of Natural Law: "Natural Jurisprudence." It is true that often the concept of natural law is stretched to include precisely these "useful" things, foreign as such to the category of good and just, which permits assigning a "given" of natural law to the entire civil law, even in those of its dispositions which more or less closely relate to "usefulness to human life." For instance, Grotius suggests a "natural jurisprudence," common to all times and places, detached from anything dependent upon an arbitrary will, a science capable of forming a complete body where one could find treated laws, tributes, judicial duty, conjectures (or presumptions of will), proofs, presumptions, etc.

That link does indeed bridge the hiatus. Natural law no longer represents—or no longer solely or principally represents—the first principles of morality, of the good, the just; it represents—or equally represents—the first principles of civil legislation in the concern for all values whatsoever with which the latter is charged, that is, not only the moral values but also the properly economic or social values, even if they be of a technical nature and in themselves morally indifferent. According to that conception, it is natural law, in the sense of the natural civil law, that will tell the jurist to what extent and in what manner he ought to intervene with his rule, or at least will offer him the first principles of his ordinance, in the same manner as natural law in the moral sense offers to the moralist the first principles of his special morals. In that way one arrives at placing under natural law not only the institution of private ownership, although "differences in wealth are not imposed by nature," but even much more contingent solutions, such as the institution of prescription, the rules of evidence, and the like, designed to bring about, sometimes with certain sacrifices of justice, the security of social relations, which is incontestably "useful to human life."

But This Extension Contradicts the Original Concept of Natural Law. But this broader interpretation rests upon a double contradiction.

What did natural law mean originally? A rule inscribed in human

---

attaches to positive law the solutions, added to natural law, *ad humanam vitam utilia* [useful to human life] . . . , *ad bene vivendum,* to the morally good life, qu. 94, art. 3 *ad resp., in fine* . . .

nature, aiming at the absolute good and just, at honesty. What does the "new style" natural law mean? A quite different concept: A rule invented by man, aiming at things useful to human life in a given social state. No doubt the nature of man is rational and therefore inventive of useful things; it is sociable and therefore concerned about things useful not only to the individual man but also to the society of men. Yet originally it was intended precisely to place in opposition to each other inventive reason and nature, and an express distinction was made between the good and the just, on the one hand, and the useful, on the other. The social was not excluded; on the contrary—but in the social the search continued to be for the absolute good and just and not the contingent useful. That the useful itself, once established, opens up the rule of the good and the just, binding as to the consequences of such establishment, changes nothing in the situation. Thus, prescription and the other rules of security in society remain what they are, to wit, useful and invented solutions, although natural law enjoins us to submit to them—as to every decision made by authority and for the public good. That the useful involves nothing contrary to natural law is obvious but does not justify any confusion. To natural law belongs what is provided by it by precept or by faculty or permission, and not what at the outset escapes its concept, such as the category of the useful.

Will it be said that in the social domain at the very least the useful rejoins the just and the good, and hence natural law? Social and political morals indeed command the rulers to make provision for everything, and the subjects to act always according to the public good, even prior to any intervention of positive law. Now the public good, which itself is a means or intermediary good finally ordered for the good of the individuals, covers all that is useful to the community. From this it follows that a morally indifferent attitude may acquire obligatory value, in the name of social justice, upon the basis of utility alone: The socially useful good merges with the just, moral, honest good. But this argument neglects a capital point: That the useful in the special case is prescribed not simply as useful but first as just, moral, honest. It is just, moral, honest, and therefore a matter of natural law, that the rulers fulfill the duty of their station, which is to dispose of everything with a view to the public good, that is to say, of general utility. It is just, moral, honest, and therefore a matter of natural law, that the subjects, members of the social whole, collaborate in that general utility. The useful becomes the just only because previously the natural, human just did command devotion by everybody, rulers and subjects, to the community.[2] Also, natural law uses restraint here: It leaves to the inventive reason of the rulers and subjects the task of discovering the socially useful solutions and attitudes. Thus, the distinction between natural law and useful invention does not yield in any way.

Those premises, then, are overthrown when, under color of "derivation" from natural law or simply of "conformity" to natural law, the rules of positive law consecrating solutions of social utility are annexed to natural law as issuing definitively from the rational and social nature of man.

The Extension Contradicts the Concept of the Legal Rule. Not only the concept of natural law, in the sense of a rule proceeding from nature, is found altered and overthrown in the system under criticism. It has been shown previously in what way the conception of a natural law of a juridical kind, dictating to the civil legislator the content of his precepts at least in a general way, violated the very concept of the civil law. It is contradictory to speak of "natural jurisprudence" because "jurisprudence," down to its most general rules and their aims—not only the useful but also the good and the just—is a matter of prudence, and prudence is a matter of rational appraisal according to the cases and not a matter of inclination of nature. Even if it is assumed, for example, that natural law prescribes to the civil law the punishment of every offense,[3] at least of every offense against the social life which is the first concern of the civil law, it remains for the prudential judgment to decide not only upon the mode of repression but also upon its social utility in the particular case. If it is said in reply that in deciding to refrain from repression in the particular case the civil law confines itself to restricting natural law without making a change in it, it is to be observed that precisely there lies the proper rôle

---

[2] In the same way, incidentally, as beneficence continues to belong to the category of morals although the benefactor endeavors to be useful to another (the useful good) or to give him pleasure (the delectable good).

[3] Cf. St. Thomas, Summa, Ia IIae, qu. 95, art. 2 ad resp., in fine, . . .

of the jurist establishing the civil law: To discern what of natural
law it is appropriate to retain and what to omit, according to the
requirements of the public good. Thus, natural law does not dictate
any decision to the jurist except negatively, to bring out no precept
contrary to moral natural law, and affirmatively, to regulate everything as a function of the possible and realizable public good, the
first principle of political natural law.

Moral and Political But No Juridical Natural Law. To sum up.
First, there exists a moral natural law which is fundamental to the
moral conduct of individuals as well as to the positive moral rule,
and in every domain including the social domain (social morals)
and without distinction between outward and inner acts. This
rule of itself obliges only in the internal forum and not before
the state, its police and its courts. Second, there also exists a political natural law which, based upon the political instinct of man,
establishes political society and all that is essential to it, especially
the public authority and the civil law, the latter being considered
not in its concrete dispositions but in its principle and its method
of elaboration. This political natural law is undoubtedly dependent upon moral natural law because morals governs everything
human. But it is in turn the starting point of a new system of
properly social (indeed, societal) institutions and rules, inspired
by the idea of the public good (at once moral, utilitarian and technical) and governing only the outward acts of man as a member
of the group. Third, there exists no juridical natural law in the
sense of solutions or even mere directives given in advance to the
authority charged with the establishment of the civil law according
to the public good. No doubt there are principles commonly accepted in the laws of the countries of the same level of civilization:
Jus gentium or "general principles of law." But one could not without ambiguity and danger credit natural law with principles which,
on the one hand, are very heterogeneous, since one finds there
commingled rules of morals, of common sense, and of social utility
—and which, on the other hand, lack the characteristics of necessity and universality inherent in the idea of nature. The practice
of civilized countries, even supported by wisdom and experience,
is not synonymous with natural inclination.[4]

---

[4] See, *contra*, on the "general principles of law," which he understands in

*The Dualism of "Natural Law—Positive Law" Replaced by
"Morals—Law."* If these views are correct, they yield an important
result concerning the statement of the problem here under discussion. One must no longer speak of relationships between natural
law and positive law (at least when by positive law one understands, as is customary, the law of the jurists, the civil law, and
not the positive moral law or rule). One must speak of relationships between morals, not only natural but also positive, and the
civil law, that is to say, the law. This statement does correspond
to reality. On the one hand, what makes its appearance throughout
natural law is indeed morals.[5] On the other hand, the law has
relationships with kinds of values other than the ethical values.
By comparison, the traditional statement errs both by lack of
precision and by confusion. It does not bring out with precision
that natural law above all signifies morals. At the same time, that
statement leads us to believe that natural law covers all values
whatever of interest to the jurist.

---

the sense of "data of natural law or of *naturalis ratio*" (at p. 156), G. del
Vecchio, *Essai sur les principes généraux du droit*, in JUSTICE, DROIT, ETAT
114 *et seq.*, esp. 155 *et seq.*
    [5] See, *contra*, F. Gény, *La laïcité du droit naturel*, in ARCHIVES DE PHILOS-
OPHIE DU DROIT (1933) nos. 3–4, p. 8, n. 1.

A. P. d'ENTREVES

Three Conceptions
of Natural Law

A. P. d'Entrèves, who teaches at the University of Turin, is the author of many studies of the history of legal and political thought. In this selection, he criticizes two conceptions of natural law and defends his own version.

Any analysis of the relationship between law and morals must lead to the recognition that there is a difference between legal and moral obligation, a difference that does not necessarily entail separation. There must be a name for the relationship between the two, for the principle that spans the chasm that divides them, thus bringing law and morals into harmony. I have suggested elsewhere[1] that this is one of the meanings, one of the essential meanings, in which the term "natural law" has been used through the ages. It is a convenient name for indicating the ground of obligation of law, which alone can ensure that the law itself is obeyed not only *propter iram* but *propter conscientiam.** And it is a no less convenient name for indicating the limits of the obligatoriness of the law, the crucial point: on it depends whether the injunction of the law is more than mere coercion.

Let me then turn back for a moment and survey our progress so

---

Reprinted by permission from A. P. d'Entrèves, "The Case for Natural Law Re-examined," *Natural Law Forum*, Vol. 1 (1956), pp. 27–46. Abridged by the editor.

[1] In the conclusion of NATURAL LAW (1951).

* [That is to say, not only because it is the law, but because of a recognition of its rightness.]

far. If we have not yet found a definition of natural law, we have
at any rate come across a number of things which seem to be implied in natural law thinking. We have found that law is no mere
command, no arbitrary choice, for it involves a problem of obligation; we have found that it is impossible to understand this problem of obligation without examining the relationship between law
and morals; and I have just suggested that, to express the "point of
intersection" between law and morals, our benighted forbears had a
name, natural law. And yet I doubt that natural law thinkers, old
and new, would rest content with a definition of natural law as
nothing but a name for the moral foundation of law, as nothing
but the attempt to explain law in terms not of force or convention,
but of obligation. They would, I surmise, consider such a definition as inadequate, and I think they would be right. For the most
important feature of natural law is to stress not only the existence
of a problem, but actually to provide an answer to it. Natural
law theorists would point out that not all solutions of the problem
of law and morals are equally valid, and that, if it were a matter
merely of explaining the obligatoriness of the law, Rousseau's
general will can do that very well. They would emphatically assert
that the only valid ground of legal obligation is given by a Law—
an unwritten law, an ideal law—to which we can and must refer
as the model or standard on which all laws depend and from which
they derive their obligation.

In brief, then, what I propose to do is to examine how, in different times and in different ways, the ideal law has been conceived
and defined. In my mind, these conceptions and definitions seem
to fall, roughly, under three main types or headings. These are and
must be purely provisional headings. I think in fact that the moment we start classifying "types" or "patterns of thought" we run
the risk of killing the very thing we are studying. But in very rough
outline it seems that the notion of natural law has been, and can
be, worked out in three different directions. The first is that of the
ideal or natural law as a kind of "technology"; the second I would
call the notion of natural law as an "ontology"; and the third might
perhaps best be described as "deontology."

The Knowledge of an Ideal Law: The Challenge of Natural Law Theories

There is no denying that the very assertion of the existence and possibility of knowledge of an ideal law is the most serious challenge which natural law theory offers modern thought. Natural law is a stumbling block, indeed perhaps a scandal to the modern: and the reason, so we are told, is that the distinction between "fact" and "value," the opposition, in other words, between what *is* and what *ought to be*, has become, after Kant, the cornerstone of modern ethics. Kant's doctrine of the "autonomy of the will" is usually taken to mark the end of the natural law tradition.

I do not propose to discuss this view at this stage, a view which— to my mind at any rate—is subject to many reservations. But I would like to point out that if we want to go back to the real source of the distinction between "fact" and "value," if we want to have before our eyes a clear and downright statement of the case, we can do no better than turn to a passage from Hume: "I cannot forbear adding to these reasonings an observation, which may, perhaps, be found of some importance. In every system of morality which I have hitherto met with, I have always remarked, that the author proceeds for some time in the ordinary way of reasoning, and establishes the being of a God, or makes observations concerning human affairs: when of a sudden I am surprised to find, that instead of the usual copulations of propositions, *is* and *is not*, I meet with no proposition that is not connected with an *ought*, or an *ought not*. This change is imperceptible; but it is, however, of the last consequence. For as this *ought*, or *ought not*, expresses some new relation or affirmation, it is necessary that it should be observed and explained; and at the same time that a reason should be given, for what seems altogether unconceivable, how this new relation can be a deduction from others, which are entirely different from it."[2]

I doubt that the main objection to natural law thinking could be put forward with more clarity and cogency than in this classic statement. It is the objection to what in the language of the mod-

[2] *Treatise of Human Nature*, bk. III ("Of Morals"), pt. I. § 1.

ern semanticists is called the passage from the indicative to the
imperative mood, an objection, one must admit, based on a perfectly accurate description of what natural law theorists are ultimately after. Rather than countering the objection forthwith, I
am inclined to accept the description, and indeed enlarge it so far
as to venture a new definition of natural law as the attempt to
bridge the chasm between *is* and *ought*, between "fact" and
"value." The classification I have proposed is in fact nothing other
than the story of these different attempts: it remains to see to
what extent they have been and can hope to be successful.

One first attempt is that of conceiving natural law as a "technology." This is an ugly word, which has gained undue popularity.
This is what makes me specially reluctant to use it. But I have
my reasons for doing so. Technology, according to the *Oxford
Dictionary*, means "science of the industrial arts." But I do not
think that I am forcing that meaning unduly by suggesting that
it is a convenient name for indicating the knowledge of the rules
of a particular art or craft (τέχνη)—the "know-how," as the phrase
now goes. And I believe that to many jurists, old and new, natural
law was just this: the knowledge of the right rule, of the correct
solution to a given problem in law, the answer that lies "in the
nature of things," and which it is only a matter of finding and applying in order to have good laws.

Such at any rate—unless I am grossly mistaken—seems to have
been in its broadest sense the Roman conception of natural law,
on the importance of which I need hardly linger. Right at the
beginning of the *Digest* we find the jurist Celsus defining law—
jus—as *ars boni et aequi.** Surely, an "art" has its rules. Surely,
therefore, there must be some means, some instrument for finding
out the *bonum et aequum*. *Jus naturale* was that instrument. I am
well aware of the ambiguities of the texts that have been handed
down to us by Justinian. They are, and always will be, a matter
of controversy. Of late, the most authoritative interpreters have
warned us against the mistake of conceiving the Roman notion
of *jus naturale* as a philosophical construction. They draw a sharp
line between the sweeping generalizations of such writers as
Cicero and Seneca, and the "professional constructions" of the

* [The art of the good and the equitable.]

lawyers who are included in Justinian's book. *Jus naturale* was to these lawyers not a complete and ready-made system of rules, but essentially a means of interpretation, almost, as it were, the "trick of the trade" which they resorted to and used in a masterly fashion. In shaping a body of laws which would apply to the whole civilized world they had no abstract theories in mind, but aimed at the workable and practical.

If we consider and compare the several definitions of natural law which are contained in the first section of the *Digest* we undoubtedly find many contradictions.[3] But these contradictions, however puzzling, are comparatively much less important than the fundamental agreement on one point, viz., on the view that there is no problem in law that cannot be solved, provided the *constans et perpetua voluntas* is there, *jus suum cuique tribuere.**
"What natural reason dictates to all men," "what nature has taught all animals"—this is what the jurist and the lawgiver must keep in mind if they are to do their job well and construct a system that may prove *semper bonum et aequum.*†

Clearly, this is not a philosophical proposition. It looks much rather like the "science of an art" according to the definition in the *Oxford Dictionary.* I cannot help being reminded, in connection with this Roman notion of natural law, of what seems to me a modern version of the same conception. I am thinking of Professor Fuller's assertion of the existence of a "natural order" underlying group life, which it is the task of the judge—and the lawgiver —to discover.[4] I would almost be tempted to apply to the Roman notion of natural law his remark, that there is "nothing mystical" about it, that our attitude in approaching this kind of natural law is not "that of one doing obeisance before an altar, but more like that of a cook trying to find the secret of a flaky pie crust, or of an engineer trying to devise a means of bridging a ravine." I rather like to think of the Roman lawyers as cooks and engineers. The pie they cooked and the bridge they built were certainly remarkably good if they proved so successful all through the ages. Their "tech-

[3] I have discussed these contradictions at length in chapter one of my NATURAL LAW.
* [The unfailing willingness to give each his due.]
† [Always good and equitable.]
[4] Fuller, *Reason and Fiat in Case Law,* 59 HARV. L. REV. 376 (1946).

40)　　　　　　　　　　　A. P. d'ENTREVES

nology" was excellent. They did find the best working law for long
centuries.

I would hardly dare to press my parallel much further. Yet, in
another place, Professor Fuller provides me with some additional
proof of what I have called the "technological" approach to our
problem.[5] "Because of the confusions invited by the term 'natural
law'" he has recently recommended a new name for the field of
study which natural law used to cover; and he suggests the term
"eunomics" for "the science, theory or study of good order and
workable arrangements." "Eunomics," Professor Fuller assures us,
"involves no commitment to 'ultimate ends.'" Its primary concern
"is with the means aspect of the means-end relation." I surmise
that one of the tasks of "eunomics" would be to discover the "natural laws of social order" as the best working laws in view of the
particular ends of a given society.

Now Professor Fuller's theory provides me with the best definition of what I have called the technological notion of natural law.
But it also provides me with the main objection which I would
move against that notion. In plain, everyday language, the objection is that the "best working" law is not necessarily the "best" law.
But that objection can also be put in more philosophical idiom by
recalling the capital distinction between "technical" and "categorical" imperatives, a distinction which, to my mind, could hardly
be more pertinent than in this case. The distinction is the one
which Kant makes in the *Foundations of the Metaphysics of
Morals*, sect. 2: "All imperatives command either hypothetically
or categorically. The former present the practical necessity of a
possible action as a means to achieving something else which one
desires (or which one may possibly desire). The categorical imperative would be one which presented an action as of itself objectively necessary, without regard to any other end." Subsequently,
Kant distinguishes hypothetical imperatives as "technical" (belonging to art), and "pragmatic" (belonging to welfare).

If anything, both the *jus naturale* of the Roman lawyers and
Professor Fuller's "natural law of the social order" are hypothetical or technical imperatives in the Kantian sense. They are hypothetical inasmuch as they are means to an end, and technical inso-

[5] *American Legal Philosophy at Mid-Century*, 6 J. LEGAL ED. 457 (1954).

far as they pertain to an "art"—though if one chose to call them "pragmatic" according to Kant's definition this would not alter their "hypothetical" character. If there were any doubts about it, here is an illustration given by Professor Fuller which clearly indicates the "technical" character of the law which, to him as to the Romans, lies in the *natura rei.** Suppose a man wants to assemble an engine: he can obviously do so only if he knows the proper rules of his job. There is no doubt that one such rule (and probably one only) exists. My comment would be that the finding out of this rule has nothing to do with the decision to do the job: our man could very well give up his attempts to assemble the engine and turn to some more congenial occupation. To determine the means for an end is a quite different matter from ascertaining the "objective necessity" of the end itself: in other words, there is no warrant for turning a technical (hypothetical) imperative into a categorical one.

To conceive natural law as a "technology" is not to help us solve our problem of obligation. There is no intention to belittle its value and use; indeed these may be great within proper limits. By the help of *jus naturale* the Roman jurists worked out a system of laws which fitted men's needs for many centuries. And the modern lawgiver must keep the "nature of things" in mind, if he wants his laws to be fitting and efficient. I guess this is what is meant by saying—in the current jargon—that laws must conform to the existing "sociological requirements." The penalty for disregarding such requirements may be a heavy one. The penalty for disregarding the "nature of things" or the "sociological requirements" does not provide any ground for asserting the absolute validity of the rules or laws deduced from them. Actually such laws are nothing more than statements of facts, even though cloaked in an "ought" proposition—as when we say: "if you want to accelerate you ought to press the pedal." It is a delusion to think that they can provide that bridge between the *is* and the *ought*, between "facts" and "values" which we are seeking.

With all its great credentials—which it would be blindness to deny—natural law as a technology does not provide the answer to our problem. Or, if it does so, it is only by assuming an end as the

* [The nature of the case.]

only right end to pursue, by surreptitiously introducing a "value"
behind the "fact," and discarding the "hypothetical" for a "categorical" imperative. Personally, I am not sure that the Roman
lawyers did not after all do something of the sort, and I am quite
willing to admit that, if this were proved to be so, my strictures
on the *jus naturale* would no longer be valid. But in that case we
would probably have to subsume the Roman theory of natural law
into the second category of natural law thinking to which I am
now turning.

The second type has a name, a name which it deliberately gives
itself. So this time I need not spend many words to justify my
terminology. It is the ontological conception of natural law—the
doctrine of natural law as an "ontology" (ὄν, ὄντος—what is). With
regard to the problem of bridging the chasm between *is* and *ought*,
between "fact" and "values," this doctrine would appear to seize
the bull by its horns, and to reply to Hume's challenge: there is no
such chasm; your distinction is a wrong one. The ontological approach welds together being and oughtness, and maintains that
the very notion of natural law stands and falls on that identification. This point is so important that I would like to clarify and
emphasize it with the help of two quotations.

My first quotation comes from Professor Rommen. "The natural law . . . depends on the science of being, on metaphysics.
Hence every attempt to establish the natural law must start from
the fundamental relation of being and oughtness, of the real and
the good." From Professor Wild I am selecting the following
sentence: "All genuine natural law philosophy . . . must be un-
reservedly ontological in character. It must be concerned with the
nature of existence in general, for it is only in the light of such
basic analysis that the moral structure of human life can be more
clearly understood."[6] The fact that two thinkers approaching the
problem from different angles agree so completely on this point
seems to me particularly eloquent. Professor Rommen has a further and important remark: "The idea of natural law obtains general acceptance only in the periods when metaphysics, queen of the
sciences, is dominant. It recedes or suffers an eclipse, on the other

[6] PLATO'S MODERN ENEMIES AND THE THEORY OF NATURAL LAW 172
(1953).

hand, when being . . . and oughtness, morality and law, are separated, when the essence of things and their ontological order are viewed as unknowable."[7]

This last contention seems indeed to have very wide implications. It might be taken to mean that the very notion of natural law is an indication of "metaphysical" thinking. Thus it would open up some very interesting lines of research on the "metaphysics" underlying some "modern" conceptions of natural law—such as the conceptions of natural law which were so prominent and indeed so effective in the seventeenth and the eighteenth century. But this is clearly not what Professor Rommen has in mind, for to him there is one system, and one system only, which bases natural law on the "ontological order of things"—and this is the system of Thomist philosophy. There is no denying that St. Thomas Aquinas' doctrine of natural law still represents the most carefully thought out presentation of the ontological view, the most complete and thoroughgoing development both of its assumptions and of its implications.

Its basis—in Professor Rommen's words—is a "conception of an order of reality" established in its essence by God's wisdom, and proceeding in its existence from God's will. It therefore provides an answer to each and every problem touched upon in this discussion: the relationship between reason and will in law, as well as the relationship between moral and legal obligation. In fact, if natural law is to be defined as the bridge between *is* and *ought*, between facts and values, St. Thomas' definition of it stands out for its cogency and conciseness: *lex naturalis nihil aliud est quam participatio legis aeternae in rationali creatura.** In the general "order of reality" man participates because he is a rational being, and hence has the possibility of attaining a knowledge of it. That knowledge thus becomes the condition and the source of all laws pertaining to men: "being themselves made participators in Providence itself, in that they control their own actions and the actions of others."[8]

---

[7] Both quotations from Rommen in this paragraph are from THE NATURAL LAW 161 (1947).

* [The natural law is nothing else than the rational creature's participation of the eternal law.]

[8] S. THEOL., Ia IIae, 91, 2, concl.

Now it seems to me that in our divided world the first and most serious stumbling block to the Thomist conception of natural law lies precisely in its premise, in that metaphysical premise which both Professor Rommen and Professor Wild tell us is essential to the proper construction of natural law. It is the premise of a divine order of the world, which St. Thomas recalls at the very beginning of his theory of law, and from which he infers, with unimpeachable logic, the most detailed and specified consequences: *supposito quod mundus divina providentia regatur, ut in Primo habitum est*.[9] Once that premise is granted, the whole majestic edifice of laws can be established on it: eternal law, the natural law, human and divine laws, all are ultimately based on and justified through the existence of a supreme, benevolent Being. In the words of a great English writer, who was also a good Thomist: "Of Law there can be no less acknowledged, than that her seat is the bosom of God, her voice the harmony of the world."

I have described this premise of the belief in God and in God's action in the world as a stumbling block. I need hardly add that I would not like to see my words misinterpreted. To be sure, such a belief, far from being a stumbling block to the Christian, is in fact the very essence of his faith. Yet even on this point, as we all well know, Christians have been, and perhaps still are divided. I had my good reasons for taking my last quotation from a Protestant writer, Richard Hooker. Protestant theology has not always been friendly towards the idea of natural law. Thomist natural law is only too often considered to be the exclusive preserve of Roman Catholics. There are, however, encouraging signs that such prejudices are gradually being overcome and the way paved for better understanding among Christians.

But the world is not peopled only by Catholics and Protestants. The modern student of law need not necessarily be a Christian. In fact, lawyers have never had a very good reputation on that score: *Juristen böse Christen!* For the agnostic jurist of the present day, and perhaps indeed for the modern man who lives in a "de-christianized world," it will be very difficult to accept the notion of natural law, if that acceptance is made conditional on the accept-

[9] S. THEOL., Iª IIae, 91, 1, concl. [Granted that the world is ruled by divine providence, as was stated in the First Part (of the SUMMA).]

ance of the metaphysical premise: *supposito quod mundus divina providentia regatur.* This, to my mind, is the first difficulty for the "ontological" theory of natural law—a difficulty which may not be a difficulty at all if we simply take the line: "Well, this is natural law. Take it or leave it." But we are here to find, if possible, a way of making the argument for natural law acceptable also to people who do not share our own premises.

Now I must limit myself to a very brief mention of one or two further points which I think can be raised—and are often raised with regard to the ontological approach to natural law. One of them is the mistake of stressing its deductive possibilities too much, and thus turning it into the "blueprint of detailed solutions" against which Dean O'Meara so rightly warns us. This is precisely the mistake Mr. Constable makes—and I hope he will not take my comment ill—in his recent essay, *What does Natural Law Jurisprudence Offer?*[10] Mr. Constable believes that, from a Thomist notion of natural law, based on the idea of "order," there can be inferred the idea of an "organic community," based on the idea of "service," "guided"—I am quoting his words—by "some persons or groups of persons" having "a clear insight into the nature of goodness."

I can only register quite frankly and openly my dissent from such views, and declare that if these were the implications of natural law, personally I would find it impossible to accept them. If not indeed of Plato's Republic, Mr. Constable's "organic community" seems to me to smack of that "corporativist" idea against which no lesser authority than Professor Maritain has warned us in his admirable essay, *The Rights of Man and Natural Law,* where he denounced it as one of the "temptations" deriving "from old concepts formerly in favor in certain Christian circles."[11]

Let us be quite chary in drawing conclusions from "natural law" which might turn into a highly controversial political program. Let us not forget that the "organic theory of society" has in recent days been a welcome excuse for the suppression of individual freedom. Let us, above all, practice a healthy distrust of

[10] 4 Cath. U. L. Rev. 1 (1954).
[11] Maritain, The Rights of Man and Natural Law 54–55 (1944).

any "persons or groups" who claim to have "a clear insight into the nature of goodness."

With these last two points, we have come to the crux of the problem. The ontological theory of natural law is a great and impressive construction. But it does not seem to take into sufficient account those aspects of natural law that have become the lasting inheritance of modern man. With its insistence on the objective notion of "order" and law, it tends to disregard or to belittle the importance of the subjective notion of a claim and a right. In one word, it does not adequately stress that idea of "natural rights" which has become part and parcel of modern civilization. "We hold . . . that all men . . . are endowed by their Creator with certain unalienable Rights." Americans, after all, have proclaimed this doctrine to the world, and have inserted it in the *Declaration of Independence*.

No doubt the "ontologist" may point out that there is no "right" without "law," and that the very notion of a subjective claim presupposes that of an objective order. And he will be perfectly justified in doing so, and this is where the ontological argument is indeed unassailable. But I seriously doubt that he can find any clear assertion of the claim—of "natural rights"—in his sources, whether in Plato or in St. Thomas Aquinas. This claim is in fact a modern development of "natural law," and for a recognition of "natural rights" the time was not ripe either in classical days or in the Middle Ages.

The same reservation should be made, I believe, with regard to the "clear insight into the nature of goodness," that is, to the authoritative interpretation of natural law which seems implied in the ontological position. Quite apart from the fact that an undue stress on the possibility of such authoritative interpretation runs the risk of converting natural law into a new kind of positivism, it is quite clear that such a notion can only be a further stumbling block to the modern.

Value Judgments and the Natural Law

If both natural law as a technology and natural law as an ontology are open to objections and encounter difficulties, is there a way

of presenting the case for natural law in a manner which might—
even if it did not ensure general acceptance—at least make that
notion less obnoxious to the modern world at large? To avoid misgivings, I might as well begin by saying that, if I borrow the name
for the third kind of approach to natural law from the founder
of utilitarianism, this should not be taken to mean that I am a
follower of Bentham and pleading a merely utilitarian approach
to our problem. It just happens that the word "deontology"
(τὸ δέον—that which is binding) seems to provide one of those
convenient labels which must, however, always be used with necessary caution.

Can we agree, at least, on certain things that are binding? The
problem is all here, in this very plain, simple question.

In order to develop my argument, I am going back first of all
to the image of the "bridge"—the bridge between fact and value,
between what *is* and what *ought to be*. This time I am taking my
text from an author who, though not very widely known in Anglo-
Saxon countries, has of late been the subject of some very admirable work here in America. He is a fellow-countryman of mine,
and his name is dear to all Italians.

At the beginning of his *Scienza Nuova* Giambattista Vico has a
remark which seems important for the problem we are discussing.
This remark is put forward in the form of two "axioms" or
Degnità—the fundamental exposition of principles by which Vico
prefaces his study of history and philosophy. I shall quote them
here in the English translation which has recently been made of
his work by two American scholars.

Degnità CXI: "The certitude of laws is an obscurity of judgment, backed only by authority, so that we find them harsh in
application, yet are obliged to apply them by their certitude. In
good Latin *certum* means 'particularized,' or, as the schools say,
'individuated'; so that, in over-elegant Latin, *certum* and *commune* are opposed to each other."

Degnità CXIII: "The truth of the laws is a certain light and
splendor with which natural reason illuminates them; so that
jurisconsults are often in the habit of saying *verum est* for
aequum est."

I am quite ready to grant that the two passages I have quoted

are far from being easy to interpret.[12] But, to put it briefly, Vico's
idea seems to be that in every law one can find an element which
he calls the *certum* (the element of authority), and an element
which he calls the *verum* (the element of "truth," which is discovered by "reason"). *Certum* and *verum*, authority and reason,
are the two facets of the law, two aspects of the same thing, two
different angles from which all law can be considered. Sometimes
the *certum* may obscure the *verum*, authority takes the place of
judgment, and laws are obeyed only because of their "certitude."
But there is no law which, illuminated by the light of reason, does
not reveal an element of *verum*, the "truth" which it contains,
like a soft kernel within the hard shell of authority that enfolds
it: though it may happen that this very authority is the value
of the law, that "certitude" is itself a valuable guarantee against
the disrupting forces of anarchy, so as to justify the old Roman
adage *dura lex sed lex**—which Vico would like to read: *lex dura
est sed certa est.*†

I believe that these ideas can shed some light on the problem
which we are discussing, that they do constitute a new approach
to the question of the bridge between *is* and *ought*, between facts
and values. For indeed, insofar as every law is a compound of
certum and *verum*, every law is in itself a bridge over that chasm
—or at any rate an attempt at bridging it. For every law is no
doubt a factual proposition, inasmuch as it is a particular authori-

[12] In order better to illustrate Vico's conception of natural law and its
relevance to the point here under discussion, I would like to quote from a recent
and excellent book on the Italian philosopher by Dr. A. R. Caponigri, of the
University of Notre Dame: "In its most immediate and concrete sense, the
natural law is [to Vico] the mediation between the truth and the certitude,
the concreteness and the universality of the law. . . . The 'certum' and the
'verum,' which natural law seeks to mediate, are dimensions, not of single laws,
but of the total process of law." "The natural law he understood to be, not
that transcendent and unenacted normative law, allegedly implied in the concept of 'human nature,' but the movement of the process of the historical
formation of the structures of positive law towards an immanent ideality." ". . .
the universality of the natural law consists, not in the fact that in all times and
in identical places identical positive law should prevail, but that in all the forms
of positive law, despite the diversity of material circumstances which dictate
the immediate force of the law, the same ideal principle is at work."
CAPONIGRI, TIME AND IDEA. THE THEORY OF HISTORY IN GIAMBATTISTA
VICO 38, 68, 116 (1953).
   * [A harsh law, but a law nonetheless.]
   † [Law is harsh, but it is certain, authoritative.]

tative statement. But it is also and at the same time—insofar as it aims at a particular end, and is not a senseless imposition—a statement about "values."

I have until now used, or tried to use, the word "value" with the utmost discretion. As I am well aware of its invidious meaning, I have put that word under a safety belt of inverted commas. But now I find that I can do no better than use that word to describe what I have in mind. Perhaps I can give it force by an example.

Take the difference between the common law and continental law in the matter of testaments. Surely it does make a difference to the father of a family if, according to the common law, he is free to dispose of his entire estate or, according to the *Code Napoléon* and to the codes that have been modelled on it, he is not allowed to do so because a portion of his estate is reserved— "earmarked" as it were—for his offspring. But surely the difference between the two systems is not merely a difference of "fact," a difference between the wording of the codes or the rules which courts will enforce in the different countries. Something else is at stake, as will be clearly shown by the reaction of any Latin *paterfamilias* when he is first told that an English father may disinherit his children and leave all his property to a charitable institution. Even though my Latin *paterfamilias* may not go so far as to say that such a practice would be against "natural law," he would certainly have strong feelings about such a patent disregard of what he considers the unity of the family and the rightful expectations of children. Is it going too far to suggest that such an example as this clearly indicates that the law embodies certain "values": in this particular case a particular notion of the comparative claims of family duty and individual freedom?

I have chosen my example at random. What I want considered is this idea: it is possible in each and every legal proposition to ascertain the "value" it contains—even down to traffic regulations if you please, since there can be no doubt about the "value" they protect, that of our own personal safety. I know full well the ambiguity of the word "value" which I am using in this context; I would be quite willing to use a different word if I could think of a better one. My point is of far greater relevance, and far more

controversial: for it amounts to nothing less than admitting that
we have gone all this long way to find the ground of obligation
of law without realizing that this ground does not lie outside, but
within the law itself, that it must be sought in the interplay of the
verum and the *certum*, in the ideal principle which is at work in
every law despite the material circumstances that engross it. For
each and every law is indeed nothing other than a "normative
translation" of a particular value: we must try and break the shell
in order to get to the kernel. And if a particular rule will not
yield an answer to our quest, it is to the general system of which
that rule is a part that we must turn, and we will no doubt find it.

Let me try to put this same argument in another way. I have
already referred to Kelsen's "pure theory of law," and I think we
would all agree that Kelsen strives at a construction and interpretation of law entirely agnostic as far as "values" are concerned.
Every legal order can, according to Kelsen, be construed as a
Stufenbau, a system of rules which derive their validity one from
the other, until we come to the "basic norm" which is the condition of validity of them all, and makes the whole system into a
coherent pattern. When I think of Kelsen's pure theory of law I
am always reminded of a passage in *Alice in Wonderland*, and
of Alice's reply to the King of Hearts. "At this moment the King,
who had been for some time busily writing in his notebook, called
out 'Silence!' and read out from his book 'Rule Forty-two. *All
Persons more than a mile high to leave the Court.*'—Everybody
looked at Alice.—'*I'm* not a mile high,' said Alice.—'You are,' said
the King.—'Nearly two miles high,' added the Queen.—'Well, I
shan't go, at any rate,' said Alice: 'besides, that's not a regular
rule. You invented it just now.'—'It's the oldest rule in the book,'
said the King.—'Then it ought to be Number One,' said Alice."

Briefly, the point I am trying to make is this. The ultimate
ground of validity of the law, the *verum* of laws as distinct from
their *certum*, the *Grundnorm* of Kelsen, the *Rule Number One*
of Alice—they are not "facts," but "values." I said in my little
book on *Natural Law* that Kelsen's "pure theory of law" can be
used to show the Achilles' heel of positivism. I do not propose
to repeat my argument here. But I would like to say that Kelsen's
insistence on the purely hypothetical character of the *Grundnorm*

can deceive nobody. Inasmuch as that hypothesis has to be endorsed by a fact, Kelsen's refined form of positivism shows its real face, the reduction of law to a mere expression of force—and even this is an assertion of "value." There have been indeed—and there always will be—political philosophies based on the assumption that force is the ultimate ground of obligation. But such philosophies, by the very fact that they glorify force, cannot avoid attributing to it an ethical value. Hobbes' *Leviathan* will free men from fear; indeed "not renouncing" trumps can have its "morality." We have only to look around to convince ourselves that to a very large number of people might *is* right. But I wonder how many of us actually take the trouble to point out to such people the revealing admission contained in the use of the word "right" in this context.

So much for the *verum* and the *certum* of the law and for the presence of a value judgment in every legal proposition. I have been very agreeably surprised to come across some interesting work lately done in this country on lines singularly akin to the one I have been indicating. I refer to Professor McDougal's program of "value clarification." I believe as he does that there is a new and fascinating line of enquiry open to jurisprudence. My only difference with Professor McDougal is, that while he seems to think of the "values" underlying a given legal proposition or a given legal order as "preferences," as "goals," as "objects of decision," I would plead that they should also and foremost be considered and studied as "grounds of obligation." In fact, I believe that it is here the notion of natural law as a "deontology" can, if at all, find its justification: for the problem of natural law is to me essentially that of the intersection between the legal proposition and the value that underlies it, the ascertainment of the element of obligation that makes us feel we are obeying the law not merely because of its "certitude,"—to use Vico's expression again—but because of the element of "truth" it contains, a truth carrying conviction. The difficulty of course is to persuade ourselves that such "values" are "objective qualities" in the law itself and not mere subjective or emotional reactions on our part, devoid of any universality.

For my part, I believe that in every human society, in fact in

"human nature" itself, there are certain ultimate standards or
values which determine approval or disapproval, assent or dissent;
and I believe that it is these same values that determine our judgment as to whether a law is "just" or "unjust": in other words—
to use a very ancient language that seems perfectly appropriate
at this point—whether we are bound in conscience to obey it or
not. To ascertain such values may be thought a modest—or an
immodest—undertaking. Yet I think that, failing all other ways,
such an undertaking is well worth attempting, and may even in
the end lead us to a much greater amount of agreement than we
might expect.

PHILIP SELZNICK

Sociology and Natural Law

Philip Selznik is a professor of sociology, and is actively en-
gaged in the work of the Center for the Study of Law and
Society at the University of California, Berkeley.

Among modern sociologists, the reputation of natural law is not
high. The phrase conjures up a world of absolutisms, of theologi-
cal fiat, of fuzzy, unoperational, "mystical" ideas, of thinking
uninformed by history and by the variety of human situations.
This is sad, because sociology should have a ready affinity for the
philosophy of natural law.

Most sociologists today, addressing themselves to the legal order,
would still agree with Ehrlich that "the center of gravity of legal
development" lies in altered ways of life and in the changing
organization of society. They would argue, however, that it is

Reprinted by permission from Philip Selznick, "Sociology and Natural Law,"
Natural Law Forum, Vol. 6 (1961), pp. 84–104. Abridged by the editor.

bootless and sterile to call every kind of order "law" and that the study of legal development, including probable future changes in law, entails no commitment to a theory of justice. There would be a fairly ready acceptance of the distinction between law as commonly understood and the *sources* of law as the whole range of influences on legal development and stability. In this way, they would hope to avoid seemingly endless terminological discussions and vexing philosophical issues.

There is much that is appealing and wholesome in this way of thinking. It does indeed apply to broad areas in the study of law and society. But in some very important respects it is a superficial and profoundly mistaken view. In this essay I shall attempt to state why I think this is so and why I believe that a modern version of natural law philosophy is needed for a proper understanding of the law as well as for the fulfillment of sociology's promise. I speak here of natural law as a legal philosophy and not as a general system of ethics.

In approaching this task, I accept two basic commitments. First is a commitment to naturalism. My approach purports to be in all respects consistent with the spirit and logic of scientific inquiry. I offer only the caveat that it is John Dewey's philosophical pragmatism, and not a narrower positivism, which frames my view of naturalism. A second commitment is to a demanding concept of natural law. We are speaking of something more than a name for the sources of law, or for the moral foundations of law. Natural law is more than "the law that ought to be." If it is to mean anything significant, natural law must be itself legally efficacious, in some sense legally authoritative.

First I shall consider two obstacles to natural law thinking in sociology—the separation of fact and value and the doctrine of moral relativism. Then I shall analyze the meaning of legality and of positive law, finally turning to some attributes of natural law as they bear on sociological inquiry.

I. Master Ideals in Sociology

The main drift of contemporary sociology has been toward positivism, especially toward an ever-greater emphasis on empirical observation and techniques of measurement. A striving for objectivity, for clarity of thought, and for scientific respectability has produced a strong feeling against speculative inquiry and especially against moral philosophy. At least, these ancient preoccupations are thought to have no place in modern sociology, whatever other value they might have as literature. This movement of thought has much to commend it. At the same time, just because it is a "movement," it harbors many illusions and often serves to close minds rather than to open them. It is a procedural canon of inquiry that the study of fact must be assiduously protected from contamination by the value preferences of the observer. From this methodological requirement has been derived a quasi-metaphysical dogma, namely, that fact and value belong to alien spheres.

The entire issue of fact and value is too large to be set forth here, but I shall try to contribute to the discussion, and at the same time advance the argument of this paper, by analyzing briefly one area in which a significant intersection of fact and value occurs. I have in mind those phenomena in the social world whose very nature encompasses the realization of values.

Social scientists are not troubled by the idea of a "norm" or standard of behavior. A great deal of anthropological and sociological writing is devoted to the description and analysis of norms and systems of norms. That a cultural prescription exists, that it changes, that it is related to other prescriptions in determinate ways—these matters of fact can be handled by the social scientist quite blandly, without an uneasy conscience. From the standpoint of the observer, norms are factual data and that is that.

But suppose we are interested in the following: friendship, scholarship, statesmanship, love, fatherhood, citizenship, consensus, reason, public opinion, culture (in its common-sense and value-laden meaning), democracy. These and a great many other similar phenomena are "normative systems," in a special and "strong" sense of that term. I have in mind more than a set of related norms. A democracy is a normative system in that much complex behavior, as well as many specific norms, is governed by a master ideal. Behavior, feeling, thought, and organization are all bound together by a commitment to the realization of democratic values. It is impossible to understand any of these phenomena without also understanding what ideal states are to be approximated. In addition we must understand what forces are produced within the system, and what pressures exerted on it which inhibit or facilitate fulfilling the ideal.[1]

In a normative system, the relation between the master ideal and discrete norms may be quite complex. For example, it might be concluded that under certain circumstances maximizing the number of people who vote, irrespective of competence or interest, would undermine rather than further the democratic ideal. This is one reason for stressing the difference between a normative system and a set of related norms. A normative system is a living reality, a cluster of problem-solving individuals and groups, and its elements are subject to change as new circumstances and new opportunities alter the relation between the system and its master ideal. Put another way, the norms applicable to friendship or democracy are derived, not directly from the master ideal, but also from knowledge of what men and institutions are like. Only thus can we know what specific norms are required to fulfill the ideal.

The study of friendship cannot long avoid an evaluation of the extent to which particular social bonds approximate the ideal. Nor can it properly escape specifying the elements of friendship —what modes of response and obligation are called for by the ideal. None of this is inconsistent with detachment on the part of the observer. The observer need not have any personal commitment to the value in question, at least at the time and in the circumstances at hand. He may assess, quite objectively and impersonally, such connections and discrepancies as may exist between the ideal and its fulfillment.

In theory, as opposed to the main trend of empirical research, some recognition of normative systems does exist. There is not much of a theory of friendship, or of love, in social science, but we do have the concept of the "primary relation," of which love and friendship are characteristic illustrations. What is a primary relation? It is a social bond marked by the free and spontaneous

---

[1] Compare the criticism of Max Weber in LEO STRAUSS, NATURAL RIGHT AND HISTORY 49 ff. (Chicago: U. of Chicago Press, 1953).

interaction of whole persons, as distinguished from the constrained and guarded arms-length contact of individuals who commit only a part of themselves to the social situation. In the primary relation, there is deep and extensive communication; individuals enter this experience as a way of directly attaining personal security and well-being, not as a mean to other ends. This rough and elliptical statement is very close to what most sociologists would accept. Yet clearly it states an ideal only incompletely realized in the actual experience of living persons.

This illustration permits us to clarify the role of assessment in the observation and analysis of normative systems. The normative concept or model tells us what are the attributes of a primary relation. Only with this in mind can we properly classify our observations or identify the significant forces at work. To formulate the ideal primary relation is part of what theory is about in social psychology. This formulation, to be sure, will avoid the language of morality. It will specify social and psychological states, such as the quality of communication. Still, the intellectual function of the model is to provide a framework for diagnosis, including standards against which to assess the experience being studied. The small nuclear family is largely based on primary relations, but where communication between generations is weakened, and where authority requires impersonal judgment and discipline, the fulfillment of the primary-relations ideal is limited.

Whatever the assessment, it is always *from the standpoint of the normative system being studied.* The student of a normative system need not have any personal commitment to the desirability of that system. We may all agree that primary relations are a good thing, and the values they realize "genuine" values, but it is precisely the role of the social scientists to avoid the moralistic fallacy that primary relations are always a good thing. Where impersonality and objectivity are needed, the intimacy and commitment associated with primary relations may well be inappropriate. A different ideal, that of "official" behavior, may be called for. This ideal, too, is a demanding one and it is likely to be fulfilled in practice only partially. The investigator, in making his assessments from the standpoint of some purportedly operating normative system, can be quite detached about whether that system's ideals should be striven for in the circumstances. Indeed, the social scientist should be able to say whether the context is appropriate for the institution and support of a particular normative system. It might well be concluded that in the circumstances the attempt to create a friendship, to sustain a university, or to establish a democracy could only result in a distortion of the ideals these phenomena embody.

These remarks about detachment are made without prejudice to the view that certain ideals may be elements of an objective moral order. Whatever we may think of the appropriateness of friendship or love in a *given* context, we may still conclude that the values inherent in primary relations are of vital importance to man's well-being, and sometimes to his survival. This is only to say that he must find them somewhere, not that they are always appropriate. It may also be argued that no normative system is possible, or at least viable, unless it contains some ideals that all men can recognize as having a general moral validity. This position has much merit, but it is not necessary to the argument I am developing here.

The study of normative systems is one way of bridging the gap between fact and value. At the same time, the objectivity and detachment of the investigator can remain unsullied. The great gain is that we can more readily perceive latent values in the world of fact. This we do when we recognize, for example, that fatherhood, sexuality, leadership, and many other phenomena have a natural potential for "envaluation." Biological parenthood is readily transferred into a relationship guided by ideals. This occurs, not because of arbitrary social convention, but because the satisfactions associated with parenthood—satisfactions which are biologically functional—are not fully realized unless a guiding ideal emerges. The same holds true for the dialectic of sex and satisfaction. On a different plane, but according to the same logic, if leadership is to be effective and satisfying, it must go beyond simple domination to encompass a sense of responsibility.

A great many such systems are normative in the sense that their organization and development are governed by certain master ideals. A familiar and widespread illustration is the governing ideal of rationality in economic and administrative systems. In normative systems, it should be noted, terms like "maintenance" and "survival" are relevant but not adequate. They do not prepare us for observing, when it occurs, the evolutionary development of the system toward increased realization of its implicit ideals.

Sociology has studied normative systems, and even the self-realization of systems, for a long time (as witness the monumental work of Max Weber on the unfolding of rationality in modern institutions), but we have not thought through the implications of this intellectual concern. When we do, it will be a matter of course to recognize that a system may be known precisely by its distinctive competence or excellence, as well as by its special inner strains and vulnerabilities.

I have offered these remarks with malice prepense. They are meant to suggest that sociological inquiry has ample warrant for the study of law as a normative order. And this is the first, indispensable step toward a rapprochement between sociology and natural law.

II. Relativism and Human Nature

A second barrier to the acceptance of natural law among social scientists is the widespread commitment to moral relativism. But whatever else it may or may not be, the natural law philosophy is not relativist. At least, it is committed to the view that universal characteristics of man, and concomitant principles of justice, are discoverable. It does not necessarily hold that such generalizations are *known*, only that they are *knowable*.

No doubt, many older efforts to identify essential traits of human nature, for example, that men are naturally acquisitive or pugnacious, have been discredited. But if older generalizations have been wrong, new and more sophisticated ones may yet be valid.

The findings of modern social science do not refute the view that generalizations about human nature are possible, despite the effects of social environment and the diversity of cultures. Nothing we know today precludes an effort to define "ends proper to man's nature" and to discover objective standards of moral judgment. This does not mean that proper ends and objective standards are knowable apart from scientific inquiry. It does mean that psychic health and well-being are, in principle, amenable to definition; and that the conditions weakening or supporting psychic health can be discovered scientifically. It also means that all such conclusions are subject to revision as our work proceeds.

Whether we are able now to say what human nature consists of, is not important. We are not completely at a loss, but any current formulations would still be very crude. The essential point is that *we must avoid any dogma that blocks inquiry.* Relativism is pernicious when it insists, on woefully inadequate theoretical and empirical grounds, that the study of human nature is a chimera, a foolish fancy. To say we "know" there is no such thing, and that there is no use looking for it, is to abandon the self-corrective method of science. It is also to ignore much evidence regarding the psychic unity of mankind.

III. Positive Law and the Legal Order

Most definitions of law—and they are not really so various as is sometimes suggested—remind us that we are dealing with a normative system and a master ideal, in the sense discussed above. Aquinas is perhaps most explicit, calling law "an ordinance of reason for the common good, made and promulgated by him who has care of the community." But even the efforts of Gray and Holmes to avoid a normative definition surely falter when they emphasize "the rules which the courts, that is, the judicial organs of that body, lay down for the determination of legal rights and duties" or, in the Holmesian formula, "the prophecies of what the courts will do in fact, and nothing more pretentious, are what I mean by the law." For the meaning of "court" or "judicial organ" is plentifully supplied with normative connotations, such as the idea of being duly constituted, independent rather than servile, and offering grounded decisions.

In framing a general concept of law it is indeed difficult to avoid terms that suggest normative standards. This is so because the phenomenon itself is defined by—it does not exist apart from —values to be realized. The name for these values is "legality."

Sometimes this is spoken of as "the rule of law" or, simply, "the legal order." Legality is a complex ideal embracing standards for assessing and criticizing decisions that purport to be legal, whether made by a legislature or a court, whether elaborating a rule or applying it to specific cases.

The essential element in legality, or the rule of law, is the governance of official power by rational principles of civic order. Official action, even at the highest levels of authority, is enmeshed in and restrained by a web of accepted general rules. Where this ideal exists, no power is immune from criticism nor completely free to follow its own bent, however well-intentioned it may be. Legality imposes an objective environment of constraint, of tests to be met, of standards to be observed, and, not less important, of ideals to be fulfilled.

This concept of legality is broad enough, but it is not so broad as the idea of justice. Justice extends beyond the legal order as such. It may have to do with the distribution of wealth, the allocation of responsibility for private harms, the definition of crimes or parental rights. Such issues may be decided politically, and law may be used to implement whatever decision is made. But the decision is not a peculiarly legal one, and many alternative arrangements are possible within the framework of the rule of law. How far government should intervene to direct social and economic life is a question of political prudence, in the light of justice, but how the government behaves if it does exercise broader controls or enter new spheres of life quickly raises questions of legality.

The ideal of legality has to do with the way rules are made and with how they are applied, but for the most part it does not prescribe the content of legal rules and doctrines. The vast majority of rules, including judge-made rules, spell out policy choices, choices not uniquely determined by the requirements of legality. Whether contracts must be supported by consideration; whether a defendant in an accident case should be spared liability because of plaintiff's contributory negligence; whether minors should be relieved of legal consequences that might otherwise apply to their actions—these and a host of other issues treated in the common law are basically matters of general public policy. For practical purposes, and especially because they arise in the course of controversies to be adjudicated, a great many of these policy matters are decided by the courts in the absence of, or as a supplement to, legislative determination. In making these decisions, and in devising substantive rules, the courts are concerned with dimensions of justice that go beyond the ideal of legality. Legality is a part of justice, but only a part. It is indeed the special province of jurists, but it is not their only concern. On the other hand, when they act outside the province where the ideal of legality is at issue, the courts share with other agencies of government the responsibility for doing justice. It is not legality alone which determines what the rule should be or how the case should be decided. That depends also on the nature of the subject matter and on the claims and interests at stake. Whether the outcome is just or unjust depends on more than legality.

However, there are times when the ideal of legality does determine the content of a legal rule or doctrine. This occurs when the purpose of the rules is precisely to implement that ideal, the most obvious illustration being the elaboration of procedural rules of pleading and evidence. In addition, principles of statutory interpretation, including much of constitutional law, directly serve the aim of creating and sustaining the "legal state." Some of these rules are "merely" procedural in the sense that they are arbitrary conveniences, chosen because some device was necessary, for which some other procedure might readily be substituted. Others are vital to just those substantial rights which the ideal of legality is meant to protect. These include all that we term civil rights, the rights of members of a polity to act as full citizens and to be free of oppressive and arbitrary official power. Again, it is not the aim of this ideal to protect the individual against all power, but only against the misuse of power by those whose actions have the color of authority. Of course, in our society we may have to extend our notions of who it is that acts "officially."

Perhaps the most difficult area governed by the ideal of legality is the process of judicial reasoning itself. Fundamentally, of course, this is part of the law of procedure, but it has a special obscurity as well as a special significance. The crucial problem here is to justify *as legal* the exercise of judicial creativity. That there is and must be creativity, whatever the name we give to it, is no longer seriously disputed. The question remains, however, whether there is something beyond the bare authority of the court, or reliance on a vague "sense of justice," to support the idea that judge-made policy has the stamp of legality.

One approach to this problem gives special weight to the legal tradition, to the received body of concepts, principles, doctrines, and rules. By working with these pre-existent legal materials, the law is in some weak sense "discovered," at the same time that creativity is permitted. Using familiar concepts establishes a link with the past and tends to create (though it does not guarantee) a smooth, gradual transition from one accepted policy to another. In this way legal craftsmanship, defined by its familiarity with the limits and potentialities of a certain body of materials and certain modes of decision, can ease social change by extending the mantle of legitimacy. A new policy, if it can be blanketed into contract doctrine or fitted into the law of torts, can have a peculiarly "legal" quality simply because of the ideas with which it is associated. It seems fair to say that this peculiar function of the law is weakening because it has become less attractive to the legal profession. This is so in part because of the modern interest in avoiding arcane language, in making policy objectives explicit, and in criticizing conventional legal categories. One may wonder, however, whether enough attention has been given to the role of legal concepts in defining an implicit delegation of power to the courts. This might be thought of as a working arrangement by which society allows the courts to make policy within areas marked out by the received body of legal ideas. It is assumed that these ideas are bounded, not limitless; that legal reasoning and judicial behavior contain some built-in restraints; and there is no contrary action by a legislature.

Another approach is to emphasize, not the "artificial reason" of the law, but the role of natural reason in the ideal of legality. Among the attributes of legality is a commitment to the search for truth, to consistency of thought, and to logical analysis of evidence as relevant, of classifications as inclusive, of analogies as persuasive. In this sense, there is no special legal reasoning; there is only the universal logic of rational assessment and scientific inquiry. The ideals of science and of legality are not the same, but they do overlap. Judicial conclusions gain in *legal* authority as they are based on good reasoning, including sound knowledge of human personality, human groups, human institutions.

The *meaning* of law includes the ideal of legality. That ideal, even though not yet completely clarified or specified, is the source of critical judgment concerning constituent parts of the legal order, especially particular rules and decisions. When a part of the law fails to meet the standards set by that ideal, it is to that extent wanting in legality. It does not necessarily cease to be law, however. It may be inferior law and yet properly command the respect and obligation of all who are committed to the legal order as a whole. At the same time, a mature legal system will develop ways of spreading the ideals of legality and of expunging offending elements.

The subtlety and scope of legal ideas, and the variety of legal materials, should give pause to any effort to define law within some simple formula. The attempt to find such a formula often leads to a disregard for more elusive parts of the law and excessive attention to specific rules. But even a cursory look at the law will remind us that a great deal more is included than rules. Legal ideas, variously and unclearly labeled "concepts," "doctrines," and "principles," have a vital place in authoritative decision. "Detrimental reliance," "attractive nuisance," "reasonable doubt," "exhaustion of remedies," "agency," and "interstate commerce" are among the many familiar concepts which purport to grasp some truth and provide a foundation for the elaboration of specific rules. In addition, of course, there are even more general ideas or principles stating, e.g., the necessary conditions of "ordered liberty" or that guilt is individual rather than collective. It would be pointless to speak of these as merely a "source" of law; they are too closely woven into the fabric of legal thought and have too direct a role in decision-making.

Variety in law is manifest in other ways, too. We may speak, for example, of variety in function: Law is called upon to organize public enterprises; to establish enforceable moral standards; to mediate differences while maintaining going concerns; to arrange contractual or marital divorces; to make public grants; to investi-

gate; to regulate some private associations, to destroy others. These
and other functions have yet to be adequately classified or systematically studied. It seems obvious that such study is a precondition for formulating a valid theory of law.

There are also well-known qualitative differences in the authority
of legal pronouncements. If opinions are divided; if there is
manifest confusion of concepts, monitored by legal scholarship;
if rules or concepts are based on received tradition alone; if a
particular rule is inconsistent with the general principles of a
particular branch of law—then the authority of opinion or judgment is weakened. If all laws are authoritative, some are more
authoritative than others.

These considerations support Lon Fuller's view that the legal
order has an implicit or internal morality,[2] a morality defined
by distinctive ideals and purposes. To say this, of course, is not to
end inquiry but virtually to begin it. We must learn to distinguish
more sharply between "bad law" that is merely bad public policy
and law that is bad because it violates or incompletely realizes
the ideals of legality. And we must attain a better understanding
of how public purpose affects legal principle, as when we recognize that society binds itself especially tightly in the administration
of criminal justice, generally requiring evidence of intent and
barring retroactive legislation.

If the legal order includes a set of standards, an internal basis
for criticism and reconstruction, then an essential foundation is
laid for a viable theory of justice. In his sympathetic treatment
of the natural law position,[3] Morris Cohen was almost right in
arguing that we must be able to appeal from the law that is to
the law that ought to be, from positive law to principles of justice. But he did not quite see that at least some principles of
justice are ingredients of the ideal of legality and are therefore
part of "the law that is." In many cases, we appeal from specific
rules or concepts in the law to other concepts and to more general
principles that are also part of the law. This is sometimes put as an

[2] Lon L. Fuller, *Positivism and Fidelity to Law—A Reply to Professor
Hart*, 71 HARVARD LAW REVIEW 645 (1958).
[3] MORRIS R. COHEN, REASON AND NATURE 408 (Glencoe, Ill.: The Free
Press, 1953).

appeal from "laws" to "the law,"[4] and there is merit in that approach. But it has the disadvantage of suggesting that "the law" is something disembodied and unspecifiable, when in fact all we mean is that general principles of legality are counterposed to more specific legal materials. Both belong to a normative system whose "existence" embraces principles of criticism and potentialities for evolution.

With this approach in mind, we can give to positive law its proper place and meaning. "Positive law" refers to those public obligations *that have been defined* by duly constituted authorities. This is not the whole of law, and it may be bad law. Law is "positive" when a particular conclusion has been reached by some authorized body—a conclusion expressed as an unambiguous rule or as a judgment duly rendered. This definition differs from the suggestion made by Holmes that law is what the courts *will* do, assuming that he meant to define positive law. I am emphasizing what the courts *have done,* because what they will do may depend on the whole body of legal materials.

Positive law is the product of legal problem solving. The legal order has the job of producing positive law as society's best effort to regulate conduct and settle disputes. What is done may be only imperfectly guided by legal principles, perhaps because those principles themselves are inadequate, but it remains law for the time being. As such, it has a claim on obedience. Positive law invokes a suspension of personal preference and judgment with regard to the *specific issue.* To suspend judgment, of course, is not necessarily to fail to have a judgment, but someone else's judgment is taken as an authoritative guide to behavior. Suspension in this sense is rightfully invoked because obedience to positive law is essential to the survival and integrity of the system as a whole. For the system to function, it is necessary that only specially appointed individuals may disregard a positive law, by changing or reinterpreting it, or by modifying its effect in a particular case when other rules can be brought to bear.

Obedience to positive law, irrespective of private judgment, is

4 See ROSCOE POUND, 2 JURISPRUDENCE 106 (St. Paul: West Publishing Co., 1959). Note also his comment at 107: "Law in the sense we are considering is made up of precepts, technique, and ideals: A body of *authoritative* precepts, developed and applied by an *authoritative* technique in the light or on the background of *authoritative* traditional ideals." (Emphasis supplied)

not an abandonment of reason. On the contrary, as has been well understood for a long time, it is a natural outcome of reasoned assent to the system as a whole. It in no way precludes criticism or testing of positive law, including the assertion that it is void and without effect. But criticism, testing, and change proceed within the broader framework of the legal order, appealing to its own ideals and purposes when they are relevant. Of special importance is the duty of legal officers, including private counsel, to respond critically to the positive law.

Plainly, positive law includes an arbitrary element. For him who must obey it, it is to some extent brute fact and brute command. But this arbitrary element, while necessary and inevitable, is repugnant to the ideal of legality. Therefore the proper aim of the legal order, and the special contribution of legal scholarship, is *progressively to reduce the degree of arbitrariness in the positive law*. This rule is comparable to that in science where the aim is to reduce the degree of empiricism, that is, the number of theoretically ungrounded factual generalizations within the corpus of scientific knowledge.

If reducing the degree of arbitrariness is accepted as the central task of jurisprudence, a long step is taken toward natural law philosophy. For whatever its variations, or its special errors, the concept of natural law has survived, and flourished periodically, precisely because of the need to minimize the role of arbitrary will in the legal order. The basic aim of this philosophy is to ground law in reason. The question then is, What shall we understand as the meaning of "reason"? I shall take it to mean what John Dewey meant by "intelligence" and, following his basic teachings, suggest that scientific inquiry, including inquiry about proper ends and values, is the road to a science of justice or natural law.

One response to the difficulty of discovering general truths about man and society is to emphasize the "flexibility" or "variable content" of natural law. (This may also be a defensive reaction to the criticism of natural law philosophy as absolutist and dogmatic.) There is an important insight here, but it must be placed in proper perspective. It is true that natural law *presumes changing legal norms*, but this does not require abandoning the quest for universals or the assertion of them when they are warranted. A grasp of this point is essential if the relation between sociology and natural law is to be rightly understood.

Why does natural law presume changing norms? The reason is that its basic commitment is to a governing ideal, not to a specific set of injunctions. This ideal is to be realized in history and not outside of it. But history makes its own demands. Even when we know the meaning of legality we must still work out the relation between general principles and the changing structure of society. New circumstances do not necessarily alter principles, but they may and do require that new rules of law be formulated and old ones changed.

In a system governed by a master ideal, many specific norms, for a time part of that system, may be expendable. The test is whether they contribute to the realization of the ideal. Many norms evolve or are devised to take account of quite specific circumstances; and when those circumstances change, the norm may lose its value for the system. Thus the governing ideal of the system may be administrative rationality, but specific norms will vary depending on the purpose of the enterprise and upon its stage of development. For example, the norm of decentralization does not always serve the end of administrative rationality. Yet that end continues to have a vital influence on the selection of appropriate norms.

There are two valid interpretations of the idea that natural law has a changing content. (1) As inquiry proceeds, it is always possible that basic premises about legality, including underlying assumptions regarding human nature and social life, will be revised. (2) As society changes, new rules and doctrines are needed in order to give effect to natural law principles by adapting them to new demands, new circumstances, new opportunities. These perspectives demand that we detach natural law from illusions of eternal stability. They also require us to reject the notion that natural law must be a directly applicable code or it is nothing. A set of principles is not a code, any more than the principle of the conservation of energy is a specific physical theory. Natural law provides the authoritative materials for devising codes and for criticizing them, in precisely the same way as constitutional principles affect legislation and judge-made rules.

Comment

ALF ROSS

A Critique of the Philosophy
of Natural Law

*Alf Ross is a professor of law at the University of Copen-
hagen. In the following selection he appears in a critical
guise; his own position is presented elsewhere in this book
(pp. 134–143).*

౾

Epistemological Points of View

A searching criticism of the philosophy of natural law would lead
into depths far beyond the limits of a general theory of law.[1] But
perhaps a glance at the history of natural law will be more helpful
than epistemological argumentation to see the arbitrariness and
emptiness of metaphysical speculation. Strictly speaking, metaphysical assertions do not admit of being disproved, precisely be-

Reprinted by permission of the author and publisher from Alf Ross, *On Law
and Justice* (London: Stevens and Sons, Ltd., 1958), pp. 258–63. Abridged by
the editor.

[1] In my *Kritik der sogenannten praktischen Erkenntnis* (1933), I attempted
to show that the very conception of a practical cognition (*i.e.*, such as is
postulated in current moral and legal philosophy) contains a logical contradiction which is again reflected in the two categories in which practical cognition
appears, namely, the idea of the good and the idea of duty. The philosophy
of natural law is predominantly conceived in the category of the good.

cause they disport themselves in a sphere beyond the reach of verification. One learns simply to by-pass them as something that has no rightful place or function in scientific thought. Has anyone ever proved that it is not Zeus or the fate goddesses who ordain the path of the sun? All that we can say is that modern astronomy manages without this assumption. Similarly the most effective way to vanquish metaphysics in law is simply to create a scientific theory of law whose self-sufficiency will push metaphysical speculations into oblivion along with other myths and legends of the childhood of civilisation.

The history of natural law reveals two striking points: the arbitrariness of the fundamental postulates concerning the nature of existence and of man; and the arbitrariness of the moral-legal ideas that are evolved on this basis. Natural law seeks the absolute, the eternal, that shall make of law something more than the handiwork of human beings and exempt the legislator from the pains and responsibility of decision. The source of the transcendent validity of law has been sought in a magical law of fate, in the will of God, or in the insight of absolute reason. But experience shows that the doctrines men have built on these sources, far from being eternal and immutable, have changed according to time, place and person. The noble guise of natural law has been used in the course of time to defend or fight for every conceivable kind of demand, obviously arising from a specific situation in life or determined by economic and political class interests, the cultural traditions of the era, its prejudices and aspirations—in short, all that goes to make what is generally called an ideology.

Is it nature's bidding that men shall be as brothers, or is it nature's law that the strong shall rule over the weak, and that therefore slavery and class distinctions are part of God's meaning for the world? Both propositions have been asserted with the same support and the same "right"; for how should anyone be able to make a choice between these absolutes except by an absolute assertion elevated above all rational argumentation: It is so, because I know that it is so! The ideology of equality was preached by the Sophists in the fifth century B.C. and by Rousseau in the eighteenth century, by both as the expression of the political aspirations of a class; likewise by the Stoics and Christians, but there against a background of religion without political intent. Plato, on the other hand, postulated the innate inequality of men, and advocated slavery and a community strictly divided into classes. Aristotle followed him with regard to the natural justification of slavery, and since then the postulate concerning the natural inequality of men has been the point of departure for many conservative doctrines of natural law and organic or totalitarian theories of government.

Carl Ludwig von Haller, a Swiss teacher of constitutional law at the beginning of the nineteenth century, maintains it is the law of nature that the strong shall rule over the weak, the husband over the wife, the father over the child, the leader over his men and the teacher over his pupils.[2] In the same way Thomas Dew, the American political theorist, declared that "it is ordained by nature and by God that the being who has the greatest abilities and learning and therefore the greater power shall rule and dispose over him who is inferior." On this basis he upheld the institution of slavery in the Southern States, and others went so far as to maintain that slavery assures the natural rights of the slaves. Liberty in its true sense is not licence. "For this reason slavery secures them in their natural rights and endows them with real liberty to the extent to which they are capable of receiving it. Were the institution of slavery to be abolished they would no longer enjoy their natural rights."

In the political field it is well known how natural law combined with the doctrine of the contract of government has been used happily to justify every kind of government from absolute power (Hobbes) to absolute democracy (Rousseau). Natural law has also similarly lent itself equally to those who wished to consolidate the existing order (Heraclitus, Aristotle, Thomas Aquinas, and others) and to those who wished to advocate revolution (Rousseau).

In the social and economic fields the natural law of the eighteenth century advocated an extreme individualism and liberalism. The inviolability of private ownership and the unfettered freedom of contract were the two dogmas which the nineteenth century inherited from natural law, and which were asserted in the practice of the American courts to obtain the reversal of a number of laws in the sphere of social welfare. As recently as

2 *Restauration der Staatswissenschaft* (1816).

1922 the United States Supreme Court (in the *Adkin's* case[3]) reversed the validity of a law concerning minimum wages for women in the District of Columbia on the grounds that this law— which had been enacted in order to assure the worst-paid women a degree of acceptable minimum subsistence and free them from the necessity of semi-prostitution—was an infringement of the natural right of these women to make contracts freely. On the other hand, natural law has also been used to provide a basis for a morality of solidarity (Grotius, Comte and other "sociologists") and, even, in Duguit's interpretation, in support of the denial of all individual rights to make way for a system of social services.

The chapter on family law always makes amusing reading in the systems of natural law, because it so clearly reflects the moral prejudices of the age. For Thomas Aquinas the indissolubility of marriage ("thou shalt not commit adultery") was of course an evident truth of reason. The ludicrous dryness of rationalism is reflected in Kant's definition of marriage as a contract between two persons of different sexes for the lifelong mutual possession of their sexual capacities; sexual intercourse is only permitted in wedlock; if one of the marriage partners gives himself or herself into another's possession, the other marriage partner is invariably entitled to "recover" the runaway, like a material object, into his possession.[4]

It would be easy to go on, but let me close by recalling St. Paul's Epistle to the Corinthians: "Judge it yourselves: is it comely that a woman pray unto God uncovered? Doth not even nature itself teach you, that, if a man have long hair, it is a shame unto him? But if a woman have long hair it is a glory to her: for her hair is given to her for a covering."[5]

Like a harlot, natural law is at the disposal of everyone. The ideology does not exist that cannot be defended by an appeal to the law of nature. And, indeed, how can it be otherwise, since the ultimate basis for every natural right lies in a private direct insight, an evident contemplation, an intuition. Cannot my intuition be just as good as yours? Evidence as a criterion of truth

[3] (1922) 261 U.S. 525.
[4] Immanuel Kant, *Metaphysische Anfangsgründe der Rechtslehre*, § 25.
[5] I. Corinthians, Chap. 11, 13–15.

explains the utterly arbitrary character of the metaphysical assertions. It raises them up above any force of inter-subjective control
and opens the door wide to unrestricted invention and dogmatics.

The historical variability of natural law supports the interpretation that metaphysical postulates are merely constructions to buttress emotional attitudes and the fulfilment of certain needs. It
must, however, be admitted that the variability is not a decisive
proof for this interpretation. It can be argued that scientific
theories also change, and (with Thomas Aquinas) that reason can
be led astray by passions, and that not all that appears as evident
is necessarily true evidence. This, however, raises the difficult problem of what is the criterion of true evidence, a problem that can
only be solved by recourse to evidence in the power, and so on
continuing *ad infinitum.*

A strong argument supporting the view that natural-law doctrines are arbitrary and subjective constructions is that evidence
cannot be a criterion of truth. What we mean by calling a proposition true is obviously different from the psychological fact that
the assertion of the proposition is accompanied by a feeling of
certainty. The assumption that evidence guarantees the truth of a
proposition cannot therefore be true analytically, that is, as a
definition of what truth means. The assumption must be taken
synthetically, that is, as asserting that the feeling of evidence always occurs together with such a state of affairs which makes the
proposition true. But what is the proof that these two phenomena
always should go together? There is none. A feeling of evidence,
to be sure, accompanies many true assertions, but there is no reason why the same feeling could not attach also to errors and
fallacies. The firm belief in the truth of a proposition always needs
justification and can never be its own justification.

The historic variability is not in itself decisive. The argument
adduced applies independently of it. Even if we all admitted
the same interpretation of the law of nature, indeed even if these
ideas should obtrude themselves upon us with the automatism of
a law of nature, the criticism would still remain unmoved. If under
the influence of poison all mankind should see visions, these
fantasies would still not be true, as long as by truth we mean
something other than psychological coercion.

Psychological Points of View

Psychological considerations supplement the epistemological criticism. The picture becomes clearer if we understand not only that moral-metaphysical speculations are empty and meaningless, but also the reasons why men persist in them.

The driving force of metaphysics in the field of morals and religion is the fear of the vicissitudes of life, the transitoriness of all things; the inexorability of death; or, conversely, the desire for the absolute, the eternally immutable which defies the law of corruption. This fear, in moral matters, is associated with the fear of having to make choices and decisions under changing circumstances and on one's own responsibility. Therefore, by seeking justification for our actions in immutable principles outside ourselves, we try to relieve ourselves of the burden of responsibility. If there is a law, independent of our own choices and pleasure, given to us as an eternal truth based in the will of God or an *a priori* insight of reason, and dictating to us the "right" course of action, then we ourselves, obeying this universal law, are but obedient parts of a cosmic order and relieved from all responsibility.

The desire for the absolute that bestows freedom from responsibility and brings peace that passeth all understanding has in the moral life of man the best conditions for developing into metaphysical beliefs, hardly to be broken down by critical thinking. The reason for this is the peculiar psychological mechanism from which the moral consciousness (the conscience) emanates presenting itself in a set of apparently blindly imperative impulses. Since these impulses make themselves felt independently of our conscious needs and desires, they are well suited to force upon us the illusionary view that in our conscience speaks a voice or a law telling us about "validity" or "rightness" radically different from, and independent of, our physical nature, its instincts, and desires. From there the way lies open to all sorts of metaphysical constructions of the nature of moral validity and the content of the moral law.

But just as an illusion of the senses is dispelled when I observe the object of it more clearly, so the *fata morgana* of the moral consciousness vanishes before a more intense psychological observation. A fuller account of the psychological mechanism which gives rise to the moral consciousness is outside the scope of this book.[6] Here it can merely be said that the moral consciousness with its mystical pathos is like manna from Heaven to the metaphysically hungry; and that it is not after all so mystical that it is not amenable to scientific explanation on a psychological basis.

What has been said here about morality and the moral consciousness similarly applies to law and legal consciousness. The law, too, is experienced as validly "binding," that is, something which I obey, not merely because of fear of the external compulsion (the sanction), but also because of respect for the inner authority (validity) of the law. The legal consciousness therefore, just like the moral consciousness, gives rise to superempirical interpretations. Natural law and moral philosophy are closely connected, whether natural law is thought of as a part of morality, or as an independent province, co-ordinate with morality, of ethics.

---

[6] For a fuller account see Alf Ross, *Kritik der sogenannten praktischen Erkenntnis* (1933), Chaps. III, 8, VII, 1, and XIII, 1.

PART II

LEGAL POSITIVISM

Austin and His Critics

JOHN AUSTIN

Law as the Sovereign's Command

The legal philosophy of John Austin (1790–1859) has had a profound effect in the English-speaking world. Austin's thought was influenced by Thomas Hobbes and Jeremy Bentham, and Austin himself occupies an important place in the history of English utilitarianism. The following selection is taken from Lectures I, V, and VI of The Province of Jurisprudence Determined, *first published in 1832, and has been abridged by the editor.*

Lecture I

The matter of jurisprudence is positive law: law, simply and strictly so called: or law set by political superiors to political inferiors. But positive law (or law, simply and strictly so called) is often confounded with objects to which it is related by *resemblance*, and with objects to which it is related in the way of *analogy*: with objects which are *also* signified, *properly* and *improperly*, by the large and vague expression *law*. To obviate the difficulties springing from that confusion, I begin my projected Course with determining the province of jurisprudence, or with distinguishing the matter of jurisprudence from those various related objects: trying to define the subject of which I intend to treat, before I endeavour to analyse its numerous and complicated parts.

A law, in the most general and comprehensive acceptation in which the term, in its literal meaning, is employed, may be said

to be a rule laid down for the guidance of an intelligent being
by an intelligent being having power over him. Under this definition are concluded, and without impropriety, several species. It
is necessary to define accurately the line of demarcation which
separates these species from one another, as much mistiness and
intricacy has been infused into the science of jurisprudence by
their being confounded or not clearly distinguished. In the comprehensive sense above indicated, or in the largest meaning which
it has, without extension by metaphor or analogy, the term *law*
embraces the following objects:—Laws set by God to his human
creatures, and laws set by men to men.

The whole or a portion of the laws set by God to men is frequently styled the law of nature, or natural law: being, in truth,
the only natural law of which it is possible to speak without a
metaphor, or without a blending of objects which ought to be
distinguished broadly. But, rejecting the appellation Law of
Nature as ambiguous and misleading, I name those laws or rules,
as considered collectively or in a mass, the *Divine law*, or the
law of God.

Laws set by men to men are of two leading or principal classes:
classes which are often blended, although they differ extremely;
and which, for that reason, should be severed precisely, and opposed distinctly and conspicuously.

Of the laws or rules set by men to men, some are established
by *political* superiors, sovereign and subject: by persons exercising
supreme and subordinate *government*, in independent nations, or
independent political societies. The aggregate of the rules thus
established, or some aggregate forming a portion of that aggregate,
is the appropriate matter of jurisprudence, general or particular.
To the aggregate of the rules thus established, or to some aggregate forming a portion of that aggregate, the term *law*, as used
simply and strictly, is exclusively applied. But, as contradistinguished to *natural* law, or to the law of *nature* (meaning, by
those expressions, the law of God), the aggregate of the rules,
established by political superiors, is frequently styled *positive* law,
or law existing *by position*. As contradistinguished to the rules
which I style *positive morality*, and on which I shall touch immediately, the aggregate of the rules, established by political superiors, may also be marked commodiously with the name of

positive law. For the sake, then, of getting a name brief and distinctive at once, and agreeably to frequent usage, I style that aggregate of rules, or any portion of that aggregate, *positive law:* though rules, which are *not* established by political superiors, are also *positive,* or exist *by position,* if they be rules or laws, in the proper signification of the term.

Though *some* of the laws or rules, which are set by men to men, are established by political superiors, *others* are *not* established by political superiors, or are *not* established by political superiors, in that capacity or character.

Closely analogous to human laws of this second class, are a set of objects frequently but *improperly* termed *laws,* being rules set and enforced by *mere opinion,* that is, by the opinions or sentiments held or felt by an indeterminate body of men in regard to human conduct. Instances of such a use of the term *law* are the expressions—"The law of honour;" "The law set by fashion;" and rules of this species constitute much of what is usually termed "International law."

The aggregate of human laws properly so called belonging to the second of the classes above mentioned, with the aggregate of objects *improperly* but by *close analogy* termed laws, I place together in a common class, and denote them by the term *positive morality.* The name *morality* severs them from *positive law,* while the epithet *positive* disjoins them from the *law of God.* And to the end of obviating confusion, it is necessary or expedient that they *should* be disjoined from the latter by that distinguishing epithet. For the name *morality* (or *morals*), when standing unqualified or alone, denotes indifferently either of the following objects: namely, positive morality *as it is,* or without regard to its merits; and positive morality *as it would be,* if it conformed to the law of God, and were, therefore, deserving of *approbation.*

Besides the various sorts of rules which are included in the literal acceptation of the term law, and those which are by a close and striking analogy, though improperly, termed laws, there are numerous applications of the term law, which rest upon a slender analogy and are merely metaphorical or figurative. Such is the case when we talk of *laws* observed by the lower animals; of *laws* regulating the growth or decay of vegetables; of *laws* determining the movements of inanimate bodies or masses. For where *intelligence* is not, or where it is too bounded to take the name of *reason*, and, therefore, is too bounded to conceive the purpose of a law, there is not the *will* which law can work on, or which duty can incite or restrain. Yet through these misapplications of a *name*, flagrant as the metaphor is, has the field of jurisprudence and morals been deluged with muddy speculation.

Having suggested the *purpose* of my attempt to determine the province of jurisprudence: to distinguish positive law, the appropriate matter of jurisprudence, from the various objects to which it is related by resemblance, and to which it is related, nearly or remotely, by a strong or slender analogy: I shall now state the essentials of *a law* or *rule* (taken with the largest signification which can be given to the term *properly*).

Every *law* or *rule* (taken with the largest signification which can be given to the term *properly*) is a *command*. Or, rather, laws or rules, properly so called, are a *species* of commands.

Now, since the term *command* comprises the term *law*, the first is the simpler as well as the larger of the two. But, simple as it is, it admits of explanation. And, since it is the *key* to the sciences of jurisprudence and morals, its meaning should be analysed with precision.

If you express or intimate a wish that I shall do or forbear from some act, and if you will visit me with an evil in case I comply not with your wish, the *expression* or *intimation* of your wish is a *command*. A command is distinguished from other significations of desire, not by the style in which the desire is signified, but by the power and the purpose of the party commanding to inflict an evil or pain in case the desire be disregarded. If you cannot or will not harm me in case I comply not with your wish, the expression of your wish is not a command, although you utter your wish in imperative phrase. If you are able and willing to harm me in case I comply not with your wish, the expression of your wish amounts to a command, although you are prompted by a spirit of courtesy to utter it in the shape of a request. "*Preces erant, sed quibus contradici non posset.*"* Such is the language of Tacitus, when speaking of a petition by the soldiery to a son and lieutenant of Vespasian.

* [They were requests, but they could not be refused.]

A command, then, is a signification of desire. But a command is distinguished from other significations of desire by this peculiarity: that the party to whom it is directed is liable to evil from the other, in case he comply not with the desire.

Being liable to evil from you if I comply not with a wish which you signify, I am *bound* or *obliged* by your command, or I lie under a *duty* to obey it. If, in spite of that evil in prospect, I comply not with the wish which you signify, I am said to disobey your command, or to violate the duty which it imposes.

Command and duty are, therefore, correlative terms: the meaning denoted by each being implied or supposed by the other. Or (changing the expression) wherever a duty lies, a command has been signified; and whenever a command is signified, a duty is imposed.

Concisely expressed, the meaning of the correlative expressions is this. He who will inflict an evil in case his desire be disregarded, utters a command by expressing or intimating his desire: He who is liable to the evil in case he disregard the desire, is bound or obliged by the command.

The evil which will probably be incurred in case a command be disobeyed or (to use an equivalent expression) in case a duty be broken, is frequently called a *sanction*, or an *enforcement of obedience*. Or (varying the phrase) the command or the duty is said to be *sanctioned* or *enforced* by the chance of incurring the evil.

Considered as thus abstracted from the command and the duty which it enforces, the evil to be incurred by disobedience is frequently styled a *punishment*. But, as punishments, strictly so called, are only a *class* of sanctions, the term is too narrow to express the meaning adequately.

I observe that Dr. Paley, in his analysis of the term *obligation*, lays much stress upon the *violence* of the motive to compliance. In so far as I can gather a meaning from his loose and inconsistent statement, his meaning appears to be this: that unless the motive to compliance be *violent* or *intense*, the expression or intimation of a wish is not a *command*, nor does the party to whom it is directed lie under a *duty* to regard it.

If he means, by a *violent* motive, a motive operating with certainty, his proposition is manifestly false. The greater the evil to be incurred in case the wish be disregarded, and the greater the chance of incurring it on that same event, the greater, no doubt, is the *chance* that the wish will *not* be disregarded. But no conceivable motive will *certainly* determine to compliance, or no conceivable motive will render obedience inevitable. If Paley's proposition be true, in the sense which I have now ascribed to it, commands and duties are simply impossible. Or, reducing his proposition to absurdity by a consequence as manifestly false, commands and duties are possible, but are never disobeyed or broken.

If he means by a *violent* motive, an evil which inspires fear, his meaning is simply this: that the party bound by a command is bound by the prospect of an evil. For that which is not feared is not apprehended as an evil: or (changing the shape of the expression) is not an evil in prospect.

The truth is, that the magnitude of the eventual evil, and the magnitude of the chance of incurring it, are foreign to the matter in question. The greater the eventual evil, and the greater the chance of incurring it, the greater is the efficacy of the command, and the greater is the strength of the obligation: Or (substituting expressions exactly equivalent), the greater is the *chance* that the command will be obeyed, and that the duty will not be broken. But where there is the smallest chance of incurring the smallest evil, the expression of a wish amounts to a command, and, therefore, imposes a duty. The sanction, if you will, is feeble or insufficient; but still there *is* a sanction, and, therefore, a duty and a command.

By some celebrated writers (by Locke, Bentham, and, I think, Paley), the term *sanction*, or *enforcement of obedience*, is applied to conditional good as well as to conditional evil: to reward as well as to punishment. But, with all my habitual veneration for the names of Locke and Bentham, I think that this extension of the term is pregnant with confusion and perplexity.

Rewards are, indisputably, *motives* to comply with the wishes of others. But to talk of commands and duties as *sanctioned* or *enforced* by rewards, or to talk of rewards as *obliging* or *constraining* to obedience, is surely a wide departure from the established meaning of the terms.

If *you* expressed a desire that *I* should render a service, and if you proffered a reward as the motive or inducement to render it, *you* would scarcely be said to *command* the service, nor should I, in ordinary language, be *obliged* to render it. In ordinary language, *you* would *promise* me a reward, on condition of my rendering the service, whilst I might be *incited* or *persuaded* to render it by the hope of obtaining the reward.

It appears, then, from what has been premised, that the ideas or notions comprehended by the term *command* are the following. 1. A wish or desire conceived by a rational being, that another rational being shall do or forbear. 2. An evil to proceed from the former, and to be incurred by the latter, in case the latter comply not with the wish. 3. An expression or intimation of the wish by words or other signs.

It also appears from what has been premised, that *command*, *duty*, and *sanction* are inseparably connected terms: that each embraces the same ideas as the others, though each denotes those ideas in a peculiar order or series.

Commands are of two species. Some are *laws* or *rules*. The others have not acquired an appropriate name, nor does language afford an expression which will mark them briefly and precisely. I must, therefore, note them as well as I can by the ambiguous and inexpressive name of "*occasional* or *particular* commands."

The term *laws* or *rules* being not unfrequently applied to occasional or particular commands, it is hardly possible to describe a line of separation which shall consist in every respect with established forms of speech. But the distinction between laws and particular commands may, I think, be stated in the following manner.

By every command, the party to whom it is directed is obliged to do or to forbear.

Now where it obliges *generally* to acts or forbearances of a *class*, a command is a law or rule. But where it obliges to a *specific* act or forbearance, or to acts or forbearances which it determines *specifically* or *individually*, a command is occasional or particular. In other words, a class or description of acts is determined by a law or rule, and acts of that class or description are enjoined or forbidden generally. But where a command is occasional or particular, the act or acts, which the command enjoins or forbids, are assigned or determined by their specific or individual natures as well as by the class or description to which they belong.

The statement which I have given in abstract expressions I will now endeavour to illustrate by apt examples.

If you command your servant to go on a given errand, or *not* to leave your house on a given evening, or to rise at such an hour on such a morning, or to rise at that hour during the next week or month, the command is occasional or particular. For the act or acts enjoined or forbidden are specially determined or assigned.

But if you command him *simply* to rise at that hour, or to rise at that hour *always*, or to rise at that hour *till further orders*, it may be said, with propriety, that you lay down a *rule* for the guidance of your servant's conduct. For no specific act is assigned by the command, but the command obliges him generally to acts of a determined class.

If a regiment be ordered to attack or defend a post, or to quell a riot, or to march from their present quarters, the command is occasional or particular. But an order to exercise daily till further orders shall be given would be called a *general* order, and *might* be called a *rule*.

If Parliament prohibited simply the exportation of corn, either for a given period or indefinitely, it would establish a law or rule: a *kind* or *sort* of acts being determined by the command, and acts of that kind or sort being *generally* forbidden. But an order issued by Parliament to meet an impending scarcity, and stopping the exportation of corn *then shipped and in port*, would not be a law or rule, though issued by the sovereign legislature. The order regarding exclusively a specified quantity of corn, the negative acts or forbearances, enjoined by the command, would be determined specifically or individually by the determinate nature of their subject.

As issued by a sovereign legislature, and as wearing the form of a law, the order which I have now imagined would probably be *called* a law. And hence the difficulty of drawing a distinct boundary between laws and occasional commands.

To conclude with an example which best illustrates the distinction, and which shows the importance of the distinction most conspicuously, *judicial commands* are commonly occasional or particular, although the commands which they are calculated to enforce are commonly laws or rules.

For instance, the lawgiver commands that thieves shall be

hanged. A specific theft and a specified thief being given, the judge commands that the thief shall be hanged, agreeably to the command of the lawgiver.

Now the lawgiver determines a class or description of acts; prohibits acts of the class generally and indefinitely; and commands, with the like generality, that punishment shall follow transgression. The command of the lawgiver is, therefore, a law or rule. But the command of the judge is occasional or particular. For he orders a specific punishment, as the consequence of a specific offence.

It appears, from what has been premised, that a law, properly so called, may be defined in the following manner.

A law is a command which obliges a person or persons.

But, as contradistinguished or opposed to an occasional or particular command, a law is a command which obliges a person or persons, and obliges *generally* to acts or forbearances of a *class*.

In language more popular but less distinct and precise, a law is a command which obliges a person or persons to a *course* of conduct.

Laws and other commands are said to proceed from *superiors*, and to bind or oblige *inferiors*. I will, therefore, analyse the meaning of those correlative expressions; and will try to strip them of a certain mystery, by which that simple meaning appears to be obscured.

Superiority is often synonymous with *precedence* or *excellence*. We talk of superiors in rank; of superiors in wealth; of superiors in virtue: comparing certain persons with certain other persons; and meaning that the former precede or excel the latter in rank, in wealth, or in virtue.

But, taken with the meaning wherein I here understand it, the term *superiority* signifies *might*: the power of affecting others with evil or pain, and of forcing them, through fear of that evil, to fashion their conduct to one's wishes.

For example, God is emphatically the *superior* of Man. For his power of affecting us with pain, and of forcing us to comply with his will, is unbounded and resistless.

To a limited extent, the sovereign One or Number is the superior of the subject or citizen: the master, of the slave or servant: the father, of the child.

In short, whoever can *oblige* another to comply with his wishes, is the *superior* of that other, so far as the ability reaches: The party who is obnoxious to the impending evil, being, to that same extent, the *inferior*.

The might or superiority of God, is simple or absolute. But in all or most cases of human superiority, the relation of superior and inferior, and the relation of inferior and superior, are reciprocal. Or (changing the expression) the party who is the superior as viewed from one aspect, is the inferior as viewed from another.

For example, To an indefinite, though limited extent, the monarch is the superior of the governed: his power being commonly sufficient to enforce compliance with his will. But the governed, collectively or in mass, are also the superior of the monarch: who is checked in the abuse of his might by his fear of exciting their anger; and of rousing to active resistance the might which slumbers in the multitude.

A member of a sovereign assembly is the superior of the judge: the judge being bound by the law which proceeds from that sovereign body. But, in his character of citizen or subject, he is the inferior of the judge: the judge being the minister of the law, and armed with the power of enforcing it.

It appears, then, that the term *superiority* (like the terms *duty* and *sanction*) is implied by the term *command*. For superiority is the power of enforcing compliance with a wish: and the expression or intimation of a wish, with the power and the purpose of enforcing it, are the constituent elements of a command.

"That *laws* emanate from *superiors*" is, therefore, an identical proposition. For the meaning which it affects to impart is contained in its subject.

If I mark the peculiar source of a given law, or if I mark the peculiar source of laws of a given class, it is possible that I am saying something which may instruct the hearer. But to affirm of laws universally "that they flow from *superiors*," or to affirm of laws universally "that *inferiors* are bound to obey them," is the merest tautology and trifling.

According to an opinion which I must notice *incidentally* here, though the subject to which it relates will be treated *directly* hereafter, *customary laws* must be excepted from the proposition "that laws are a species of commands."

By many of the admirers of customary laws (and, especially, of their German admirers), they are thought to oblige legally (independently of the sovereign or state), *because* the citizens or subjects have observed or kept them. Agreeably to this opinion, they are not the *creatures* of the sovereign or state, although the sovereign or state may abolish them at pleasure. Agreeably to this opinion, they are positive law (or law, strictly so called), inasmuch as they are enforced by the courts of justice: But, that notwithstanding, they exist *as positive law* by the spontaneous adoption of the governed, and not by position or establishment on the part of political superiors. Consequently, customary laws, considered as positive law, are not commands. And, consequently, customary laws, considered as positive law, are not laws or rules properly so called.

An opinion less mysterious, but somewhat allied to this, is not uncommonly held by the adverse party: by the party which is strongly opposed to customary law; and to all law made judicially, or in the way of judicial legislation. According to the latter opinion, all judge-made law, or all judge-made law established by *subject* judges, is purely the creature of the judges by whom it is established immediately. To impute it to the sovereign legislature, or to suppose that it speaks the will of the sovereign legislature, is one of the foolish or knavish *fictions* with which lawyers, in every age and nation, have perplexed and darkened the simplest and clearest truths.

I think it will appear, on a moment's reflection, that each of these opinions is groundless: that customary law is *imperative*, in the proper signification of the term; and that all judge-made law is the creature of the sovereign or state.

At its origin, a custom is a rule of conduct which the governed observe spontaneously, or not in pursuance of a law set by a political superior. The custom is transmuted into positive law, when it is adopted as such by the courts of justice, and when the judicial decisions fashioned upon it are enforced by the power of the state. But before it is adopted by the courts, and clothed with the legal sanction, it is merely a rule of positive morality: a rule generally observed by the citizens or subjects; but deriving the only force, which it can be said to possess, from the general disapprobation falling on those who transgress it.

Now when judges transmute a custom into a legal rule (or make a legal rule not suggested by a custom), the legal rule which they establish is established by the sovereign legislature. A subordinate or subject judge is merely a minister. The portion of the sovereign power which lies at his disposition is merely delegated. The rules which he makes derive their legal force from authority given by the state: an authority which the state may confer expressly, but which it commonly imparts in the way of acquiescence. For, since the state may reverse the rules which he makes, and yet permits him to enforce them by the power of the political community, its sovereign will "that his rules shall obtain as law" is clearly evinced by its conduct, though not by its express declaration.

The admirers of customary law love to trick out their idol with mysterious and imposing attributes. But to those who can see the difference between positive law and morality, there is nothing of mystery about it. Considered as rules of positive morality, customary laws arise from the consent of the governed, and not from the position or establishment of political superiors. But, considered as moral rules turned into positive laws, customary laws are established by the state: established by the state directly, when the customs are promulged in its statutes; established by the state circuitously, when the customs are adopted by its tribunals.

The opinion of the party which abhors judge-made laws, springs from their inadequate conception of the nature of commands.

Like other significations of desire, a command is express or tacit. If the desire be signified by *words* (written or spoken), the command is express. If the desire be signified by conduct (or by any signs of desire which are *not* words), the command is tacit.

Now when customs are turned into legal rules by decisions of subject judges, the legal rules which emerge from the customs are *tacit* commands of the sovereign legislature. The state, which is able to abolish, permits its ministers to enforce them: and it, therefore, signifies its pleasure, by that its voluntary acquiescence, "that they shall serve as a law to the governed."

My present purpose is merely this: to prove that the positive law styled *customary* (and all positive law made judicially) is established by the state directly or circuitously, and, therefore, is *imperative.* I am far from disputing, that law made judicially (or in the way of improper legislation) and law made by statute (or in the properly legislative manner) are distinguished by weighty differences. I shall inquire, in future lectures, what those differences are; and why subject judges, who are properly ministers of the law, have commonly shared with the sovereign in the business of making it.

I assume, then, that the only laws which are not imperative, and which belong to the subject-matter of jurisprudence, are the following:—1. Declaratory laws, or laws explaining the import of existing positive law. 2. Laws abrogating or repealing existing positive law. 3. Imperfect laws, or laws of imperfect obligation (with the sense wherein the expression is used by the Roman jurists).

But the space occupied in the science by these improper laws is comparatively narrow and insignificant. Accordingly, although I shall take them into account so often as I refer to them directly, I shall throw them out of account on other occasions. Or (changing the expression) I shall limit the term *law* to laws which are imperative, unless I extend it expressly to laws which are not.

Lecture V

Positive laws, or laws strictly so called, are established directly or immediately by authors of three kinds:—by monarchs, or sovereign bodies, as supreme political superiors: by men in a state of subjection, as subordinate political superiors: by subjects, as private persons, in pursuance of legal rights. But every positive law, or every law strictly so called, is a direct or circuitous command of a monarch or sovereign number in the character of political superior: that is to say, a direct or circuitous command of a monarch or sovereign number to a person or persons in a state of subjection to its author. And being a *command* (and therefore flowing from a *determinate* source), every positive law is a law proper, or a law properly so called.

Besides the human laws which I style positive law, there are human laws which I style positive morality, rules of positive morality, or positive moral rules.

The generic character of laws of the class may be stated briefly in the following negative manner:—No law belonging to the class is a direct or circuitous command of a monarch or sovereign number in the character of political superior. In other words, no law belonging to the class is a direct or circuitous command of a monarch or sovereign number to a person or persons in a state of subjection to its author.

But of positive moral rules, some are laws proper, or laws properly so called: others are laws improper, or laws improperly so called. Some have all the essentials of an *imperative* law or rule: others are deficient in some of those essentials, and are styled *laws* or *rules* by an analogical extension of the term.

The positive moral rules which are laws properly so called, are distinguished from other laws by the union of two marks:—1. They are imperative laws or rules set by men to men. 2. They are not set by men as political superiors, nor are they set by men as private persons, in pursuance of legal rights.

Inasmuch as they bear the latter of these two marks, they are not commands of sovereigns in the character of political superiors. Consequently, they are not positive laws: they are not clothed with legal sanctions, nor do they oblige legally the persons to whom they are set. But being *commands* (and therefore being established by *determinate* individuals or bodies), they are laws properly so called: they are armed with sanctions, and impose duties, in the proper acceptation of the terms.

The positive moral rules which are laws improperly so called, are *laws set* or *imposed by general opinion*: that is to say, by the general opinion of any class or any society of persons. For example, Some are set or imposed by the general opinion of persons who are members of a profession or calling: others, by that of persons who inhabit a town or province: others, by that of a nation or independent political society: others, by that of a larger society formed of various nations.

A few species of the laws which are set by general opinion have gotten appropriate names.—For example, There are laws or rules imposed upon gentlemen by opinions current amongst gentlemen. And these are usually styled *the rules of honour*, or *the laws* or *law of honour*.—There are laws or rules imposed upon people of fashion by opinions current in the fashionable world. And these are usually styled *the law set by fashion*.—There are laws which regard the conduct of independent political societies in their various relations to one another: Or, rather, there are laws which regard the conduct of sovereigns or supreme governments in their various relations to one another. And laws or rules of this species, which are imposed upon nations or sovereigns by opinions current amongst nations, are usually styled *the law of nations* or *international law*.

Now a law set or imposed by general opinion is a law improperly so called. It is styled a *law* or *rule* by an analogical extension of the term. When we speak of a law set by general opinion, we denote, by that expression, the following fact:—Some *indeterminate* body or *uncertain* aggregate of persons regards a kind of conduct with a sentiment of aversion or liking: Or (changing the expression) that indeterminate body opines unfavourably or favourably of a given kind of conduct. In *consequence* of that sentiment, or in *consequence* of that opinion, it is likely that they or some of them will be displeased with a party who shall pursue or not pursue conduct of that kind. And, in *consequence* of that displeasure, it is likely that *some* party (*what* party being undetermined) will visit the party provoking it with some evil or another.

The body by whose opinion the law is said to be set, does not *command*, expressly or tacitly, that conduct of the given kind shall be forborne or pursued. For, since it is not a body precisely determined or certain, it cannot, *as a body*, express or intimate a wish. *As a body*, it cannot *signify* a wish by oral or written words, or by positive or negative deportment. The so called *law* or *rule* which its opinion is said to impose, is merely the *sentiment* which it feels, or is merely the *opinion* which it holds, in regard to a kind of conduct.

In the foregoing analysis of a law set by general opinion, the meaning of the expression "*indeterminate* body of persons" is indicated rather than explained. To complete my analysis of a law set by general opinion (and to abridge that analysis of sovereignty which I shall place in my sixth lecture), I will here insert a concise exposition of the following pregnant distinction: namely, the distinction between a *determinate*, and an *indeterminate* body of single or individual persons.—If my exposition of the distinction shall appear obscure and crabbed, my hearers (I hope) will recollect that the distinction could hardly be expounded in lucid and flowing expressions.

I will first describe the distinction in general or abstract terms, and will then exemplify and illustrate the general or abstract description.

If a body of persons be determinate, *all* the persons who compose it are determined and assignable, or *every* person who belongs to it is determined and may be indicated.

But determinate bodies are of two kinds.

A determinate body of one of those kinds is distinguished by the following marks:—1. The body is composed of persons determined specifically or individually, or determined by characters or descriptions respectively appropriate to themselves. 2. Though every individual member must of necessity answer to many generic descriptions, every individual member is a member of the determinate body, not by reason of his answering to any generic description but by reason of his bearing his specific or appropriate character.

A determinate body of the other of those kinds is distinguished by the following marks:—1. It comprises *all* the persons who belong to a given class, or who belong respectively to two or more of such classes. In other words, *every* person who answers to a given generic description, or to any of two or more given generic descriptions, is also a member of the determinate body. 2. Though every individual member is of necessity determined by a specific or appropriate character, every individual member is a member of the determinate body, not by reason of his bearing his specific or appropriate character, but by reason of his answering to the given generic description.

If a body be indeterminate, *all* the persons who compose it are not determined and assignable. Or (changing the expression) *every* person who belongs to it is not determined, and, therefore, cannot be indicated.—For an indeterminate body consists of *some* of the persons who belong to another and larger aggregate. But *how many of those persons* are members of the indeterminate body, or *which of those persons in particular* are members of the indeterminate body, is not and cannot be known completely and exactly.

Lecture VI

I shall finish, in the present lecture, the purpose mentioned above, by explaining the marks or characters which distinguish positive laws, or laws strictly so called. And, in order to an explanation of the marks which distinguish positive laws, I shall analyze the expression *sovereignty*, the correlative expression *subjection*, and the inseparably connected expression *independent political society*. With the ends or final causes for which governments *ought* to exist, or with their different degrees of fitness to attain or approach those ends, I have no concern. I examine the notions of *sovereignty* and *independent political society*, in order that I may finish the purpose to which I have adverted above: in order that I may distinguish completely the appropriate province of jurisprudence from the regions which lie upon its confines, and by which it is encircled. It is necessary that I should examine those notions, in order that I may finish that purpose. For the essential difference of a positive law (or the difference that severs it from a law which is not a positive law) may be stated thus. Every positive law, or every law simply and strictly so called, is set by a sovereign person, or a sovereign body of persons, to a member or members of the independent political society wherein that person or body is sovereign or supreme. Or (changing the expression) it is set by a monarch, or sovereign number, to a person or persons in a state of subjection to its author. Even though it sprung directly from another fountain or source, it *is* a positive law, or a law strictly so called, by the institution of that present sovereign in the character of political superior. Or (borrowing the language of Hobbes) "the legislator is he, not by whose authority the law was first made, but by whose authority it continues to be a law."

The superiority which is styled sovereignty, and the independent political society which sovereignty implies, is distinguished from other superiority, and from other society, by the following marks or characters:—1. The *bulk* of the given society are in a *habit* of obedience or submission to a *determinate* and *common* superior: let that common superior be a certain individual person, or a certain body or aggregate of individual persons. 2. That certain individual, or that certain body of individuals, is *not* in a habit of obedience to a determinate human superior. Laws (improperly so called) which opinion sets or imposes, may permanently affect the conduct of that certain individual or body. To express or tacit commands of other determinate parties, that certain individual or body may yield occasional submission. But there is no determinate person, or determinate aggregate of persons, to whose commands, express or tacit, that certain individual or body renders habitual obedience.

Or the notions of sovereignty and independent political society may be expressed concisely thus.—If a *determinate* human superior, *not* in a habit of obedience to a like superior, receive *habitual* obedience from the *bulk* of a given society, that determinate superior is sovereign in that society, and the society (including the superior) is a society political and independent.

To that determinate superior, the other members of the society are *subject*: or on that determinate superior, the other members of the society are *dependent*. The position of its other members towards that determinate superior, is *a state of subjection*, or *a state of dependence*. The mutual relation which subsists between that superior and them, may be styled *the relation of sovereign and subject*, or *the relation of sovereignty and subjection*.

Hence it follows, that it is only through an ellipsis, or an abridged form of expression, that the *society* is styled *independent*. The party truly independent (independent, that is to say, of a determinate human superior), is not the society, but the sovereign portion of the society: that certain member of the society, or that certain body of its members, to whose commands, expressed or intimated, the generality or bulk of its members render habitual obedience. Upon that certain person, or certain body of persons, the other members of the society are *dependent*: or to that certain person, or certain body of persons, the other members of the society are *subject*. By "an independent political society," or "an independent and sovereign nation," we mean a political society consisting of a sovereign and subjects, as opposed to a political society which is merely subordinate: that is to say, which is merely a limb or member of another political society, and which therefore consists entirely of persons in a state of subjection.

In order that a given society may form a society political and independent, the two distinguishing marks which I have mentioned above must unite. The *generality* of the given society must be in the *habit* of obedience to a *determinate* and *common* superior: whilst that determinate person, or determinate body of persons must *not* be habitually obedient to a determinate person or body. It is the union of that positive, with this negative mark, which renders that certain superior sovereign or supreme, and which renders that given society (including that certain superior) a society political and independent.

In order that a given society may form a society political and independent, the positive and negative marks which I have mentioned above must unite. The *generality* or *bulk* of its members must be in a *habit* of obedience to a *certain* and *common* superior: whilst that certain person, or certain body of persons, must *not* be habitually obedient to a certain person or body.

But, in order that the *bulk* of its members may render obedience to a *common* superior, *how many* of its members, or *what proportion* of its members, must render obedience to *one and the same* superior? And, assuming that the bulk of its members render obedience to a common superior, *how often* must they render it, and *how long* must they render it, in order that that obedience may be *habitual*?—Now since these questions cannot be answered precisely, the positive mark of sovereignty and independent political society is a fallible test of specific or particular cases.

Note*—on the prevailing tendency to confound what is with what ought to be law or morality, that is, 1st, to confound positive law with the science of legislation, and positive morality with deontology; and 2ndly, to confound positive law with positive morality, and both with legislation and deontology.

The existence of law is one thing; its merit or demerit is another. Whether it be or be not is one enquiry; whether it be or be not conformable to an assumed standard, is a different enquiry. A law, which actually exists, is a law, though we happen to dislike it, or though it vary from the text, by which we regulate our approbation and disapprobation. This truth, when formally announced as an abstract proposition, is so simple and glaring that it seems idle to insist upon it. But simple and glaring as it is, when enunciated in abstract expressions the enumeration of the instances in which it has been forgotten would fill a volume.

Sir William Blackstone, for example, says in his "Commentaries," that the laws of God are superior in obligation to all other laws; that no human laws should be suffered to contradict them; that

* [Appended to Lecture V.]

human laws are of no validity if contrary to them; and that all valid laws derive their force from that Divine original.

Now, he *may* mean that all human laws ought to conform to the Divine laws. If this be his meaning, I assent to it without hesitation. The evils which we are exposed to suffer from the hands of God as a consequence of disobeying His commands are the greatest evils to which we are obnoxious; the obligations which they impose are consequently paramount to those imposed by any other laws, and if human commands conflict with the Divine law, we ought to disobey the command which is enforced by the less powerful sanction; this is implied in the term *ought*: the proposition is identical, and therefore perfectly indisputable—it is our interest to choose the smaller and more uncertain evil, in preference to the greater and surer. If this be Blackstone's meaning, I assent to his proposition, and have only to object to it, that it tells us just nothing. Perhaps, again, he means that human lawgivers are themselves obliged by the Divine laws to fashion the laws which they impose by that ultimate standard, because if they do not, God will punish them. To this also I entirely assent: for if the index to the law of God be the principle of utility, that law embraces the whole of our voluntary actions in so far as motives applied from without are required to give them a direction conformable to the general happiness.

But the meaning of this passage of Blackstone, if it has a meaning, seems rather to be this: that no human law which conflicts with the Divine law is obligatory or binding; in other words, that no human law which conflicts with the Divine law *is a law*, for a law without an obligation is a contradiction in terms. I suppose this to be his meaning, because when we say of any transaction that it is invalid or void, we mean that it is not binding: as, for example, if it be a contract, we mean that the political law will not lend its sanction to enforce the contract.

Now, to say that human laws which conflict with the Divine law are not binding, that is to say, are not laws, is to talk stark nonsense. The most pernicious laws, and therefore those which are most opposed to the will of God, have been and are continually enforced as laws by judicial tribunals. Suppose an act innocuous, or positively beneficial, be prohibited by the sovereign under the penalty of death; if I commit this act, I shall be tried and condemned, and if I object to the sentence, that it is contrary to the law of God, who has commanded that human lawgivers shall not prohibit acts which have no evil consequences, the Court of Justice will demonstrate the inconclusiveness of my reasoning by hanging me up, in pursuance of the law of which I have impugned the validity. An exception, demurrer, or plea, founded on the law of God was never heard in a Court of Justice, from the creation of the world down to the present moment.

But this abuse of language is not merely puerile, it is mischievous. When it is said that a law ought to be disobeyed, what is meant is that we are urged to disobey it by motives more cogent and compulsory than those by which it is itself sanctioned. If the laws of God are certain, the motives which they hold out to disobey any human command which is at variance with them are paramount to all others. But the laws of God are not always certain. All divines, at least all reasonable divines, admit that no scheme of duties perfectly complete and unambiguous was ever imparted to us by revelation. As an index to the Divine will, utility is obviously insufficient. What appears pernicious to one person may appear beneficial to another. And as for the moral sense, innate practical principles, conscience, they are merely convenient cloaks for ignorance or sinister interest: they mean either that I hate the law to which I object and cannot tell why, or that I hate the law, and that the cause of my hatred is one which I find it incommodious to avow. If I say openly, I hate the law, *ergo*, it is not binding and ought to be disobeyed, no one will listen to me; but by calling my hate my conscience or my moral sense, I urge the same argument in another and more plausible form: I seem to assign a reason for my dislike, when in truth I have only given it a sounding and specious name. In times of civil discord the mischief of this detestable abuse of language is apparent. In quiet times the dictates of utility are fortunately so obvious that the anarchical doctrine sleeps, and men habitually admit the validity of laws which they dislike. To prove by pertinent reasons that a law is pernicious is highly useful, because such process may lead to the abrogation of the pernicious law. To incite the public to resistance by determinate views of *utility* may be useful, for re-

sistance, grounded on clear and definite prospects of good, is
sometimes beneficial. But to proclaim generally that all laws which
are pernicious or contrary to the will of God are void and not to
be tolerated, is to preach anarchy, hostile and perilous as much
to wise and benign rule as to stupid and galling tyranny.

HENRY SUMNER MAINE

The Limits of the Analytical System

*Recognized as the founder of the English historical school of
jurisprudence, Sir Henry Sumner Maine (1822–88) con-
tributed to the development of anthropology, as well. The following selection is taken from Maine's Lectures on the* Early
History of Institutions, *7th ed., London, 1897, pp. 375–86
and has been abridged by the editor.*

8~

The laws with which the student of Jurisprudence is concerned
in our own day are undoubtedly either the actual commands of
Sovereigns, understood as the portion of the community endowed
with irresistible coercive force, or else they are practices of mankind brought under the formula "a law is a command," by help of
the formula, "whatever the Sovereign permits, is his command."
From the point of view of the Jurist, law is only associated with
order through the necessary condition of every true law that it
must prescribe a class of acts or omissions, or a number of acts
and omissions determined generally; the law which prescribes a
single act not being a true law, but being distinguished as an
"occasional" or "particular" command. Law, thus defined and
limited, is the subject-matter of Jurisprudence as conceived by the
Analytical Jurists. At present we are only concerned with the
foundations of their system; and the questions which I wish to

raise in the present Lecture are these: has the force which compels obedience to a law always been of such a nature that it can reasonably be identified with the coercive force of the Sovereign, and have laws always been characterised by that generality which, it is said, alone connects them with physical laws or general formulas describing the facts of nature? These enquiries may seem to you to lead us far afield, but I trust you will perceive in the end that they have interest and importance, and that they throw light on the limits which must be assigned in certain cases, not to the theoretical soundness, but to the practical value, of the speculations we have been discussing.

Let me recur to Sovereignty, as conceived by the Analytical Jurists. The readers of Austin's treatise will remember his examination of a number of existing governments or (as he would say), forms of political superiority and inferiority, for the purpose of determining the exact seat of sovereignty in each of them. This is among the most interesting parts of his writings, and his sagacity and originality are nowhere more signally demonstrated. The problem had become much more complex than it was when Hobbes wrote, and even than it was at the date of Bentham's earlier publications.

Nevertheless Austin fully recognises the existence of communities, or aggregates of men, in which no dissection could disclose a person or group answering to his definition of a Sovereign. The passage occurs at p. 237 of the first volume of the third edition:*—

"Let us suppose that a single family of savages lives in absolute estrangement from every other community. And let us suppose that the father, the chief of this insulated family, receives habitual obedience from the mother and children. Now, since it is not a limb of another and larger community, the society formed by the parents and children, is clearly an independent society, and, since the rest of its members habitually obey its chief, this independent society would form a society political, in case the number of its members were not extremely minute. But, since the number of its members *is* extremely minute, it would, I believe, be esteemed a society in a state of nature; that is, a society consisting of persons not in a state of subjection. Without an application of the terms,

* [LECTURES ON JURISPRUDENCE.]

which would somewhat smack of the ridiculous, we could hardly style the society a society *political* and independent, the imperative father and chief a *monarch* or *sovereign*, or the obedient mother and children *subjects*."

And then Austin quotes from Montesquieu the doctrine that "Political power necessarily implies the union of several families."

The effect of this passage then is that a society may be too small to admit of the application of the theory. The employment, Austin says, of his terminology would be ridiculous in such a case. I believe I shall be able to point out to you the significance of this appeal to our sense of absurdity, generally a most dangerous criterion; but at present I merely ask you to note the seriousness of the admission, since the form of authority about which it is made, the authority of the Patriarch or Paterfamilias over his family, is, at least according to one modern theory, the element or germ out of which all permanent power of man over man has been gradually developed.

There are, however, another set of cases, known to us from sources of knowledge of which it is perhaps fair to say that (though Austin is in one sense a modern writer) they were hardly open when he wrote—cases in which the application of his principles is at least difficult and doubtful. It is from no special love of Indian examples that I take one from India, but because it happens to be the most modern precedent in point. My instance is the Indian Province called the Punjaub, the Country of the Five Rivers, in the state in which it was for about a quarter of a century before its annexation to the British Indian Empire. After passing through every conceivable phase of anarchy and dormant anarchy, it fell under the tolerably consolidated dominion of a half-military, half-religious oligarchy, known as the Sikhs. The Sikhs themselves were afterwards reduced to subjection by a single chieftain belonging to their order, Runjeet Singh. At first sight, there could be no more perfect embodiment than Runjeet Singh of Sovereignty, as conceived by Austin. He was absolutely despotic. Except occasionally on his wild frontier, he kept the most perfect order. He could have commanded anything: the smallest disobedience to his commands would have been followed by death or mutilation, and this was perfectly well known to the enormous majority of his subjects. Yet I doubt whether once in all his life he issued a command which Austin would call a law. He took, as his revenue, a prodigious share of the produce of the soil. He harried villages which recalcitrated at his exactions, and he executed great numbers of men. He levied great armies; he had all material of power, and exercised it in various ways. But he never made a law. The rules which regulated the life of his subjects were derived from their immemorial usages, and these rules were administered by domestic tribunals, in families or village-communities—that is, in groups no larger or little larger than those to which the application of Austin's principles cannot be effected, on his own admission, without absurdity.

I do not for a moment assert that the existence of such a state of political society falsifies Austin's theory, as a theory. The great maxim by which objections to it are disposed of is, as I have so often said before, "What the Sovereign permits, he commands." The Sikh despot permitted heads of households and village-elders to prescribe rules, therefore these rules were his commands and true laws. Now we can see that an answer of this kind might have some force if it were made to an English lawyer who denied that the Sovereign in England had ever commanded the Common law. The Crown and Parliament command it, because the Crown and Parliament permit it; and the proof that they permit it is that they could change it. As a matter of fact, since the objection was first advanced, the Common law has been largely encroached upon by Act of Parliament, and, in our own day, it is possible that it may come to owe the whole of its binding force to statute. But my Oriental example shows that the difficulty felt by the old lawyers about the Common law may have once deserved more respect than it obtained from Hobbes and his successors. Runjeet Singh never did or could have dreamed of changing the civil rules under which his subjects lived. Probably he was as strong a believer in the independent obligatory force of such rules as the elders themselves who applied them. An Eastern or Indian theorist in law, to whom the assertion was made that Runjeet Singh commanded these rules, would feel it stinging him exactly in that sense of absurdity to which Austin admits the appeal to be legitimate. The theory remains true in such a case, but the truth is only verbal.

You must not suppose that I have been indulging in a merely curious speculation about a few extreme cases to which the theory of Sovereignty, and of Law founded on it, will not apply without straining of language. In the first place, the Punjaub under Runjeet Singh may be taken as a type of all Oriental communities in their native state, during their rare intervals of peace and order. They have ever been despotisms, and the commands of the despots at their head, harsh and cruel as they might be, have always been implicitly obeyed. But then these commands, save in so far as they served to organise administrative machinery for the collection of revenue, have not been true laws; they have been of the class called by Austin occasional or particular commands. The truth is that the one solvent of local and domestic usage in those parts of the world of which we have any real knowledge has been not the command of the Sovereign but the supposed command of the Deity. In India, the influence of the Brahminical treatises on mixed law and religion in sapping the old customary law of the country has always been great, and in some particulars, as I tried to explain on a former occasion, it has become greater under English rule.

It is important to observe that, for the purposes of the present enquiry, the state of political society which I have described as Indian or Oriental is a far more trustworthy clue to the former condition of the greatest part of the world than is the modern social organisation of Western Europe, as we see it before our eyes. It is a perhaps not unreasonable impression that Sovereignty was simpler and more easily discovered in the ancient than in the modern world. We know something of the Assyrian and Babylonian Empires from Jewish records, and something of the Median and Persian Empires from Greek records. We learn from these that they were in the main tax-taking empires. We know that they raised enormous revenues from their subjects. We know that, for occasional wars of conquest, they levied vast armies from populations spread over immense areas. We know that they exacted the most implicit obedience to their occasional commands, or punished disobedience with the utmost cruelty. We know that the monarchs at their head were constantly dethroning petty kings and even transplanting whole communities. But amid all this, it is clear that in the main they interfered but little with the every day religious or civil life of the groups to which their subjects belonged. They did not legislate. The "royal statute" and "firm decree" which has been preserved to us as a sample of "law of the Medes and Persians which altereth not" is not a law at all in the modern juridical acceptation of the term. It is what Austin would call a "particular command," a sudden, spasmodic, and temporary interference with ancient multifarious usage left in general undisturbed. What is even more instructive is that the famous Athenian Empire belonged to the same class of sovereignties as the Empire of the Great King. The Athenian Assembly made true laws for residents on Attic territory, but the dominion of Athens over her subject cities and islands was clearly a tax-taking as distinguished from a legislating Empire.

The difficulty of employing Austin's terminology of these great governments is obvious enough. How can it conduce to clear thinking to speak of the Jewish law as commanded at one period by the Great King at Susa? The cardinal rule of the Analytical Jurists, "what the Sovereign permits, he commands," remains verbally true, but against its application in such a case there lies an appeal to a higher tribunal of which Austin allows the jurisdiction, our sense of the ridiculous.

I have now reached the point at which I can conveniently state my own opinion of the practical limitations which must be given to the system of the Analytical Jurists, in order that it may possess, I will not say theoretical truth, but practical value. The Western world, to which they confined their attention, must be conceived as having undergone two sets of changes. The States of modern Europe must be conceived as having been formed in a manner different from the great empires of antiquity (save one), and from the modern empires and kingdoms of the East, and a new order of ideas on the subject of *legislation* must be conceived as having been introduced into the world through the empire of the Romans. Unless these changes had taken place, I do not believe that the system would ever have been engendered in the brain of its authors. Wherever these changes have not taken place, I do not believe the application of the system to be of value.

H. L. A. HART

Obligation and Coercion

The author of many important books and articles, H. L. A. Hart, professor of jurisprudence at the University of Oxford, is one of the leading contemporary philosophers of law. In his book The Concept of Law *(see the selection below, pp. 144–160), Hart develops his own positivist position by means of showing the inadequacies of the austinian theory. At the same time, Hart tries to preserve what he regards as the essential insights of the natural law tradition. An instructive discussion on positivism and morals is contained in the exchange between Hart and Lon L. Fuller (see biblography).*

ॐ

We have yet to discuss in detail what most people would regard as *the* salient feature of an obligation and to some extent of duties: this is the important connection between obligation and coercion or compulsion. If we have an obligation to do something there is some sense in which we are bound to do it, and where we are bound there is some sense in which we are or may be compelled to do it. To probe these notions it is important to distinguish three things: (1) being physically compelled to do something, (2) being obliged to do something, (3) having an obligation to do something. The difficulty of the topic is that of stating without exaggeration the relation between the third member of this trio and the others, and Austin, who made in the introductory sections of *The Province of Jurisprudence Determined* the most painstaking effort to understand the notion of obligation, did

Reprinted by permission of the publishers from H. L. A. Hart, "Legal and Moral Obligation," in A. I. Melden (ed.), *Essays in Moral Philosophy* (Seattle: University of Washington Press, 1958), pp. 95–99. Abridged by the editor.

fatally exaggerate this relation. He perceived correctly that when a man is dragged to prison, and so in some sense compelled to enter it, this is not a case of having an obligation or duty to go there. But, though he avoided this mistake, Austin defined obligation and duty in terms of the sanction or evil which one who commands (signifies his desire to another that he should do something) threatens to inflict in the event of disobedience. To have a duty or an obligation, according to Austin, is to be liable or obnoxious to an evil so threatened where "liable" or "obnoxious" means "likely to incur." The most obvious defect of this definition is that it would be satisfied by the case of a gunman's ordering me to hand over my purse at the point of a gun, where we would *not* say, "I had an obligation to hand over my purse"; what encourages the mistake is that we *would* say in such a case, "I was *obliged* to hand over my purse." So at first sight Austin's account looks like a fairly accurate definition of "being obliged" to do something and a very poor definition of "having an obligation" to do something. But we must take into account Austin's additions to and refinements upon his starting point. His account of specifically *legal* obligation differs from the primitive example of the gunman in a number of respects. Instead of the gunman, we have the sovereign defined as the person or persons whom the bulk of society generally obey, and who is himself not in a like habit of obedience to anyone else; further, commands of the sovereign are to follow "general" courses of conduct and are addressed usually to numbers of persons. Apart from these qualifications for the special case of legal obligation, Austin also insists that his definition would be satisfied even if the chance of incurring the threatened evil was very small, and the evil itself was very small: "the slightest chance of the slightest evil" is enough to constitute obligation or duty. Lastly, Austin, albeit with hesitation, suggests that if a person has an obligation or duty he must have the threatened evil "in prospect," i.e., fear it, though certainly this psychological element is little stressed.

Unfortunately these additions and refinements cause Austin's analysis to fall between two stools. It ceases to be a plausible analysis of "being obliged" to do something and remains an inadequate analysis of "having an obligation." To see precisely where it fails we must concede something which may be disputed: Austin would not allow any system of rules to count as a legal system unless its rules provided for the infliction of evil in the case of disobedience. We may for the purpose of the argument concede this as a part of the definition of "legal," though it was deduced by Austin from propositions that we might wish to reject: he thought laws were commands, and he thought commands were significations of desire by one who had the intention and some ability to inflict some evil in the event of disobedience. But, even if we concede the analytical connection between the notion of a legal system and that of a sanction in the form of evil or harm, the definition of having an obligation in terms of the *chance* of incurring the threatened evil, and of the individual's having this evil in prospect, leads to absurdities.

We may deal first with the psychological element (prospect of evil), which Austin only very uncertainly uses. The statement that a thief has a legal obligation not to take the purse is not a psychological statement about him. He may have no fear at all of the threatened evil, and yet his obligation remains. If he is deterred by fear we may say, rather oddly, that he was obliged to leave it alone. Second, the statement that a person has an obligation on a particular occasion is quite independent of any assessment of the chances of his incurring the evil though these may be very important in considering where he could be said to be obliged to do something that he did on a particular occasion. There is no contradiction or even oddity in saying, "It's your duty to report for military service, but, since you're living in Monte Carlo and there's no extradition treaty, there's not the slightest chance of their getting you."

Third, there is something quite ludicrous in Austin's first stressing the importance of the threatened evil and then reducing it to "the slightest chance of the slightest evil." This ruins his analysis as an analysis even of being obliged to do something. Only where a choice is made less eligible by some substantial disadvantage do we speak of being obliged.

The important connection between the concept of coercion and obligation cannot be clearly stated in Austinian terms with its impoverished vocabulary of habit and its inadequate analysis of a command in terms of the expression of a wish that people should act in certain ways made by one who intends and has some power to visit disobedience with some evil. The coercion in question may indeed take the form of the infliction of evil as it does in the case of a municipal legal system, but if it does the application of the evil must be something for which the rules of the system itself provide. However clear the actual power of a legislator was to visit certain conduct with pains, his threat and even use of force to coerce people to obey him would not constitute an obligation unless these were provided for by means of the appropriate legislative forms. At the most people would be obliged to do what he said. So the essential element of coercion is not the fact (the chance or the prospect) that evil will follow disobedience, but there should be an existing system of rules conferring authority on persons to prohibit behavior and to visit breaches of the prohibition with the appropriate coercive, repressive, or punitory techniques of the system.

Some qualification though not abandonment must be made of this last point. In all municipal legal systems there are some cases where there is no provision for sanctions in the event of a breach of a rule. Though perhaps no logical vice or infinite regress would attach to a self-referring rule that all officials should exact sanctions for all offenses including any breach of this rule itself, it is quite common for legal rules to require officials to do certain things and for the system to provide no sanction in the case of their breach. This is for example the case with the obligation imposed by the United States Constitution on the President to take care for the due execution of the laws. Yet we do not hesitate to refer to such cases as cases of official duty or obligation. They show that even within a legal system the complex features that characterize the standard case of obligation may come apart. This is reflected in juristic terminology, such as that of "duties of imperfect obligation," which the Romans invented for just such cases; and it helps to generate part of the skeptical doubts whether international law is "really" law or better classified as a branch of morality.

Recent Formulations

HANS KELSEN

The Pure Theory of Law

Hans Kelsen was born in Prague in 1881, and served as the head of the school of law at Vienna. In 1940 he moved to the United States, and is now emeritus professor of political science at the University of California. A prolific writer on jurisprudence, Kelsen is probably the most influential legal philosopher in the 20th century. Kelsen maintains his theory of law to be "pure" in two senses: (1) the analysis of "legal norm" is independent of any conception of just law and of any ideological considerations; and (2) the study of political, economic, or historical influences on the development of law and the sociological study of legal institutions are held to be beyond the purview of an investigation of the nature of law as such.

ॐ

The Concept of Law

SCIENTIFIC AND POLITICAL DEFINITION OF LAW. Any attempt to define a concept must take for its starting-point the common usage of the word, denoting the concept in question. In defining the

Reprinted by permission of the publisher from Hans Kelsen, *General Theory of Law and State* (trans. by A. Wedberg) (New York: Russell & Russell, 1961), pp. 4–5, 15, 18–19, 28–30, 35–7, 39–46, 110–20, 122, 399–401. Abridged by the editor.

THE PURE THEORY OF LAW

(109

concept of law, we must begin by examining the following questions: Do the social phenomena generally called "law" present a common characteristic distinguishing them from other social phenomena of a similar kind? And is this characteristic of such importance in the social life of man that it may be made the basis of a concept serviceable for the cognition of social life? For reasons of economy of thought, one must start from the broadest possible usage of the word "law." Perhaps no such characteristic as we are looking for can be found. Perhaps the actual usage is so loose that the phenomena called "law" do not exhibit any common characteristic of real importance. But if such a characteristic can be found, then we are justified in including it in the definition.

This is not to say that it would be illegitimate to frame a narrower concept of law, not covering all the phenomena usually called "law." We may define at will those terms which we wish to use as tools in our intellectual work. The only question is whether they will serve the theoretical purpose for which we have intended them. A concept of law whose extent roughly coincides with the common usage is obviously—circumstances otherwise being equal—to be preferred to a concept which is applicable only to a much narrower class of phenomena. Let us take an example. Even since the rise of Bolshevism, National Socialism, and Fascism, one speaks of Russian, German, and Italian "law." Nothing would prevent us, however, from including in our definition of a legal order a certain minimum of personal freedom and the possibility of private property. One result of adopting such a definition would be that the social orders prevailing in Russia, Italy and Germany could no longer be recognized as legal orders, although they have very important elements in common with the social orders of democratic-capitalistic States.

The above-mentioned concept—which actually appears in recent works on legal philosophy—also shows how a political bias can influence the definition of law. The concept of law is here made to correspond to a specific ideal of justice, namely, of democracy and liberalism. From the standpoint of science, free from any moral or political judgments of value, democracy and liberalism are only two possible principles of social organization, just as autocracy and socialism are. There is no scientific reason why the concept of law should be defined so as to exclude the latter. As used in these investigations, the concept of law has no moral connotation whatsoever. It designates a specific technique of social organization. The problem of law, as a scientific problem, is the problem of social technique, not a problem of morals. The statement: "A certain social order has the character of law, is a legal order," does not imply the moral judgment that this order is good or just. There are legal orders which are, from a certain point of view, unjust. Law and justice are two different concepts. Law as distinguished from justice is positive law. It is the concept of positive law which is here in question; and a science of positive law must be clearly distinguished from a philosophy of justice.

The Criterion of Law (Law as a Specific Social Technique)

If we confine our investigation to positive law, and if we compare all those social orders, past and present, that are generally called "law," we shall find that they have one characteristic in common which no social orders of another kind present. This characteristic constitutes a fact of supreme importance for social life and its scientific study. And this characteristic is the only criterion by which we may clearly distinguish law from other social phenomena such as morals and religion. What is this criterion?

It is the function of every social order, of every society—because society is nothing but a social order—to bring about a certain reciprocal behavior of human beings: to make them refrain from certain acts which, for some reason, are deemed detrimental to society, and to make them perform others which, for some reason, are considered useful to society.

According to the manner in which the socially desired behavior is brought about, various types of social orders can be distinguished. These types—it is ideal types that are to be presented here—are characterized by the specific motivation resorted to by the social order to induce individuals to behave as desired. The motivation may be indirect or direct. The order may attach certain advantages to its observance and certain disadvantages to its non-observance, and, hence, make desire for the promised advantage or fear of the threatened disadvantage a motive for behavior. Behavior conforming to the established order is achieved by a sanction provided in the order itself. The principle of reward and punishment—the principle of retribution—fundamental for social life, consists in associating conduct in accordance with the established order and conduct contrary to the order with a promised advantage or a threatened disadvantage respectively, as sanctions.

The social order can, however, even without promise of an advantage in case of obedience, and without threat of a disadvantage in case of disobedience, i.e. without decreeing sanctions, require conduct that appeals directly to the individuals as advantageous, so that the mere idea of a norm decreeing this behavior suffices as a motive for conduct conforming to the norm. This type of direct motivation in its full purity is seldom to be met with in social reality.

LAW AS A COERCIVE ORDER. The evil applied to the violator of the order when the sanction is socially organized consists in a deprivation of possessions—life, health, freedom, or property. As the possessions are taken from him against his will, this sanction has the character of a measure of coercion. This does not mean that in carrying out the sanction physical force must be applied. This is necessary only if resistance is encountered in applying the sanction. This is only exceptionally the case, where the authority applying the sanction possesses adequate power. A social order that seeks to bring about the desired behavior of individuals by the enactment of such measures of coercion is called a coercive order. Such it is because it threatens socially harmful deeds with measures of coercion, decrees such measures of coercion. As such it presents a contrast to all other possible social orders—those that provide reward rather than punishment as sanctions, and especially those that enact no sanctions at all, relying on the technique of direct motivation. In contrast to the orders that enact coercive measures as sanctions, the efficacy of the others rests not on coercion but on voluntary obedience. Yet this contrast is not so distinct as it might at first sight appear. This follows from the fact that the technique of reward, as a technique of indirect motivation, has its place between the technique of indirect motivation through punishment, as a technique of coercion, and the technique of direct motivation, the technique of voluntary obedience. Voluntary obedience is itself a form of motivation, that is, of coercion, and hence is not freedom, but it is coercion in the psychological sense. If coercive orders are contrasted with those that have no coercive character, that rest on voluntary obedience, this is possible only in the sense that one provides measures of coercion as sanctions whereas the other does not. And these sanctions are only coercive measures in the sense that certain possessions are taken from the individuals in question against their will, if necessary by the employment of physical force.

In this sense, the law is a coercive order.

If the social orders, so extraordinarily different in their tenors, which have prevailed at different times and among the most different peoples, are all called legal orders, it might be supposed that one is using an expression almost devoid of meaning. What could the so-called law of ancient Babylonians have in common with the law that prevails today in the United States? What could the social order of a negro tribe under the leadership of a despotic chieftain—an order likewise called "law"—have in common with the constitution of the Swiss Republic? Yet there is a common element, that fully justifies this terminology, and enables the word "law" to appear as the expression of a concept with a socially highly significant meaning. For the word refers to that specific social technique of a coercive order which, despite the vast differences existing between the law of ancient Babylon and that of the United States of today, between the law of the Ashantis in West Africa and that of the Swiss in Europe, is yet essentially the same for all these peoples differing so much in time, in place, and in culture: the social technique which consists in bringing about the desired social conduct of men through the threat of a measure of coercion which is to be applied in case of contrary conduct. What the social conditions are that necessitate this technique, is an important sociological question. I do not know whether we can answer it satisfactorily.

THE NEVER-ENDING SERIES OF SANCTIONS. An argument against the doctrine that coercion is an essential element of law, or that sanctions form a necessary element within the legal structure, runs as follows: if it is necessary to guarantee the efficacy of a norm prescribing a certain behavior by another norm prescribing a sanction in the case the former is not obeyed, a never-ending series of sanctions, a *regressus ad infinitum*, is inevitable. For "in order to secure the efficacy of a rule of the nth degree, a rule of the $n + 1$ degree is necessary."[1] Since the legal order can be composed only by a definite number of rules, the norms prescribing sanctions presuppose norms which prescribe no sanctions. Coercion is not a necessary but only a possible element of law.

The assertion that in order to secure the efficacy of a rule of the nth degree, a rule of the $n + 1$th degree is necessary, and that therefore it is impossible to secure the efficacy of all legal rules by rules providing for sanctions, is correct; but the rule of law is not a rule the efficacy of which is secured by another rule providing for a sanction, even if the efficacy of this rule is not secured by another rule. A rule is a legal rule not because its efficacy is secured by another rule providing for a sanction; a rule is a legal rule because it provides for a sanction. The problem of coercion (constraint, sanction) is not the problem of securing the efficacy of rules, but the problem of the content of the rules. The fact that it is impossible to secure the efficacy of all rules of a legal order by rules providing for sanctions does not exclude the possibility of considering only rules providing for sanctions as legal rules. All the norms of a legal order are coercive norms, i.e. norms providing for sanctions; but among these norms there are norms the efficacy of which is not secured by other coercive norms. Norm n, e.g., runs as follows: If an individual steals, another individual, an organ of the community, shall punish him. The efficacy of this norm is secured by the norm $n + 1$: If the organ does not punish a thief, another organ shall punish the organ who violates his duty of punishing the thief. There is no norm $n + 2$, securing the efficacy of the norm $n + 1$. The coercive norm $n + 1$: If the organ does not punish the thief, another organ shall punish the law-violating organ, is not guaranteed by a norm of the

[1] N. S. TIMASHEFF, AN INTRODUCTION TO THE SOCIOLOGY OF LAW (1939) 264, according to L. PETRAZHITSKY, THEORY OF LAW AND STATE (in Russian: 2d ed. 1909) 273–285.

$n + 2$nd degree. But all the norms of this legal order are coercive norms.[2]

Finally, one objects to the doctrine that coercion is an essential element of law by alleging that among the norms of a legal order there are many rules which provide for no sanctions at all. The norms of the constitution are frequently pointed out as legal norms although they provide for no sanctions. We shall deal with this argument in a later chapter.

Validity and Efficacy

The element of "coercion" which is essential to law thus consists, not in the so-called "psychic compulsion," but in the fact that specific acts of coercion, as sanctions, are provided for in specific cases by the rules which form the legal order. The element of coercion is relevant only as part of the contents of the legal norm, only as an act stipulated by this norm, not as a process in the mind of the individual subject to the norm. The rules which constitute a system of morality do not have any such import. Whether or not men do actually behave in a manner to avoid the sanction threatened by the legal norm, and whether or not the sanction is actually carried out in case its conditions are fulfilled, are issues concerning the efficacy of the law. But it is not the efficacy, it is the validity of the law which is in question here.

THE "NORM." What is the nature of the validity, as distinguished from the efficacy of law? The difference may be illustrated by an example: A legal rule forbids theft, prescribing that every thief must be punished by the judge. This rule is "valid" for all people, to whom theft is thereby forbidden, the individuals who have to obey the rule, the "subjects." The legal rule is "valid" particularly for those who actually steal and in so doing "violate" the rule. That is to say, the legal rule is valid even in those cases where it lacks "efficacy." It is precisely in those cases that it has to be "applied" by the judge. The rule in question is valid not only for the subjects but also for the law-applying organs. But the rule retains its validity, even if the thief should succeed in escaping, and the

[2] This does not mean that the execution of the sanction stipulated in a legal norm has always the character of a legal duty.

judge, therefore, should be unable to punish him and thus apply the legal rule. Thus, in the particular case, the rule is valid for the judge even if it is without efficacy, in the sense that the conditions of the sanction prescribed by the rule are fulfilled and yet the judge finds himself unable to order the sanction. What is now the significance of the statement that the rule is valid even if, in a concrete case, it lacks efficacy, is not obeyed, or is not applied?

By "validity" we mean the specific existence of norms. To say that a norm is valid, is to say that we assume its existence or—what amounts to the same thing—we assume that it has "binding force" for those whose behavior it regulates. Rules of law, if valid, are norms. They are, to be more precise, norms stipulating sanctions. But what is a norm?

THE "OUGHT." When laws are described as "commands" or expressions of the "will" of the legislator, and when the legal order as such is said to be the "command" or the "will" of the State, this must be understood as a figurative mode of speech. As usual, an analogy is responsible for the figurative statement. The situation when a rule of law "stipulates," "provides for," or "prescribes" a certain human conduct is in fact quite similar to the situation when one individual wants another individual to behave in such-and-such a way and expresses this will in the form of a command. The only difference is that when we say that a certain human conduct is "stipulated," "provided for," or "prescribed" by a rule of law, we are employing an abstraction which eliminates the psychological act of will which is expressed by a command. If the rule of law is a command, it is, so to speak, a de-psychologized command, a command which does not imply a "will" in a psychological sense of the term. The conduct prescribed by the rule of law is "demanded" without any human being having to "will" it in a psychological sense. This is expressed by the statement that one "shall," one "ought" to observe the conduct prescribed by the law. A "norm" is a rule expressing the fact that somebody ought to act in a certain way, without implying that anybody really "wants" the person to act that way.

The statement that an individual "ought to" behave in a certain way implies neither that some other individual "wills" or "commands" so, nor that the individual who ought to behave in a certain way actually behaves in this way. The norm is the expression of the idea that something ought to occur, especially that an individual ought to behave in a certain way. By the norm, nothing is said about the actual behavior of the individual concerned. The statement that an individual "ought to" behave in a certain way means that this behavior is prescribed by a norm—it may be a moral or a legal norm or some other norm. The "ought" simply expresses the specific sense in which human behavior is determined by a norm. All we can do to describe this sense is to state that it is different from the sense in which we say that an individual actually behaves in a certain way, that something actually occurs or exists. A statement to the effect that something ought to occur is a statement about the existence and the contents of a norm, not a statement about natural reality, i.e. actual events in nature.

A norm expressing the idea that something ought to occur—although, possibly, it does not actually occur—is "valid." And if the occurrence referred to is the behavior of a certain individual, if the norm says that a certain individual ought to behave in a certain way, then the norm is "binding" upon that individual. Only by the help of the concept of a norm and the correlated concept of "ought" can we grasp the specific meaning of rules of law. Only thus can we understand their relevance to those for whose behavior they "provide," for whom they "prescribe" a certain course of conduct. Any attempt to represent the meaning of legal norms by rules describing the actual behavior of men—and thus to render the meaning of legal norms without having recourse to the concept of "ought"—must fail. Neither a statement about the actual behavior of those creating the norm, nor a statement about the actual behavior of those subject to the norm, can reproduce the specific meaning of the norm itself.

In summary: To say that a norm is "valid" for certain individuals is not to say that a certain individual or certain individuals "want" other individuals to behave in a certain way; for the norm is valid also if no such will exists. To say that a norm is valid for certain individuals is not to say that individuals actually behave in a certain way; for the norm is valid for these individuals even if they do not behave in that way. The distinction between the "ought" and the "is" is fundamental for the description of law.

EFFICACY AS CONFORMITY OF THE BEHAVIOR TO THE NORM. In the foregoing, we have tried to clarify the difference between the validity and the efficacy of the law. Validity of law means that the legal norms are binding, that men ought to behave as the legal norms prescribe, that men ought to obey and apply the legal norms. Efficacy of law means that men actually behave as, according to the legal norms, they ought to behave, that the norms are actually applied and obeyed. The validity is a quality of law; the so-called efficacy is a quality of the actual behavior of men and not, as linguistic usage seems to suggest, of law itself. The statement that law is effective means only that the actual behavior of men conforms with the legal norms. Thus, validity and efficacy refer to quite different phenomena. The common parlance, implying that validity and efficacy are both attributes of law, is misleading, even if by the efficacy of law is meant that the idea of law furnishes a motive for lawful conduct. Law as valid norm finds its expression in the statement that men ought to behave in a certain manner, thus in a statement which does not tell us anything about actual events. The efficacy of law, understood in the last-mentioned way, consists in the fact that men are led to observe the conduct required by a norm by their idea of this norm. A statement concerning the efficacy of law so understood is a statement about actual behavior. To designate both the valid norm and the idea of the norm, which is a psychological fact, by the same word "norm" is to commit an equivocation which may give rise to grave fallacies. However, as I have already pointed out, we are not in a position to say anything with exactitude about the motivating power which men's idea of law may possess. Objectively, we can ascertain only that the behavior of men conforms or does not conform with the legal norms. The only connotation attached to the term "efficacy" of law in this study is therefore that the actual behavior of men conforms to the legal norms.

EFFICACY AS CONDITION OF VALIDITY. The statement that a norm is valid and the statement that it is efficacious are, it is true, two different statements. But although validity and efficacy are two entirely different concepts, there is nevertheless a very important relationship between the two. A norm is considered to be valid only on the condition that it belongs to a system of norms, to an order which, on the whole, is efficacious. Thus, efficacy is a condition of validity; a condition, not the reason of validity. A norm is not valid *because* it is efficacious; it is valid *if* the order to which it belongs is, on the whole, efficacious. This relationship between validity and efficacy is cognizable, however, only from the point of view of a dynamic theory of law dealing with the problem of the reason of validity and the concept of the legal order. From the point of view of a static theory, only the validity of law is in question.

SPHERE OF VALIDITY OF THE NORMS. Since norms regulate human behavior, and human behavior takes place in time and space, norms are valid for a certain time and for a certain space. The validity of a norm may begin at one moment and end at another. The norms of Czechoslovakian law began to be valid on a certain day of 1918, the norms of Austrian law ceased to be valid on the day when the Austrian Republic had been incorporated into the German Reich in 1938. The validity of a norm has also a relation to space. In order to be valid at all, it must be valid, not only for a certain time, but also for a certain territory. The norms of French law are valid only in France, the norms of Mexican law only in Mexico. We may therefore speak of the temporal and the territorial sphere of validity of a norm.

Occasionally it is asserted that norms can have validity not for the past but only for the future. That is not so, and the assertion appears to be due to a failure to distinguish between the validity of a norm and the efficacy of the idea of a norm. The idea of a norm as a psychic fact can become efficacious only in the future, in the sense that this idea must temporally precede the behavior conforming to the norm, since the cause must temporally precede the effect. But the norm may refer also to past behavior. Past and future are relative to a certain moment in time. The moment which those who argue that a norm is valid only for the future have in mind is evidently the moment when the norm was created. What they mean is that norms cannot refer to events which had taken place before that moment. But this does not hold if we are considering the validity of a norm as distinguished from the efficacy of its idea. Nothing prevents us from applying a norm

as a scheme of interpretation, a standard of evaluation, to facts
which occurred before the moment when the norm came into
existence. What someone did in the past we may evaluate according to a norm which assumed validity only after it had been done.

RETROACTIVE LAWS AND *Ignorantia Juris*. The moral and political value of retroactive laws may be disputed, but their possibility
cannot be doubted. The constitution of the United States, for
instance, says in Article I, section 9, clause 3: "No . . . *ex post
facto* law shall be passed." The term *"ex post facto* law" is interpreted as penal law with retroactive force. Retroactive laws are
considered to be objectionable and undesirable because it hurts
our feeling of justice to inflict a sanction, especially a punishment,
upon an individual because of an action or omission of which this
individual could not know that it would entail this sanction. However, on the other hand, we recognize the principle—a fundamental principle of all positive legal orders—*ignorantia juris
neminem excusat*, ignorance of the law excuses no one. The fact
that an individual does not know that the law attaches a sanction
to his action or omission is no reason for not inflicting the sanction upon him. Sometimes the principle in question is interpreted
restrictively: ignorance of the law is no excuse if the individual
did not know the law although it was possible to know the law.
Then this principle seems not incompatible with the rejection of
retroactive laws. For in case of a retroactive law it is indeed impossible to know the law at the moment when the act is performed
to which the retroactive law attaches a sanction. The distinction,
however, between a case in which the individual can know the law
valid at the moment he commits the delict and a case in which
the individual cannot know the law is more than problematical.
In fact, it is generally presupposed that a law which is valid can
be known by the individuals whose behavior is regulated by the
law. In fact, it is a *presumptio juris et de jure*, i.e. an "irrebuttable
presumption," a legal presumption against which no evidence is
permitted, a legal hypothesis the incorrectness of which must not
be proved, that all the norms of a positive legal order can be
known by the individuals subject to this order. This is obviously
not true; the presumption in question is a typical legal fiction.
Hence, with respect to the possibility or impossibility of knowing

the law, there is no essential difference between a retroactive law and many cases in which a non-retroactive law is not, and cannot, be known by the individual to whom this law has to be applied.

The Legal Norm

LEGAL NORM AND RULE OF LAW IN A DESCRIPTIVE SENSE. If "coercion" in the sense here defined is an essential element of law, then the norms which form a legal order must be norms stipulating a coercive act, i.e. a sanction. In particular, the general norms must be norms in which a certain sanction is made dependent upon certain conditions, this dependence being expressed by the concept of "ought." This does not mean that the law-making organs necessarily have to give the norms the form of such hypothetical "ought" statements. The different elements of a norm may be contained in very different products of the law-making procedure, and they may be linguistically expressed in very different ways. When the legislator forbids theft, he may, for instance, first define the concept of theft in a number of sentences which form an article of a statute, and then stipulate the sanction in another sentence, which may be part of another article of the same statute or even part of an entirely different statute. Often the latter sentence does not have the linguistic form of an imperative or an "ought" sentence but the form of a prediction of a future event. The legislator frequently makes use of the future tense, saying that a thief "will be" punished in such and such a way. He then presupposes that the question as to who is a thief has been answered somewhere else, in the same or in some other statute. The phrase "will be punished" does not imply the prediction of a future event—the legislator is no prophet—but an "imperative" or a "command," these terms taken in a figurative sense. What the norm-creating authority means is that the sanction "ought" to be executed against the thief, when the conditions of the sanction are fulfilled.

It is the task of the science of law to represent the law of a community, i.e. the material produced by the legal authority in the law-making procedure, in the form of statements to the effect that "if such and such conditions are fulfilled, then such and such a sanction shall follow." These statements, by means of which the science of law represents law, must not be confused with the norms created by the law-making authorities. It is preferable not to call these statements norms, but legal rules. The legal norms enacted by the law creating authorities are prescriptive; the rules of law formulated by the science of law are descriptive. It is of importance that the term "legal rule" or "rule of law" be employed here in a descriptive sense.

RULE OF LAW AND LAW OF NATURE. The rule of law, the term used in a descriptive sense, is a hypothetical judgment attaching certain consequences to certain conditions. This is the logical form of the law of nature, too. Just as the science of law, the science of nature describes its object in sentences which have the character of hypothetical judgments. And like the rule of law, the law of nature, too, connects two facts with one another as condition and consequence. The condition is here the "cause," the consequence the "effect." The fundamental form of the law of nature is the law of causality. The difference between the rule of law and the law of nature seems to be that the former refers to human beings and their behavior, whilst the latter refers to things and their reactions. Human behavior, however, may also be the subject-matter of natural laws, insofar as human behavior, too, belongs to nature. The rule of law and the law of nature differ not so much by the elements they connect as by the manner of their connection. The law of nature establishes that if A is, B is (or will be). The rule of law says: If A is, B ought to be. The rule of law is a norm (in the descriptive sense of that term). The meaning of the connection established by the law of nature between two elements is the "is," whereas the meaning of the connection between two elements established by the rule of law is the "ought." The principle according to which natural science describes its object is causality; the principle according to which the science of law describes its object is normativity.

The Unity of a Normative Order

THE REASON OF VALIDITY: THE BASIC NORM. The legal order is a system of norms. The question then arises: What is it that makes a system out of a multitude of norms? When does a norm belong to a certain system of norms, an order? This question is in close connection with the question as to the reason of validity of a norm.

In order to answer this question, we must first clarify the grounds on which we assign validity to a norm. When we assume the truth of a statement about reality, it is because the statement corresponds to reality, because our experience confirms it. The statement "A physical body expands when heated" is true, because we have repeatedly and without exception observed that physical bodies expand when they are heated. A norm is not a statement about reality and is therefore incapable of being "true" or "false," in the sense determined above. A norm is either valid or non-valid. Of the two statements: "You shall assist a fellowman in need," and "You shall lie whenever you find it useful," only the first, not the second, is considered to express a valid norm. What is the reason?

The reason for the validity of a norm is not, like the test of the truth of an "is" statement, its conformity to reality. As we have already stated, a norm is not valid because it is efficacious. The question why something ought to occur can never be answered by an assertion to the effect that something occurs, but only by an assertion that something ought to occur. In the language of daily life, it is true, we frequently justify a norm by referring to a fact. We say, for instance: "You shall not kill because God has forbidden it in one of the Ten Commandments"; or a mother says to her child: "You ought to go to school because your father has ordered it." However, in these statements the fact that God has issued a command or the fact that the father has ordered the child to do something is only apparently the reason for the validity of the norms in question. The true reason is norms tacitly presupposed because taken for granted. The reason for the validity of the norm, You shall not kill, is the general norm, You shall obey the commands of God. The reason for the validity of the norm, You ought to go to school, is the general norm, Children ought to obey their father. If these norms are not presupposed, the references to the facts concerned are not answers to the questions why we shall not kill, why the child ought to go to school.

The fact that somebody commands something is, in itself, no reason for the statement that one ought to behave in conformity with the command, no reason for considering the command as a valid norm, no reason for the validity of the norm the contents of which corresponds to the command. The reason for the validity of a norm is always a norm, not a fact. The quest for the reason of validity of a norm leads back, not to reality, but to another norm from which the first norm is derivable in a sense that will be investigated later. Let us, for the present, discuss a concrete example. We accept the statement "You shall assist a fellowman in need," as a valid norm because it follows from the statement "You shall love your neighbor." This statement we accept as a valid norm, either because it appears to us as an ultimate norm whose validity is self-evident, or—for instance—Christ has bidden that you shall love your neighbor, and we postulate as an ultimate valid norm the statement "You shall obey the commandments of Christ." The statement "You shall lie whenever you find it useful," we do not accept as a valid norm, because it is neither derivable from another valid norm nor is it in itself an ultimate, self-evidently valid norm.

A norm the validity of which cannot be derived from a superior norm we call a "basic" norm. All norms whose validity may be traced back to one and the same basic norm form a system of norms, or an order. This basic norm constitutes, as a common source, the bond between all the different norms of which an order consists. That a norm belongs to a certain system of norms, to a certain normative order, can be tested only by ascertaining that it derives its validity from the basic norm constituting the order. Whereas an "is" statement is true because it agrees with the reality of sensuous experience, an "ought" statement is a valid norm only if it belongs to such a valid system of norms, if it can be derived from a basic norm presupposed as valid. The ground of truth of an "is" statement is its conformity to the reality of our experience; the reason for the validity of a norm is a presupposition, a norm presupposed to be an ultimately valid, that is, a basic norm. The quest for the reason of validity of a norm is not—like the quest for the cause of an effect—a *regressus ad infinitum*; it is terminated by a highest norm which is the last reason of validity within the normative system, whereas a last or first cause has no place within a system of natural reality.

THE STATIC SYSTEM OF NORMS. According to the nature of the basic norm, we may distinguish between two different types of orders or normative systems: static and dynamic systems. Within an order of the first kind the norms are "valid" and that means, we assume that the individuals whose behavior is regulated by the norms "ought" to behave as the norms prescribe, by virtue of their contents: Their contents has an immediately evident quality that guarantees their validity, or, in other terms: the norms are valid because of their inherent appeal. This quality the norms have because they are derivable from a specific basic norm as the particular is derivable from the general. The binding force of the basic norm is itself self-evident, or at least presumed to be so. Such norms as "You must not lie," "You must not deceive," "You shall keep your promise," follow from a general norm prescribing truthfulness. From the norm "You shall love your neighbor" one may deduce such norms as "You must not hurt your neighbor," "You shall help him in need," and so on. If one asks why one has to love one's neighbor, perhaps the answer will be found in some still more general norm, let us say the postulate that one has to live "in harmony with the universe." If that is the most general norm of whose validity we are convinced, we will consider it as the ultimate norm. Its obligatory nature may appear so obvious that one does not feel any need to ask for the reason of its validity. Perhaps one may also succeed in deducing the principle of truthfulness and its consequences from this "harmony" postulate. One would then have reached a norm on which a whole system of morality could be based. However, we are not interested here in the question of what specific norm lies at the basis of such and such a system of morality. It is essential only that the various norms of any such system are implicated by the basic norm as the particular is implied by the general, and that, therefore, all the particular norms of such a system are obtainable by means of an intellectual operation, viz., by the inference from the general to the particular. Such a system is of a static nature.

THE DYNAMIC SYSTEM OF NORMS. The derivation of a particular norm may, however, be carried out also in another way. A child,

THE PURE THEORY OF LAW (125

asking why it must not lie, might be given the answer that its father has forbidden it to lie. If the child should further ask why it has to obey its father, the reply would perhaps be that God has commanded that it obey its parents. Should the child put the question why one has to obey the commands of God, the only answer would be that this is a norm beyond which one cannot look for a more ultimate norm. That norm is the basic norm providing the foundation for a system of dynamic character. Its various norms cannot be obtained from the basic norm by any intellectual operation. The basic norm merely establishes a certain authority, which may well in turn vest norm-creating power in some other authorities. The norms of a dynamic system have to be created through acts of will by those individuals who have been authorized to create norms by some higher norm. This authorization is a delegation. Norm creating power is delegated from one authority to another authority; the former is the higher, the latter the lower authority. The basic norm of a dynamic system is the fundamental rule according to which the norms of the system are to be created. A norm forms part of a dynamic system if it has been created in a way that is—in the last analysis—determined by the basic norm. A norm thus belongs to the religious system just given by way of example if it is created by God or originates in an authority having its power from God, "delegated" by God.

The Law as a Dynamic System of Norms

THE POSITIVITY OF LAW. The system of norms we call a legal order is a system of the dynamic kind. Legal norms are not valid because they themselves or the basic norm have a content the binding force of which is self-evident. They are not valid because of their inherent appeal. Legal norms may have any kind of content. There is no kind of human behavior that, because of its nature, could not be made into a legal duty corresponding to a legal right. The validity of a legal norm cannot be questioned on the ground that its contents are incompatible with some moral or political value. A norm is a valid legal norm by virtue of the fact that it has been created according to a definite rule and by virtue thereof only. The basic norm of a legal order is the postulated ultimate rule according to which the norms of this order are established and annulled, receive and lose their validity. The statement "Any man who manufactures or sells alcoholic liquors as beverages shall be punished" is a valid legal norm if it belongs to a certain legal order. This it does if this norm has been created in a definite way ultimately determined by the basic norm of that legal order, and if it has not again been nullified in a definite way, ultimately determined by the same basic norm. The basic norm may, for instance, be such that a norm belongs to the system provided that it has been decreed by the parliament or created by custom or established by the courts, and has not been abolished by a decision of the parliament or through custom or a contrary court practice. The statement mentioned above is no valid legal norm if it does not belong to a valid legal order—it may be that no such norm has been created in the way ultimately determined by the basic norm, or it may be that, although a norm has been created in that way, it has been repealed in a way ultimately determined by the basic norm.

Law is always positive law, and its positivity lies in the fact that it is created and annulled by acts of human beings, thus being independent of morality and similar norm systems. This constitutes the difference between positive law and natural law, which, like morality, is deduced from a presumably self-evident basic norm which is considered to be the expression of the "will of nature" or of "pure reason." The basic norm of a positive legal order is nothing but the fundamental rule according to which the various norms of the order are to be created. It qualifies a certain event as the initial event in the creation of the various legal norms. It is the starting point of a norm-creating process and, thus, has an entirely dynamic character. The particular norms of the legal order cannot be logically deduced from this basic norm, as can the norm "Help your neighbor when he needs your help" from the norm "Love your neighbor." They are to be created by a special act of will, not concluded from a premise by an intellectual operation.

The Basic Norm of a Legal Order

THE BASIC NORM AND THE CONSTITUTION. The derivation of the norms of a legal order from the basic norm of that order is performed by showing that the particular norms have been created in accordance with the basic norm. To the question why a certain act of coercion—e.g., the fact that one individual deprives another individual of his freedom by putting him in jail—is a legal act, the answer is: because it has been prescribed by an individual norm, a judicial decision. To the question why this individual norm is valid as part of a definite legal order, the answer is: because it has been created in conformity with a criminal statute. This statute, finally, receives its validity from the constitution, since it has been established by the competent organ in the way the constitution prescribes.

If we ask why the constitution is valid, perhaps we come upon an older constitution. Ultimately we reach some constitution that is the first historically and that was laid down by an individual usurper or by some kind of assembly. The validity of this first constitution is the last presupposition, the final postulate, upon which the validity of all the norms of our legal order depends. It is postulated that one ought to behave as the individual, or the individuals, who laid down the first constitution have ordained. This is the basic norm of the legal order under consideration. The document which embodies the first constitution is a real constitution, a binding norm, only on the condition that the basic norm is presupposed to be valid. Only upon this presupposition are the declarations of those to whom the constitution confers norm-creating power binding norms. It is this presupposition that enables us to distinguish between individuals who are legal authorities and other individuals whom we do not regard as such, between acts of human beings which create legal norms and acts which have no such effect. All these legal norms belong to one and the same legal order because their validity can be traced back—directly or indirectly—to the first constitution. That the first constitution is a binding legal norm is presupposed, and the formulation of the presupposition is the basic norm of this legal order. The basic norm of a religious norm system says that one ought to behave as God and the authorities instituted by Him command. Similarly, the basic norm of a legal order prescribes that one ought to behave as the "fathers" of the constitution and the individuals—directly or indirectly—authorized (delegated) by the constitution command. Expressed in the form of a legal norm: coercive acts ought to be carried out only under the conditions and in the way determined by the "fathers" of the constitution or the organs delegated by them. This is, schematically formulated, the basic norm of the legal order of a single State, the basic norm of a national legal order. It is to the national legal order that we have here limited our attention. Later, we shall consider what bearing the assumption of an international law has upon the question of the basic norm of national law.

THE SPECIFIC FUNCTION OF THE BASIC NORM. That a norm of the kind just mentioned is the basic norm of the national legal order does not imply that it is impossible to go beyond that norm. Certainly one may ask why one has to respect the first constitution as a binding norm. The answer might be that the fathers of the first constitution were empowered by God. The characteristic of so-called legal positivism is, however, that it dispenses with any such religious justification of the legal order. The ultimate hypothesis of positivism is the norm authorizing the historically first legislator. The whole function of this basic norm is to confer law-creating power on the act of the first legislator and on all the other acts based on the first act. To interpret these acts of human beings as legal acts and their products as binding norms, and that means to interpret the empirical material which presents itself as law as such, is possible only on the condition that the basic norm is presupposed as a valid norm. The basic norm is only the necessary presupposition of any positivistic interpretation of the legal material.

The basic norm is not created in a legal procedure by a law-creating organ. It is not—as a positive legal norm is—valid because it is created in a certain way by a legal act, but it is valid because it is presupposed to be valid; and it is presupposed to be valid because without this presupposition no human act could be interpreted as a legal, especially as a norm-creating, act.

By formulating the basic norm, we do not introduce into the science of law any new method. We merely make explicit what all jurists, mostly unconsciously, assume when they consider positive law as a system of valid norms and not only as a complex of facts, and at the same time repudiate any natural law from which positive law would receive its validity. That the basic norm really exists in the juristic consciousness is the result of a simple analysis of actual juristic statements. The basic norm is the answer to the question: how—and that means under what condition—are all these juristic statements concerning legal norms, legal duties, legal rights, and so on, possible?

CHANGE OF THE BASIC NORM. It is just the phenomenon of revolution which clearly shows the significance of the basic norm. Suppose that a group of individuals attempt to seize power by force, in order to remove the legitimate government in a hitherto monarchic State, and to introduce a republican form of government. If they succeed, if the old order ceases, and the new order begins to be efficacious, because the individuals whose behavior the new order regulates actually behave, by and large, in conformity with the new order, then this order is considered as a valid order. It is now according to this new order that the actual behavior of individuals is interpreted as legal or illegal. But this means that a new basic norm is presupposed. It is no longer the norm according to which the old monarchical constitution is valid, but a norm according to which the new republican constitution is valid, a norm endowing the revolutionary government with legal authority. If the revolutionaries fail, if the order they have tried to establish remains inefficacious, then, on the other hand, their undertaking is interpreted, not as a legal, a law-creating act, as the establishment of a constitution, but as an illegal act, as the crime of treason, and this according to the old monarchic constitution and its specific basic norm.

THE PRINCIPLE OF EFFECTIVENESS. If we attempt to make explicit the presupposition on which these juristic considerations rest, we find that the norms of the old order are regarded as devoid of validity because the old constitution and, therefore, the legal norms based on this constitution, the old legal order as a whole, has lost its efficacy; because the actual behavior of men does no longer conform to this old legal order. Every single norm loses its validity when the total legal order to which it belongs loses its efficacy as a whole. The efficacy of the entire legal order is a necessary condition for the validity of every single norm of the order. A *conditio sine qua non*, but not a *conditio per quam*. The efficacy of the total legal order is a condition, not the reason for the validity of its constituent norms. These norms are valid not because the total order is efficacious, but because they are created in a constitutional way. They are valid, however, only on the condition that the total order is efficacious; they cease to be valid, not only when they are annulled in a constitutional way, but also when the total order ceases to be efficacious. It cannot be maintained that, legally, men have to behave in conformity with a certain norm, if the total legal order, of which that norm is an integral part, has lost its efficacy. The principle of legitimacy is restricted by the principle of effectiveness.

DESUETUDO. This must not be understood to mean that a single legal norm loses its validity, if that norm itself and only that norm is rendered ineffective. Within a legal order which as a whole is efficacious there may occur isolated norms which are valid and which yet are not efficacious, that is, are not obeyed and not applied even when the conditions which they themselves lay down for their application are fulfilled. But even in this case efficacy has some relevance to validity. If the norm remains permanently inefficacious, the norm is deprived of its validity by "desuetudo."

The relation between validity and efficacy thus appears to be the following: A norm is a valid legal norm if (a) it has been created in a way provided for by the legal order to which it belongs, and (b) if it has not been annulled either in a way provided for by that legal order or by way of desuetudo or by the fact that the legal order as a whole has lost its efficacy.

The Static and the Dynamic Concept of Law

If one looks upon the legal order from the dynamic point of view, as it has been expounded here, it seems possible to define the concept of law in a way quite different from that in which we have tried to define it in this theory. It seems especially possible to ignore the element of coercion in defining the concept of law.

It is a fact that the legislator can enact commandments without considering it necessary to attach a criminal or civil sanction to their violation. If such norms are also called legal norms, it is because they were created by an authority which, according to the constitution, is competent to create law. They are law because they issue from a law-creating authority. According to this concept, law is anything that has come about in the way the constitution prescribes for the creation of law. This dynamic concept differs from the concept of law defined as a coercive norm. According to the dynamic concept, law is something created by a certain process, and everything created in this way is law. This dynamic concept, however, is only apparently a concept of law. It contains no answer to the question of what is the essence of law, what is the criterion by which law can be distinguished from other social norms. This dynamic concept furnishes an answer only to the question whether or not and why a certain norm belongs to a system of valid legal norms, forms a part of a certain legal order. And the answer is, a norm belongs to a certain legal order if it is created in accordance with a procedure prescribed by the constitution fundamental to this legal order.

The Static Principle of Natural Law and the Dynamic Principle of Positive Law*

The essential relation of unity which prevails among the norms of one system with regard to their basic norm may be of different types. Static and dynamic systems may be distinguished by the method of "derivation" prevailing in them. The norms of an order may be directly or indirectly "derived" from its basic norm and thus obtain their validity. In the former case, the basic norm unfolds itself into norms of varying content, just as a general concept issues special concepts which are subsumed under it. The basic norm of truth or truthfulness yields the norms: "you shall

* [This section of Kelsen's *Die Philosophischen Grundlagen der Naturrechtslehre und des Rechtspositivismus*, 1929, was translated by W. H. Kraus.]

not defraud," "you shall keep your promise," etc.; the basic norm
of love: "you shall not injure anyone," "you shall help the needy,"
etc. From these particular norms more special ones follow, for
instance: that the merchant must not conceal defects of his goods
which are known to him, that the buyer shall pay the promised
purchase price at the agreed time, that one must not injure anyone's reputation or inflict physical injury on anyone, etc. All these
norms follow from the basic norm without requiring a special act
of norm-making, an act of human will. They are all contained in
the basic norm from the outset and are derivable from it by a mere
intellectual operation. A dynamic system is different. Its basic
norm merely empowers a specific human will to create norms.
"Obey your parents" is such a basic norm. No mere intellectual
operation can derive a single special norm from it. A parental
order with a specific content is needed (for instance: "go to
school"), that is, a special act of norm-creation or law-making.
This particular norm does not have "validity" simply because its
content is consistent with the basic norm, as a special thing is
related to a general one, but only because the act of its creation
is in keeping with the rule enunciated by the basic norm, because
it was made as the basic norm prescribed. The authority which
has received its power from the basic norm can, in turn, delegate
its jurisdiction either for the whole or for a part of its sphere.
Thus parents may delegate a teacher for the education of their
children, and this delegation may continue further down the
line. The unity of the dynamic system is the unity of a system of
delegation.

It follows that natural law ideally tends to be a static system of
norms, even though the question remains, whether that is possible
in view of man's inadequate qualities of will and intellect. It is also
evident from the preceding discussion that positive law, whose
basic norm consists in the delegation of a law-making authority,
constitutes a dynamic system. "Positivity" actually consists in this
dynamic principle. The whole contrast between natural and positive law may, in a certain sense, be presented as the contrast
between a static and a dynamic system of norms. To the extent
that natural law theory ceases to develop its natural order according to a static principle and substitutes a dynamic one, that is, as

it is impelled to introduce the principle of delegation because it has to realize itself in application to actual human conditions, it imperceptibly changes into positive law.

The static principle, on the other hand, in turn gains access to the system of positive law. This is not because the authority constituted by the basic norm cannot itself create other than pure norms of delegation. The constitutional legislator does not determine merely organs for legislation, but also a legislative procedure; and, at times, his norms, that is the constitution, determine in the so-called fundamental rights and bills of liberty the content of the laws, when they prescribe a minimum of what they should and should not contain. The ordinary legislator in particular is by no means content with the establishment of agencies for adjudication and administration. He issues norms to regulate the procedure of these agencies and others by which he largely determines the content of those individual norms which law-applying agencies are called upon to create. The application of a general norm of positive law to a concrete case involves the same intellectual operation as the deduction of an individual from a general norm of natural law. Yet no individual norm, as a positive norm, simply emanates from a general legal norm (such as: "a thief should be punished") as the particular from the general, but only in so far as such an individual norm has been created by the law-applying organs. Within the system of positive law no norm, not even the material one, is valid, unless it has been created in a manner ultimately prescribed by the basic norm. The existence of other than purely delegating norms does not signify a limitation of the dynamic principle in positive law. Such a limitation comes from another direction.

Above all, even the validity of the basic norm of a given positive legal order does not rest on the dynamic principle. This principle makes its first appearance in and through the basic norm. The basic norm is not itself a made, but a hypothetical, presupposed norm; it is not positive law, but only its condition. Even this clearly shows the limitation of the idea of legal "positivity." The basic norm is not valid because it has been created in a certain way, but its validity is assumed by virtue of its content. It is valid, then, like a norm of natural law, apart from its merely

hypothetical validity. The idea of a pure positive law, like that
of natural law, has its limitation.

ALF ROSS

Directives and the "Validity" of Law

*Alf Ross (see pp. 68–74) is a professor of law at the University
of Copenhagen. His thought has affinities with both legal
positivism and legal realism, and this selection also could
have been placed in the third section of this reader. Ross is
a member of a group of writers called "Scandinavian realists."*

Observing the law as it functions in society we find that a large
number of human actions are interpreted as a coherent whole of
meaning and motivation by means of legal norms as the scheme of
interpretation. A purchases a house from B. It turns out that the
house is full of termites. A asks B for a reduction in the purchase
price, but B will not agree. A brings an action against B, and the
judge in accordance with the law of contract orders B to pay to A
a certain sum of money within a given time. B does not do this.
A has the sheriff levy upon the personal property of B which is then
sold in auction. This sequence of events comprises a whole series
of human actions, from the establishment of the law of contract to
the auction. A biological-physical consideration of these actions
cannot reveal any causal connection between them. Such connec-

Reprinted by permission of the author and publishers from Alf Ross, *On Law
and Justice* (London: Stevens and Sons, Ltd., 1958), pp. 17–18, 32–8, 70.
Abridged by the editor.

tions lie within each single individual. But we interpret them with the aid of the reference scheme "valid law" as legal phenomena constituting a coherent whole of meaning and motivation. Each one of these actions acquires its legal character only when this is done. A's purchase of the house happens by word of mouth or with the aid of written characters. But these become a "purchase" only when seen in relation to the legal norms. The various actions are mutually motivating just like the moves in chess. The judge, for example, is motivated by A's and B's parts in the deal (and the further circumstances in connection with it, the condition of the house), and by the precedents establishing the law of contract. The whole proceeding has the character of a "game," only according to norms which are far more complicated than the norms of the game of chess.

On the basis of what has been said, the following hypothesis is advanced: The concept "valid (Illinois, California, common) law" can be explained and defined in principle in the same manner as the concept "valid (for any two players) norm of chess." That is to say, "valid law" means the abstract set of normative ideas which serve as a scheme of interpretation for the phenomena of law in action, which again means that these norms are effectively followed, and followed because they are experienced and felt to be socially binding.[1]

This conclusion may perhaps be thought commonplace, and it may seem that a vast apparatus of reasoning has been employed to this end. This might be true if the problems were approached by a person with no preconceived notions. But it would not be true for an historical approach. By far the greater part of all writers on jurisprudence up to the present have maintained that the concept "valid law" cannot be explained without recourse to the metaphysical. The law according to this view is not merely an empirical phenomenon. When we say that a rule of law is "valid" we refer not only to something factual, that can be observed, but also to a "validity" of a metaphysical character. This validity is alleged to be a pure concept of reason of divine origin or existing *a priori* (independent of experience) in the rational nature of man. And eminent writers on jurisprudence who deny such spiritual

[1] By the judge and other legal authorities applying the law.

metaphysics have nevertheless been of the opinion that the "validity" of the law can only be explained by means of specific postulates.

Seen in this light our preliminary conclusion will, I trust, not be called commonplace. This analysis of a simple model is calculated to raise doubts as to the necessity of metaphysical explanations of the concept of law. Who would ever think of tracing the valid norms of chess back to an *a priori* validity, a pure idea of chess, bestowed upon man by God or deduced by man's eternal reason? The thought is ridiculous, because we do not take chess as seriously as law—because stronger emotions are bound up with the concepts of law. But this is no reason for believing that logical analysis should adopt a fundamentally different attitude in each of the two cases.

A national law system, like the norms of chess, constitutes an individual system determined by "an inner coherence of meaning," and our task is to indicate what this consists of. As far as the rules of chess are concerned, the case is simple. Coherence of meaning is given by the fact that they all, directly or indirectly, have reference to the moves made by the persons playing the game of chess. If the rules of law are in like manner to constitute a system, they must in like manner have reference to definite actions performed by definite persons. But what and who are these? This question can only be answered by finding out, by an analysis of the rules commonly regarded as a national law system, to whom they are directed and what their purport is.

The norms of law may be divided according to their immediate content into two groups, norms of conduct and norms of competence or procedure. The first group includes those norms which prescribe a certain course of action—for example, the rule in the Uniform Negotiable Instruments Act, s. 62, which prescribes that the acceptor of a negotiable instrument engages that he will pay it according to the tenor of his acceptance. The second group contains those which create a competence (power, authority)—they are directives to the effect that norms which come into existence in conformity with a declared mode of procedure shall be regarded as norms of conduct. A norm of competence is thus an indirectly expressed norm of conduct. The norms of the Constitution concerning the legislature, for example, are indirectly expressed norms of conduct which prescribe behaviour in accordance with the further norms of conduct which come into being by way of legislation.

To whom are the norms of conduct directed? The Uniform Negotiable Instruments Act, s. 62, for example, apparently prescribes how a person who has accepted a bill shall behave. But this is not an exhaustive statement of the normative meaning of the regulation; indeed, it does not get anywhere near what is really relevant. Section 62 is at the same time a directive to the courts as to how in a case under this rule they are to exercise their authority. Obviously, this alone is of interest to the jurist. If it must be assumed of any statutory provision that it does not contain a directive to the courts it can be regarded only as a moral-ideological pronouncement without legal relevance. Conversely, if it is established that a provision does contain a directive to the courts, then there is no need to give the private individual any further instructions as to his conduct. These are two sides of the same matter. The instruction to the private individual is implicit in the fact that he knows what reactions on the part of the courts he can expect in given conditions. If he wants to avoid these reactions, this knowledge constitutes a challenge to him to arrange his conduct accordingly.

The provisions of the criminal law are drafted in this way. They say nothing about citizens being forbidden to commit homicide, but merely indicate to the judge what his judgment shall be in such a case. In principle there is nothing to prevent the rules in the Negotiable Instruments Act, or any other norms of conduct, from being drafted after the same pattern. This shows that the real content of a norm of conduct is a directive to the judge, while the instruction to the private individual is a derived and figurative legal norm deduced from it.

The norms of competence are reducible to norms of conduct and must therefore also be interpreted as directives to the courts.

The judgment is the basis for execution. Whatever form execution may take, it constitutes potentially the exercise of physical force against a person not willing to act according to the tenor of the judgment.

A "judge" is a person qualified under the rules governing the organisation of the courts and the appointment or election of judges. In this way the rules of private law (directed to the judges) are integrated with the rules of public law. The law in its entirety determines not only—in the rules of conduct—under what conditions the exercise of force shall be ordered but also the public authorities, the courts, established to order the exercise of force.[2]

The natural corollary of this, and that which gives the public exercise of force its special meaning and effect, is that the right to the exercise of physical force is in all essentials the monopoly of public authorities. Where the machinery for the monopoly of the exercise of force exists, we speak of a State.

Summarising then: A national law system is an integrated body of rules, determining the conditions under which physical force shall be exercised against a person; the national law system sets up a machinery of public authorities (the courts and the executive agencies) whose function it is to order and carry out the exercise of force accordingly in specific cases; or shorter: A national law system is the rules for the establishment and functioning of the State machinery of force.

The Validity of the Legal System

The point from which we set out is the hypothesis that a system of norms is "valid" if it is able to serve as a scheme of interpretation for a corresponding set of social actions in such a way that it becomes possible for us to comprehend this set of actions as a coherent whole of meaning and motivation, and within certain limits to predict them. This capacity within the system is based on the fact that the norms are effectively complied with, because they are felt to be socially binding.

What, now, are those social facts which as legal phenomena constitute the counterpart of the legal norms? They must be the human actions regulated by the legal norms. These, as we have

---

[2] Facts are a little more complicated than described here, because in some, relatively infrequent cases, force may be ordered directly by administrative agencies without the intervention of the courts.

seen, are in the last analysis norms determining the conditions under which force shall be exercised through the machinery of the State; or—briefly—norms for the ordering by the courts of the exercise of force. It follows that the legal phenomena as the counterpart of the norms must be the decisions of the courts. It is here that we must seek for the effectiveness that is the validity of law.

A national law system, considered as a valid system of norms, can accordingly be defined as the norms which actually are operative in the mind of the judge, because they are felt by him to be socially binding and therefore obeyed. The test of the validity is that on this hypothesis—that is, accepting the system of norms as a scheme of interpretation—we can comprehend the actions of the judge (the decisions of the courts) as meaningful responses to given conditions and within certain limits predict them—in the same way as the norms of chess enable us to understand the moves of the players as meaningful responses and predict them.

The action of the judge is a response to a number of conditions determined by the legal norms—that a contract of sale has been performed, that the seller has not delivered, that the buyer has given notice in due time, and so on. Also these conditioning facts acquire their specific meaning as legal acts through an interpretation in the light of the ideology of the norms. For this reason they might be included under the term legal phenomena in the wider sense or law in action.

Only the legal phenomena in the narrower sense, however— the application of the law by the courts—are decisive in determining the validity of the legal norms. In contrast to generally accepted ideas it must be emphasised that the law provides the norms for the behaviour of the courts, and not of private individuals. The effectiveness which conditions the validity of the norms can therefore be sought solely in the judicial application of the law, and not in the law in action among private individuals. If, for example, criminal abortion is prohibited, the true content of the law consists in a directive to the judge that he shall under certain conditions impose a penalty for criminal abortion. The decisive factor determining that the prohibition is valid law is solely the fact that it is effectively upheld by the courts where breaches of the law are brought to light and prosecuted.[3] It makes no difference whether the people comply with or frequently ignore the prohibition. This indifference results in the apparent paradox that the more effectively a rule is complied with in extrajudicial legal life, the more difficult it is to ascertain whether the rule possesses validity, because the courts have that much less opportunity to manifest their reaction.

In the foregoing, the terms "the judge" and "the courts" have been used indiscriminately. When we are speaking of a national law system, it is assumed that we are dealing with a set of norms which are supraindividual in the sense that they are particular to the nation, varying from nation to nation, not from one individual judge to another. For this reason it makes no difference whether one refers to "the judge" or to "the courts." So far as the individual judge is motivated by particular, personal ideas, these cannot be assigned to the law of the nation, although they are a factor which must be considered by anyone interested in forecasting a concrete legal decision.

When the basis for the validity of the law is sought in the decisions of the courts, the chain of reasoning may appear to be working in a circle. For it may be adduced that the qualification of judge is not merely a factual quality but can only be assigned by reference to valid law, in particular to the rules of public law governing the organisation of the courts and the appointment of judges. Before I can ascertain whether a certain rule of private law is valid law, therefore, I have to establish what is valid law in these other respects. And what is the criterion for this?

The answer to this problem is that the legal system forms a whole integrating the rules of private law with the rules of public law. Fundamentally, validity is a quality ascribed to the system as a whole. The test of the validity is that the system in its entirety, used as a scheme of interpretation, makes us to comprehend, not only the manner in which the judges act, but also that they

[3] The term "courts" is here understood as a comprehensive term for the authorities which combine to administer the criminal prosecutions: police, prosecuting authority and court. If the police regularly omit to investigate certain breaches of the law, or if the prosecuting authority regularly omits to bring a prosecution, the penal law loses its character of valid law, notwithstanding its application at rare intervals in the courts.

are acting in the capacity as "judges." There is no Archimedes point for the verification, no part of the law which is verified before any other part.[4]

The fact that fundamentally the entire legal system undergoes verification need not exclude the possibility of investigating whether a definite individual rule is valid law. It merely implies that the problem cannot be solved without reference to "valid law" as a whole.

The concept of the validity of the law rests, according to the explanation offered in this section, on hypotheses concerning the spiritual life of the judge. What is valid law cannot be ascertained by purely behaviouristic means, that is, by external observation of regularity in the reactions (customs) of the judges. Throughout a lengthy period the judge may have exhibited a certain typical reaction; for example, he may have imposed penalties for criminal abortion. Suddenly this reaction changes, because a new law has been promulgated. Validity cannot be ascertained by recourse to a more general, externally observable custom, namely, that of "obeying the legislator." For it is not possible from external observation to identify the "legislator" who is being obeyed. Purely external observation might lead one to the conclusion that obedience was paid to the persons, mentioned by their names, who at the time of observation were members of the legislature. But one day this too is changed. One can continue in this way right up to the constitution, but there is nothing to prevent the constitution from being changed too one day.

A behaviouristic interpretation, then, achieves nothing. The changing behaviour of the judge can only be comprehended and predicted through ideological interpretation, that is, by means of the hypothesis of a certain ideology which animates the judge and motivates his actions.

Another way of expressing the same thing is to say that law

[4] There is nothing peculiar in the fact that the system as a whole comes up for verification. The same principle also applies in natural science. The verification of one particular natural law takes place on the assumption that a number of others are true. The question is whether the particular law is compatible with the hitherto accepted system. But nothing is established beyond doubt. There is nothing to prevent fresh experience compelling us to revise all hitherto accepted starting points. It is always the entire systematic whole which remains the final criterion in deciding what shall be held to be true.

presupposes, not only regularity in the judge's mode of action, but also his experience of being bound by the rules. In the concept of validity two points are involved: partially the outward observable and regular compliance with a pattern of action, and partly the experience of this pattern of action as being a socially binding norm. Not every outward observable custom in the game of chess is an expression of a valid norm of chess, as, for example, not to open with a rook's pawn; in the same way not every outward and observable regularity in the reactions of the judge is the expression of a valid norm of law. It may be, for example, that a custom has developed of imposing only fines as the penalties for certain breaches of the law even though imprisonment is also authorised. Now it must, to be sure, be added that the customs of judges show a strong inclination to develop into binding norms, and that a custom will, in that case, be construed as the expression of valid law. But this is not the case so long as it is nothing more than a factual custom.

This twofold point in the concept of validity explains the dualism which has always marked this concept in current metaphysical theory of law. According to this theory valid law means both an order which is in fact effective and an order which possesses "binding force" derived from *a priori* principles; law is at the same time something factual in the world of reality and something valid in the world of ideas. It is not difficult to see that this dualism of viewpoint may lead to both logical and epistemological complications which find expression in a number of antinomies in the theory of law.[5] It leads consistently to a metaphysical assertion that existence itself in its innermost being is valid (Hegel.)[6] Like most metaphysical constructions, the construction of the immanent validity of positive law rests on a misinterpretation of certain experiences, in this case the experience that the law is not merely a factual, customary order, but an order which is experienced as being socially binding. The traditional conception, therefore, with the metaphysics removed, can be ap-

---

[5] The demonstration of such antinomies is the main theme of my book, *Towards a Realistic Jurisprudence* (1946).

[6] *Ibid.*, p. 42, and Alf Ross, *Kritik der sogenannten praktischen Erkenntnis* (1933), Chap. XII, 4.

propriated in support of my own view so far as it is opposed to a purely behaviouristic interpretation of the validity of the law.

Finally, if one radically rejects every ethical censure, as Kelsen does, and simply accepts as valid law the order which is actually upheld, specific validity as a categorical form becomes a superfluous drape. The impossibility of Kelsen's attempt, in determining the nature of positive law, to ignore psychological and social reality becomes apparent when we reach the initial hypothesis (basic norm or *Grundnorm*). As long as we remain on the lower steps of the legal system, it is possible to postpone the problem of the validity of the norm by referring back to a superior norm. But this procedure cannot be employed when we come to the initial hypothesis. At this point the question of the relation of the norm to reality becomes inescapably urgent. If the system is to make sense, it is clear that the initial hypothesis cannot be chosen arbitrarily. Kelsen himself says that it must be chosen in such a way that it covers the system which is actually in effect. But it is then clear that, in reality, effectivity is the criterion for positive law; and that the initial hypothesis, once we know what is positive law, in reality only has the function of investing it with the "validity" which is demanded by the metaphysical interpretation of legal consciousness, though no one knows what it is. The initial hypothesis is the ultimate source from which validity wells forth and branches out through the whole system. It might be possible to pass this over as a superfluous but harmless construction were it not that it results in shutting the eyes to a closer analysis of the criterion of effectivity. By making validity an internormative relation (deriving the validity of one norm from the validity of another) Kelsen has at the outset precluded himself from dealing with the heart of the problem of the validity of the law—the relation between the normative idea content and the social reality.[7]

[7] For further detail see Ross, *Towards a Realistic Jurisprudence* (1946), Chap. II, sec. 6, and review of Hans Kelsen, *What is Justice?* in *California L.R.* 45 (1957), 564 *et seq.*

H. L. A. HART

Law as the Union of
Primary and Secondary Rules

In this selection H. L. A. Hart (see above, p. 104) describes the steps that take us from "the pre-legal into the legal world."

ॐ

The Elements of Law

It is, of course, possible to imagine a society without a legislature, courts or officials of any kind. Indeed, there are many studies of primitive communities which not only claim that this possibility is realized but depict in detail the life of a society where the only means of social control is that general attitude of the group towards its own standard modes of behaviour in terms of which we have characterized rules of obligation.* A social structure of this kind is often referred to as one of "custom"; but we shall not use this term, because it often implies that the customary rules are very old and supported with less social pressure than other rules. To avoid these implications we shall refer to such a social structure as one of primary rules of obligation. If a society is to live by such primary rules alone, there are certain conditions which, granted a

---

Reprinted from H. L. A. Hart, *The Concept of Law* (1961), pp. 89–96, 98–107, by permission of the Clarendon Press, Oxford. Abridged by the editor.

* [When the members of a group have a reflective critical attitude towards certain of its modes of behavior, *i.e.*, regard them as standards, the members have adopted (what Hart calls) "the inner point of view." Demands for compliance are made and deviation from a standard is generally regarded as a fault open to criticism. Deviation is also generally accepted as a good reason for making a criticism. When the general demand for conformity is insistent and the social pressure brought to bear upon those who deviate or threaten to deviate is great, such standards are conceived of as rules imposing obligations.]

few of the most obvious truisms about human nature and the world we live in, must clearly be satisfied. The first of these conditions is that the rules must contain in some form restrictions on the free use of violence, theft, and deception to which human beings are tempted but which they must, in general, repress, if they are to coexist in close proximity to each other. Such rules are in fact always found in the primitive societies of which we have knowledge, together with a variety of others imposing on individuals various positive duties to perform services or make contributions to the common life. Secondly, though such a society may exhibit the tension, already described, between those who accept the rules and those who reject the rules except where fear of social pressure induces them to conform, it is plain that the latter cannot be more than a minority, if so loosely organized a society of persons, approximately equal in physical strength, is to endure: for otherwise those who reject the rules would have too little social pressure to fear. This too is confirmed by what we know of primitive communities where, though there are dissidents and malefactors, the majority live by the rules seen from the internal point of view.

More important for our present purpose is the following consideration. It is plain that only a small community closely knit by ties of kinship, common sentiment, and belief, and placed in a stable environment, could live successfully by such a régime of unofficial rules. In any other conditions such a simple form of social control must prove defective and will require supplementation in different ways. In the first place, the rules by which the group lives will not form a system, but will simply be a set of separate standards, without any identifying or common mark, except of course that they are the rules which a particular group of human beings accepts. They will in this respect resemble our own rules of etiquette. Hence if doubts arise as to what the rules are or as to the precise scope of some given rule, there will be no procedure for settling this doubt, either by reference to an authoritative text or to an official whose declarations on this point are authoritative. For, plainly, such a procedure and the acknowledgement of either authoritative text or persons involve the existence of rules of a type different from the rules of obligation or duty which *ex hypothesi* are all that the group has. This defect in the simple social structure of primary rules we may call its *uncertainty*.

A second defect is the *static* character of the rules. The only mode of change in the rules known to such a society will be the slow process of growth, whereby courses of conduct once thought optional become first habitual or usual, and then obligatory, and the converse process of decay, when deviations, once severely dealt with, are first tolerated and then pass unnoticed. There will be no means, in such a society, of deliberately adapting the rules to changing circumstances, either by eliminating old rules or introducing new ones: for, again, the possibility of doing this presupposes the existence of rules of a different type from the primary rules of obligation by which alone the society lives. In an extreme case the rules may be static in a more drastic sense. This, though never perhaps fully realized in any actual community, is worth considering because the remedy for it is something very characteristic of law. In this extreme case, not only would there be no way of deliberately changing the general rules, but the obligations which arise under the rules in particular cases could not be varied or modified by the deliberate choice of any individual. Each individual would simply have fixed obligations or duties to do or abstain from doing certain things. It might indeed very often be the case that others would benefit from the performance of these obligations; yet if there are only primary rules of obligation they would have no power to release those bound from performance or to transfer to others the benefits which would accrue from performance. For such operations of release or transfer create changes in the initial positions of individuals under the primary rules of obligation, and for these operations to be possible there must be rules of a sort different from the primary rules.

The third defect of this simple form of social life is the *inefficiency* of the diffuse social pressure by which the rules are maintained. Disputes as to whether an admitted rule has or has not been violated will always occur and will, in any but the smallest societies, continue interminably, if there is no agency specially empowered to ascertain finally, and authoritatively, the fact of violation. Lack of such final and authoritative determinations is to be distinguished from another weakness associated with it. This is the fact that punishments for violations of the rules, and other forms of social pressure involving physical effort or the use of force, are not administered by a special agency but are left to the individuals affected or to the group at large. It is obvious that the waste of time involved in the group's unorganized efforts to catch and punish offenders, and the smouldering vendettas which may result from self help in the absence of an official monopoly of "sanctions," may be serious. The history of law does, however, strongly suggest that the lack of official agencies to determine authoritatively the fact of violation of the rules is a much more serious defect; for many societies have remedies for this defect long before the other.

The remedy for each of these three main defects in this simplest form of social structure consists in supplementing the *primary* rules of obligation with *secondary* rules which are rules of a different kind. The introduction of the remedy for each defect might, in itself, be considered a step from the pre-legal into the legal world; since each remedy brings with it many elements that permeate law: certainly all three remedies together are enough to convert the régime of primary rules into what is indisputably a legal system. We shall consider in turn each of these remedies and show why law may most illuminatingly be characterized as a union of primary rules of obligation with such secondary rules. Before we do this, however, the following general points should be noted. Though the remedies consist in the introduction of rules which are certainly different from each other, as well as from the primary rules of obligation which they supplement, they have important features in common and are connected in various ways. Thus they may all be said to be on a different level from the primary rules, for they are all *about* such rules; in the sense that while primary rules are concerned with the actions that individuals must or must not do, these secondary rules are all concerned with the primary rules themselves. They specify the ways in which the primary rules may be conclusively ascertained, introduced, eliminated, varied, and the fact of their violation conclusively determined.

The simplest form of remedy for the *uncertainty* of the régime of primary rules is the introduction of what we shall call a "rule of recognition." This will specify some feature or features possession of which by a suggested rule is taken as a conclusive affirmative indication that it is a rule of the group to be supported by the social pressure it exerts. The existence of such a rule of recognition may take any of a huge variety of forms, simple or complex. It may, as in the early law of many societies, be no more than that an authoritative list or text of the rules is to be found in a written document or carved on some public monument. No doubt as a matter of history this step from the pre-legal to the legal may be accomplished in distinguishable stages, of which the first is the mere reduction to writing of hitherto unwritten rules. This is not itself the crucial step, though it is a very important one: what is crucial is the acknowledgement of reference to the writing or inscription as *authoritative*, i.e. as the *proper* way of disposing of doubts as to the existence of the rule. Where there is such an acknowledgement there is a very simple form of secondary rule: a rule for conclusive identification of the primary rules of obligation.

In a developed legal system the rules of recognition are of course more complex; instead of identifying rules exclusively by reference to a text or list they do so by reference to some general characteristic possessed by the primary rules. This may be the fact of their having been enacted by a specific body, or their long customary practice, or their relation to judicial decisions. Moreover, where more than one of such general characteristics are treated as identifying criteria, provision may be made for their possible conflict by their arrangement in an order of superiority, as by the common subordination of custom or precedent to statute, the latter being a "superior source" of law. Such complexity may make the rules of recognition in a modern legal system seem very different from the simple acceptance of an authoritative text: yet even in this simplest form, such a rule brings with it many elements distinctive of law. By providing an authoritative mark it introduces, although in embryonic form, the idea of a legal system: for the rules are now not just a discrete unconnected set but are, in a simple way, unified. Further, in the simple operation of identifying a given rule as possessing the required feature of being an item on an authoritative list of rules we have the germ of the idea of legal validity.

The remedy for the *static* quality of the régime of primary rules consists in the introduction of what we shall call "rules of change." The simplest form of such a rule is that which empowers an individual or body of persons to introduce new primary rules for the conduct of the life of the group, or of some class within it, and to eliminate old rules. It is in terms of such a rule, and not in terms of orders backed by threats, that the ideas of legislative enactment and repeal are to be understood. Such rules of change may be very simple or very complex: the powers conferred may be unrestricted or limited in various ways: and the rules may, besides specifying the persons who are to legislate, define in more or less rigid terms the procedure to be followed in legislation. Plainly, there will be a very close connexion between the rules of change and the rules of recognition: for where the former exists the latter will necessarily incorporate a reference to legislation as an identifying feature of the rules, though it need not refer to all the details of procedure involved in legislation. Usually some official certificate or official copy will, under the rules of recognition, be taken as a sufficient proof of due enactment. Of course if there is a social structure so simple that the only "source of law" is legislation, the rule of recognition will simply specify enactment as the unique identifying mark or criterion of validity of the rules.

The third supplement to the simple régime of primary rules, intended to remedy the *inefficiency* of its diffused social pressure, consists of secondary rules empowering individuals to make authoritative determinations of the question whether, on a particular occasion, a primary rule has been broken. The minimal form of adjudication consists in such determinations, and we shall call the secondary rules which confer the power to make them "rules of adjudication." Besides identifying the individuals who are to adjudicate, such rules will also define the procedure to be followed. Like the other secondary rules these are on a different level from the primary rules: though they may be reinforced by further rules imposing duties on judges to adjudicate, they do not impose duties but confer judicial powers and a special status on judicial declarations about the breach of obligations. Again these rules, like the other secondary rules, define a group of important legal concepts: in this case the concepts of judge or court, jurisdiction and judgment. Besides these resemblances to the other secondary rules, rules of adjudication have intimate connexions with them. Indeed, a system which has rules of adjudication is necessarily also committed to a rule of recognition of an elementary and imperfect sort. This is so because, if courts are empowered to make authoritative determinations of the fact that a rule has been broken, these cannot avoid being taken as authoritative determinations of what the rules are. So the rule which confers jurisdiction will also be a rule of recognition, identifying the primary rules through the judgments of the courts and these judgments will become a "source" of law. It is true that this form of rule of recognition, inseparable from the minimum form of jurisdiction, will be very imperfect. Unlike an authoritative text or a statute book, judgments may not be couched in general terms and their use as authoritative guides to the rules depends on a somewhat shaky inference from particular decisions, and the reliability of this must fluctuate both with the skill of the interpreter and the consistency of the judges.

It need hardly be said that in few legal systems are judicial powers confined to authoritative determinations of the fact of violation of the primary rules. Most systems have, after some delay, seen the advantages of further centralization of social pressure; and have partially prohibited the use of physical punishments or violent self help by private individuals. Instead they have supplemented the primary rules of obligation by further secondary rules, specifying or at least limiting the penalties for violation, and have conferred upon judges, where they have ascertained the fact of violation, the exclusive power to direct the application of penalties by other officials. These secondary rules provide the centralized official "sanctions" of the system.

If we stand back and consider the structure which has resulted from the combination of primary rules of obligation with the secondary rules of recognition, change and adjudication, it is plain that we have here not only the heart of a legal system, but a most powerful tool for the analysis of much that has puzzled both the jurist and the political theorist.

Not only are the specifically legal concepts with which the

lawyer is professionally concerned, such as those of obligation and rights, validity and source of law, legislation and jurisdiction, and sanction, best elucidated in terms of this combination of elements. The concepts (which bestride both law and political theory) of the state, of authority, and of an official require a similar analysis if the obscurity which still lingers about them is to be dissipated. The reason why an analysis in these terms of primary and secondary rules has this explanatory power is not far to seek. Most of the obscurities and distortions surrounding legal and political concepts arise from the fact that these essentially involve reference to what we have called the internal point of view: the view of those who do not merely record and predict behaviour conforming to rules, but *use* the rules as standards for the appraisal of their own and others' behaviour. This requires more detailed attention in the analysis of legal and political concepts than it has usually received. Under the simple régime of primary rules the internal point of view is manifested in its simplest form, in the use of those rules as the basis of criticism, and as the justification of demands for conformity, social pressure, and punishment. Reference to this most elementary manifestation of the internal point of view is required for the analysis of the basic concepts of obligation and duty. With the addition to the system of secondary rules, the range of what is said and done from the internal point of view is much extended and diversified. With this extension comes a whole set of new concepts and they demand a reference to the internal point of view for their analysis. These include the notions of legislation, jurisdiction, validity and, generally, of legal powers, private and public. There is a constant pull towards an analysis of these in the terms of ordinary or "scientific," fact-stating or predictive discourse. But this can only reproduce their external aspect: to do justice to their distinctive, internal aspect we need to see the different ways in which the law-making operations of the legislator, the adjudication of a court, the exercise of private or official powers, and other "acts-in-the-law" are related to secondary rules.

In the next chapter we shall show how the ideas of the validity of law and sources of law, and the truths latent among the errors of the doctrines of sovereignty may be rephrased and clarified in terms of rules of recognition. But we shall conclude this chapter with a warning: though the combination of primary and secondary rules merits, because it explains many aspects of law, the central place assigned to it, this cannot by itself illuminate every problem. The union of primary and secondary rules is at the centre of a legal system; but it is not the whole, and as we move away from the centre we shall have to accommodate, in ways indicated in later chapters, elements of a different character.

Rule of Recognition and Legal Validity

In the day-to-day life of a legal system its rule of recognition is very seldom expressly formulated as a rule; though occasionally, courts in England may announce in general terms the relative place of one criterion of law in relation to another, as when they assert the supremacy of Acts of Parliament over other sources or suggested sources of law. For the most part the rule of recognition is not stated, but its existence is *shown* in the way in which particular rules are identified, either by courts or other officials or private persons or their advisers. There is, of course, a difference in the use made by courts of the criteria provided by the rule and the use of them by others: for when courts reach a particular conclusion on the footing that a particular rule has been correctly identified as law, what they say has a special authoritative status conferred on it by other rules. In this respect, as in many others, the rule of recognition of a legal system is like the scoring rule of a game. In the course of the game the general rule defining the activities which constitute scoring (runs, goals, &c.) is seldom formulated; instead it is *used* by officials and players in identifying the particular phases which count towards winning. Here too, the declarations of officials (umpire or scorer) have a special authoritative status attributed to them by other rules. Further, in both cases there is the possibility of a conflict between these authoritative applications of the rule and the general understanding of what the rule plainly requires according to its terms. This, as we shall see later, is a complication which must be catered for in any account of what it is for a system of rules of this sort to exist.

The use of unstated rules of recognition, by courts and others, in identifying particular rules of the system is characteristic of the internal point of view. Those who use them in this way thereby manifest their own acceptance of them as guiding rules and with this attitude there goes a characteristic vocabulary different from the natural expressions of the external point of view. Perhaps the simplest of these is the expression, "It is the law that . . . ," which we may find on the lips not only of judges, but of ordinary men living under a legal system, when they identify a given rule of the system. This, like the expression "Out" or "Goal," is the language of one assessing a situation by reference to rules which he in common with others acknowledges as appropriate for this purpose. This attitude of shared acceptance of rules is to be contrasted with that of an observer who records *ab extra* the fact that a social group accepts such rules but does not himself accept them. The natural expression of this external point of view is not "It is the law that . . ." but "In England they recognize as law . . . whatever the Queen in Parliament enacts. . . ." The first of these forms of expression we shall call an *internal statement* because it manifests the internal point of view and is naturally used by one who, accepting the rule of recognition and without stating the fact that it is accepted, applies the rule in recognizing some particular rule of the system as valid. The second form of expression we shall call an *external statement* because it is the natural language of an external observer of the system who, without himself accepting its rule of recognition, states the fact that others accept it.

If this use of an accepted rule of recognition in making internal statements is understood and carefully distinguished from an external statement of fact that the rule is accepted, many obscurities concerning the notion of legal "validity" disappear. For the word "valid" is most frequently, though not always, used, in just such internal statements, applying to a particular rule of a legal system, an unstated but accepted rule of recognition. To say that a given rule is valid is to recognize it as passing all the tests provided by the rule of recognition and so as a rule of the system. We can indeed simply say that the statement that a particular rule is valid means that it satisfies all the criteria provided by the rule of recognition. This is incorrect only to the extent that it might obscure the internal character of such statements; for, like the cricketers' "Out," these statements of validity normally apply to a particular case a rule of recognition accepted by the speaker and others, rather than expressly state that the rule is satisfied.

Some of the puzzles connected with the idea of legal validity are said to concern the relation between the validity and the "efficacy" of law. If by "efficacy" is meant that the fact that a rule of law which requires certain behaviour is obeyed more often than not, it is plain that there is no necessary connexion between the validity of any particular rule and *its* efficacy, unless the rule of recognition of the system includes among its criteria, as some do, the provision (sometimes referred to as a rule of obsolescence) that no rule is to count as a rule of the system if it has long ceased to be efficacious.

From the inefficacy of a particular rule, which may or may not count against its validity, we must distinguish a general disregard of the rules of the system. This may be so complete in character and so protracted that we should say, in the case of a new system, that it had never established itself as the legal system of a given group, or, in the case of a once-established system, that it had ceased to be the legal system of the group. In either case, the normal context or background for making any internal statement in terms of the rules of the system is absent. In such cases it would be generally *pointless* either to assess the rights and duties of particular persons by reference to the primary rules of a system or to assess the validity of any of its rules by reference to its rules of recognition. To insist on applying a system of rules which had either never actually been effective or had been discarded would, except in special circumstances mentioned below, be as futile as to assess the progress of a game by reference to a scoring rule which had never been accepted or had been discarded.

One who makes an internal statement concerning the validity of a particular rule of a system may be said to *presuppose* the truth of the external statment of fact that the system is generally efficacious. For the normal use of internal statements is in such a context of general efficacy. It would however be wrong to say that statements of validity "mean" that the system is generally efficacious. For though it is normally pointless or idle to talk of the validity of a rule of a system which has never established itself or has been discarded, none the less it is not meaningless nor is it always pointless. One vivid way of teaching Roman Law is to speak *as if* the system were efficacious still and to discuss the validity of particular rules and solve problems in their terms; and one way of nursing hopes for the restoration of an old social order destroyed by revolution, and rejecting the new, is to cling to the criteria of legal validity of the old régime. This is implicitly done by the White Russian who still claims property under some rule of descent which was a valid rule of Tsarist Russia.

A grasp of the normal contextual connexion between the internal statement that a given rule of a system is valid and the external statement of fact that the system is generally efficacious, will help us see in its proper perspective the common theory that to assert the validity of a rule is to predict that it will be enforced by courts or some other official action taken. In many ways this theory is similar to the predictive analysis of obligation which we considered and rejected in the last chapter. In both cases alike the motive for advancing this predictive theory is the conviction that only thus can metaphysical interpretations be avoided: that either a statement that a rule is valid must ascribe some mysterious property which cannot be detected by empirical means or it must be a prediction of future behaviour of officials. In both cases also the plausibility of the theory is due to the same important fact: that the truth of the external statement of fact, which an observer might record, that the system is generally efficacious and likely to continue so, is normally presupposed by anyone who accepts the rules and makes an internal statement of obligation or validity. The two are certainly very closely associated. Finally, in both cases alike the mistake of the theory is the same: it consists in neglecting the special character of the internal statement and treating it as an external statement about official action.

This mistake becomes immediately apparent when we consider how the judge's own statement that a particular rule is valid functions in judicial decision; for, though here too, in making such a statement, the judge presupposes but does not state the general efficacy of the system, he plainly is not concerned to predict his own or others' official action. His statement that a rule is valid is an internal statement recognizing that the rule satisfies the tests for identifying what is to count as law in his court, and constitutes not a prophecy of but part of the *reason* for his decision. There is indeed a more plausible case for saying that a statement that a rule is valid is a prediction when such a statement is made by a private person; for in the case of conflict between unofficial statements of validity or invalidity and that of a court in deciding a case, there is often good sense in saying that the former must then be withdrawn. Yet even here, as we shall see when we come in Chapter VII to investigate the significance of such conflicts between official declarations and the plain requirements of the rules, it may be dogmatic to assume that it is withdrawn as a statement now shown to be *wrong*, because it has falsely *predicted* what a court would say. For there are more reasons for withdrawing statements than the fact that they are wrong, and also more ways of being wrong than this allows.

The rule of recognition providing the criteria by which the validity of other rules of the system is assessed is in an important sense, which we shall try to clarify, an *ultimate* rule: and where, as is usual, there are several criteria ranked in order of relative subordination and primacy one of them is *supreme*. These ideas of the ultimacy of the rule of recognition and the supremacy of one of its criteria merit some attention. It is important to disentangle them from the theory, which we have rejected, that somewhere in every legal system, even though it lurks behind legal forms, there must be a sovereign legislative power which is legally unlimited.

Of these two ideas, supreme criterion and ultimate rule, the first is the easiest to define. We may say that a criterion of legal validity or source of law is supreme if rules identified by reference to it are still recognized as rules of the system, even if they conflict with rules identified by reference to the other criteria, whereas rules identified by reference to the latter are not so recognized if they conflict with the rules identified by reference to the supreme criterion. A similar explanation in comparative terms can be given of the notions of "superior" and "subordinate" criteria which we have already used. It is plain that the notions of a superior and a supreme criterion merely refer to a *relative* place on a scale and do not import any notion of legally *unlimited* legislative power. Yet "supreme" and "unlimited" are easy to confuse —at least in legal theory. One reason for this is that in the simpler forms of legal system the ideas of ultimate rule of recognition, supreme criterion, and legally unlimited legislature seem to converge. For where there is a legislature subject to no constitutional limitations and competent by its enactment to deprive all other rules of law emanating from other sources of their status as law, it is part of the rule of recognition in such a system that enactment by that legislature is the supreme criterion of validity. This is, according to constitutional theory, the position in the United Kingdom. But even systems like that of the United States in which there is no such legally unlimited legislature may perfectly well contain an ultimate rule of recognition which provides a set of criteria of validity, one of which is supreme. This will be so, where the legislative competence of the ordinary legislature is limited by a constitution which contains no amending power, or places some clauses outside the scope of that power. Here there is no legally unlimited legislature, even in the widest interpretation of "legislature"; but the system of course contains an ultimate rule of recognition and, in the clauses of its constitution, a supreme criterion of validity.

The sense in which the rule of recognition is the *ultimate* rule of a system is best understood if we pursue a very familiar chain of legal reasoning. If the question is raised whether some suggested rule is legally valid, we must, in order to answer the question, use a criterion of validity provided by some other rule. Is this purported by-law of the Oxfordshire County Council valid? Yes: because it was made in exercise of the powers conferred, and in accordance with the procedure specified, by a statutory order made by the Minister of Health. At this first stage the statutory order provides the criteria in terms of which the validity of the by-law is assessed. There may be no practical need to go farther; but there is a standing possibility of doing so. We may query the validity of the statutory order and assess its validity in terms of the statute empowering the minister to make such orders. Finally when the validity of the statute has been queried and assessed by reference to the rule that what the Queen in Parliament enacts is law, we are brought to a stop in inquiries concerning validity: for we have reached a rule which, like the intermediate statutory order and statute, provides criteria for the assessment of the validity of other rules; but it is also unlike them in that there is no rule providing criteria for the assessment of its own legal validity.

There are, indeed, many questions which we can raise about
this ultimate rule. We can ask whether it is the practice of
courts, legislatures, officials, or private citizens in England actually
to use this rule as an ultimate rule of recognition. Or has our
process of legal reasoning been an idle game with the criteria
of validity of a system now discarded? We can ask whether it is a
satisfactory form of legal system which has such a rule at its
root. Does it produce more good than evil? Are there prudential
reasons for supporting it? Is there a moral obligation to do so?
These are plainly very important questions; but, equally plainly,
when we ask about the rule of recognition, we are no longer
attempting to answer the same kind of question about it as those
which we answered about other rules with its aid. When we move
from saying that a particular enactment is valid, because it satisfies
the rule that what the Queen in Parliament enacts is law, to saying that in England this last rule is used by courts, officials, and
private persons as the ultimate rule of recognition, we have moved
from an internal statement of law asserting the validity of a rule
of the system to an external statement of fact which an observer
of the system might make even if he did not accept it. So too
when we move from the statement that a particular enactment is
valid, to the statement that the rule of recognition of the system
is an excellent one and the system based on it is one worthy of
support, we have moved from a statement of legal validity to
a statement of value.

Some writers, who have emphasized the legal ultimacy of the
rule of recognition, have expressed this by saying that, whereas
the legal validity of other rules of the system can be demonstrated by reference to it, its own validity can not be demonstrated but is "assumed" or "postulated" or is a "hypothesis."
This may, however, be seriously misleading. Statements of legal
validity made about particular rules in the day-to-day life of a
legal system whether by judges, lawyers, or ordinary citizens
do indeed carry with them certain presuppositions. They are
internal statements of law expressing the point of view of those
who accept the rule of recognition of the system and, as such,
leave unstated much that could be stated in external statements
of fact about the system. What is thus left unstated forms the
normal background or context of statements of legal validity

and is thus said to be "presupposed" by them. But it is important to see precisely what these presupposed matters are, and not to obscure their character. They consist of two things. First, a person who seriously asserts the validity of some given rule of law, say a particular statute, himself makes use of a rule of recognition which he accepts as appropriate for identifying the law. Secondly, it is the case that this rule of recognition, in terms of which he assesses the validity of a particular statute, is not only accepted by him but is the rule of recognition actually accepted and employed in the general operation of the system. If the truth of this presupposition were doubted, it could be established by reference to actual practice: to the way in which courts identify what is to count as law, and to the general acceptance of or acquiescence in these identifications.

Neither of these two presuppositions are well described as "assumptions" of a "validity" which cannot be demonstrated. We only need the word "validity," and commonly only use it, to answer questions which arise *within* a system of rules where the status of a rule as a member of the system depends on its satisfying certain criteria provided by the rule of recognition. No such question can arise as to the validity of the very rule of recognition which provides the criteria; it can neither be valid nor invalid but is simply accepted as appropriate for use in this way. To express this simple fact by saying darkly that its validity is "assumed but cannot be demonstrated," is like saying that we assume, but can never demonstrate, that the standard metre bar in Paris which is the ultimate test of the correctness of all measurement in metres, is itself correct.

A more serious objection is that talk of the "assumption" that the ultimate rule of recognition is valid conceals the essentially factual character of the second presupposition which lies behind the lawyers' statements of validity. No doubt the practice of judges, officials, and others, in which the actual existence of a rule of recognition consists, is a complex matter. As we shall see later, there are certainly situations in which questions as to the precise content and scope of this kind of rule, and even as to its existence, may not admit of a clear or determinate answer. None the less it is important to distinguish "assuming the validity" from "presupposing the existence" of such a rule; if only because failure to do this obscures what is meant by the assertion that such a rule *exists*.

In the simple system of primary rules of obligation sketched in the last chapter, the assertion that a given rule existed could only be an external statement of fact such as an observer who did not accept the rules might make and verify by ascertaining whether or not, as a matter of fact, a given mode of behaviour was generally accepted as a standard and was accompanied by those features which, as we have seen, distinguish a social rule from mere convergent habits. It is in this way also that we should now interpret and verify the assertion that in England a rule—though not a legal one—exists that we must bare the head on entering a church. If such rules as these are found to exist in the actual practice of a social group, there is no separate question of their validity to be discussed, though of course their value or desirability is open to question. Once their existence has been established as a fact we should only confuse matters by affirming or denying that they were valid or by saying that "we assumed" but could not show their validity. Where, on the other hand, as in a mature legal system, we have a system of rules which includes a rule of recognition so that the status of a rule as a member of the system now depends on whether it satisfies certain criteria provided by the rule of recognition, this brings with it a new application of the word "exist." The statement that a rule exists may now no longer be what it was in the simple case of customary rules—an external statement of the *fact* that a certain mode of behaviour was generally accepted as a standard in practice. It may now be an internal statement apply-ing an accepted but unstated rule of recognition and meaning (roughly) no more than "valid given the system's criteria of validity." In this respect, however, as in others a rule of recogni-tion is unlike other rules of the system. The assertion that it exists can only be an external statement of fact. For whereas a sub-ordinate rule of a system may be valid and in that sense "exist" even if it is generally disregarded, the rule of recognition exists only as a complex, but normally concordant, practice of the courts, officials, and private persons in identifying the law by reference to certain criteria. Its existence is a matter of fact.

Comment

LON L. FULLER

Reason and Fiat

Lon L. Fuller is a professor at the Harvard Law School. In this selection, Gray and Holmes (who are represented below in the third section) are critically discussed, as well as such positivists as Austin and Kelsen. An instructive discussion on positivism and morals is contained in the exchange between Fuller and H. L. A. Hart (see bibliography). The issue is also pursued in Fuller's book, The Morality of Law *(1964).*

ॐ

[I]

In order to get a clear view of the judicial process, we have to begin, I think, by elminating provisionally certain complications that surround it and obscure its nature as it actually functions in our society. To see the process in its simplest form, we have to imagine how it would function in a society newly founded, without precedents, or statutes, or customary ways of doing things. In order to give concreteness to this problem, let us for a moment indulge ourselves in the intellectual fashion of another century and imagine a group of shipwrecked men isolated in some corner of the earth. So that this detached community may in fact present the social *tabula rasa* that our inquiry demands, let us imagine that its members have been visited by an amnesia that has wiped

Reprinted by permission of the author from Lon L. Fuller, "Reason and Fiat in Case Law," *Harvard Law Review*, Vol. 59 (1946), pp. 377–89. Abridged by the editor.

out the memory of their previous social existence and the laws and conventions which they observed in their original homes.

Disputes arise among the members of the group and it is seen that some means must be provided for their settlement. Accordingly, one of the company is designated as arbitrator or judge. Since our inquiry is directed to general problems rather than to the investigation of individual aberrations, we shall assume that the man chosen for this office is sane and reasonably intelligent, and that he feels a sense of responsibility for advancing the prosperity of the group and preserving its morale.

It would be folly to suppose that the decisions of such a judge or arbitrator could properly be viewed as the mere expression of his personal predilections. From the very beginning of his judicial office, it would be apparent to him that the nature of his task imposed certain limitations on him. If he knew anything of human nature, he would know that his decisions would come to be looked on as precedents, if not on first utterance, at least as soon as a recurring pattern could be discerned in them. He would foresee that there would emerge from his treatment of individual cases a body of rules, and that the community would tend in some degree to adjust itself to those rules. He would realize that it was his responsibility to see that his decisions were *right*—right for the group, *right* in the light of the group's purposes and the things that its members sought to achieve through common effort. Such a judge would find himself driven into an attempt to discover the natural principles underlying group life, so that his decisions might conform to them. He would properly feel that he, no less than the engineers and carpenters and cooks of the company, was faced with the task of mastering a segment of reality and of discovering and utilizing its regularities for the benefit of the group.

Though our judge would see that his task was one that demanded study and reflection, he would at the same time realize that no study, however intense, could ever answer all the questions he would be called upon to solve. His insight into the ways in which men live together in groups might make it clear to him, for example, that certain acts would have to be punished if the morale of the group was to be preserved. But if the question were one of imprisonment, should the sentence be set at seven days, or

eight days, or perhaps two weeks, or even a month? Here obviously
is an area, and a wide and important area, where law cannot be discovered, but must be made by the judge who applies it. In this
area the judge functions not as one who seeks to conform his will
to an external order, but as one whose will itself creates the order
to which men must conform.

In my description of the judicial process there is nothing so
far, I think, that would incite challenge. I have said in effect
that the law laid down by our desert-island judge would represent
a combination of reason and fiat; that it would be, in other words,
in part the discovery of an order and in part the imposition of an
order. In the language of legal philosophy, we might say the
same thing by describing it as a system of "positive law" that
approaches to an indefinite degree "natural law." This would,
however, be a dangerous way of speaking, because for many the
term "natural law" still has about it a rich, deep odor of the
witches' caldron, and the mere mention of it suffices to unloose a
torrent of emotions and fears. But our aversion to the term should
not be allowed to obscure the fact which the term has been used
to describe. The fact in this case is simply that our judge would
believe, and would be justified in believing, that there are external
criteria, found in the conditions required for successful group living, that furnish some standard against which the rightness of
his decisions should be measured. He would be puzzled to learn
that so innocent a belief could instill fear or give rise to invective.
Certainly it would never occur to him to describe the natural law
he sought to discover, and felt bound to respect, as a "brooding
omnipresence in the skies." Rather for him it would be a hard
and earthy reality that challenged his best intellectual efforts to
capture it. The emotional attitude with which he approached his
task would not be that of one doing obeisance before an altar, but
more like that of a cook trying to find the secret of a flaky pie
crust, or of an engineer trying to devise a means of bridging a
ravine.

If, continuing our illustration, we remove our judge from his
desert island and put him down in a society that is already a real
and going concern, his functions may seem at first to have been
complicated beyond recognition. He must now move within a

framework of statutes, precedents, accepted values and meanings, professional traditions, and customary ways of doing things. The influences that bear upon him have been enormously multiplied. Yet it is important to see that essentially only one new factor has been introduced into the judging process. This new factor lies in the circumstance that the force of established institutions has now become one of the realities the judge must respect in making his decisions. If the conditions of successful group living determine the rules we ought to apply to the group, the rules already applied themselves determine in part what those conditions are. Man's nature consists partly of what he has made of himself, and natural law, therefore, demands that we must within certain limits respect established positive law.

As my first illustration was intended to show, even if we could imagine the judicial function operating in a kind of historical vacuum, it would still contain within itself the antinomy of reason and fiat. In a going society, joined fore and aft with history, this antinomy becomes aggravated and compounded, as it were, because established fiat is itself a reality that reason bids us take into account in our reckonings. There is no denying that this complication permeates our whole legal system; and the perplexities it causes crop out in the remotest corners of the law. Yet it is well to see the common source of these difficulties, for otherwise it is easy to forget that the basic problem of the judicial process remains that of discovering and applying those principles that will best promote the ends men seek to attain by collective action. This problem tends to get obscured in a going society because there are so many competing "sources of positive law" from which a judge may draw, or appear to draw, his decision. For example, a court decides that an established precedent is having an injurious effect, and acting on this conviction, overrules it. A very common way of describing such an event is that which assumes that the precedent was overruled because it had become contrary to "prevailing conceptions of morality." The court therefore had its choice of two recognized sources of law, the first lying in established judicial precedent, the second in received conceptions of morality, and it gave preference to the second. There is usually much that is fictitious in this description, for the reason that the "prevailing conceptions of morality" in question often have existence only in the mind of the commentator. Often—perhaps usually—the problem in issue is one with which society as a whole is unfamiliar, and, in any event, is generally one on which society could have formed no opinion for lack of an acquaintance with the interests involved.

I am reminded in this connection of the comments David Cavers has made on the judicial process as it functions in the conflict of laws.[1] Where the court seems to decide whether, according to the principles of the conflict of laws, it is the law of State A or State B that controls a transaction, back of this choice there often lies an unacknowledged but more determinative choice: Which rule will furnish the most desirable and workable standard of decision? If the rule of State A is preferred the real reason may be because it is thought to be a better rule than that of State B, rather than because it is "the law of the place of contracting," or whatever other formal ground may, in accordance with received doctrine, be assigned for the preference. So on a larger scale when courts seem to be choosing among various recognized "sources of law"—precedent, business custom, learned treatises, received conceptions of morality—the really determinative choice may simply be: Which rule is best? Which rule most closely respects the facts of men's social existence and tends most to promote an effective and satisfactory life in common? Though the existence of this problem tends to get obscured in the converging streams of fiat in modern society, it remains a constant reality in the judicial process.

[II]

Men have never been very ready to acknowledge that their thinking contains anything like an unresolved state of tension. They have never been very happy with what Morris Cohen calls "the principle of polarity," according to which notions apparently contradictory form indispensable complements for one another. In dealing with the antinomy of reason and fiat, the main effort of the various schools of legal philosophy has been to obliterate one of its branches.

[1] *A Critique of the Choice-of-Law Problem* (1933) 47 HARV. L. REV. 173.

Extremists of the "law of nature" school have tried to eliminate the branch of fiat by maintaining that the whole of law is, or at least can be, the expression of reason. This school has always rested more on assertion than demonstration, and the fact that it has to help itself over all the difficult points with liberal doses of rhetoric serves as a sufficient warning of its inadequacies. The opposing school, that of the extreme positivists, is hard at work to cut the fiat branch loose from reason, though in recent years the adherents of this school have asserted that this severance is "provisional" only and for certain unspecified "methodological purposes." To convert the whole of law into fiat, it is, of course, necessary to make it the fiat of some person or thing. So we find this school insisting, for example, that custom, no matter how widespread, reasonable and clearly promotive of the social welfare it may be, can never be "law" until it has been stamped as such by the judge,[2] or the state[3] or the sovereign,[4] or the *Rechtsmacht*,[5] or the basic norm,[6] or whatever standard of authoritativeness the particular faction of the school happens to sponsor. Cardozo revealed his attitude toward this school when he said, concerning the controversy whether moral precepts can be "law" before they have been acted on by a court: "Such verbal disputations do not greatly interest me."[7]

When we deal with law, not in terms of definitions and authoritative sources, but in terms of problems and functions, we inevitably see that it is compounded of reason and fiat, of order discovered and order imposed, and that to attempt to eliminate either of these aspects of the law is to denature and falsify it.

No one has ever worked with concepts like "right," "title" and "ownership," without being struck at some time by the extent to which these concepts appear to involve a circle in reasoning. For example, when the owner of Blackacre is permitted recovery against a trespasser we say that his "ownership" is protected by

[2] GRAY, NATURE AND SOURCES OF THE LAW (1909).
[3] HEARN, THE THEORY OF LEGAL DUTIES AND RIGHTS (1883).
[4] AUSTIN, LECTURES ON JURISPRUDENCE (4th ed. 1879).
[5] SOMLO, JURISTISCHE GRUNDLEHRE (2d ed. 1927).
[6] KELSEN, REINE RECHTSLEHRE (1934).
[7] THE NATURE OF THE JUDICIAL PROCESS (1921) 133.

the suit in trespass; his "ownership" is the thing that "gives rise to" the cause of action. Asked what his "ownership" consists of we respond that it is made up of certain legal rights, including the right to sue trespassers. In brief, he can sue because he is owner; he is owner because he can sue. Both of these statements seem to contain a degree of truth, yet it is difficult to see how both can be true at once. The explanation for this paradox is that in the one case we are viewing law from its reason side, and "ownership" stands as an ellipsis for the considerations of policy that justify a court in granting a recovery in trespass. In the other case we are viewing law from its fiat side, and "ownership" is an elliptical description of the power relationships created by existing rules. The concept of "ownership," in other words, contains within itself the antinomy of reason and fiat that lies at the heart of the whole legal order.

This will be seen a little more clearly, perhaps, if we analyze in greater detail the meaning of "ownership" in its two senses. Viewing it as the thing that "gives rise to" the remedy, if it has any meaning at all it is, as I have said, an ellipsis for the considerations of policy that justify a court in granting a recovery to the owner. If we undertake to supply the elements that were dropped in the ellipsis we shall find that we are driven into a consideration of the whole philosophy of private property. In such an inquiry we would encounter much that was founded on reason, but we would also discover that like all human creations this institution has its arbitrary qualities, its sharp corners that violate the fluid contours of nature. In other words, an analysis of "ownership" as an elliptical statement of the reason for the recovery leads us inevitably across the dividing line of the antinomy and into the branch of fiat.

We shall have a similar experience if we approach the concept of ownership from the other side. Holmes has made generally familiar the notion that legal rights and duties may be viewed as ways of describing the fact that certain legal remedies are available. ". . . a legal duty so called is nothing but a prediction that if a man does or omits certain things, he will be made to suffer in this or that way by judgment of the court; and so of a

legal right."[8] According to this view, "ownership" is merely a
way of expressing a prediction that courts under certain circumstances will act in ways advantageous to the person who is called
owner. The avowed purpose of this theory is to cut the law loose
from the ethical considerations that have shaped it or, in other
words, from its underlying reasons.

Though this theory of Holmes has enjoyed a great popularity,
remarkably little attempt has been made to examine what it actually means. Certainly Holmes did not mean that saying John Doe
has a right carries exactly the same meaning as saying he has
a remedy. If this were true the notion of "right" would be a
tautology wholly lacking in the descriptive value Holmes ascribed
to the term. The introduction of the term "right" must add
something that is absent when it is not used. It is not difficult
to see what Holmes intended this to be. The term "right" is a
generalized statement of the circumstances under which the remedy is available. When we say that the owner of Blackacre has
"a right" to sue we mean to express a prediction that he, *and
others in a similar position,* will be granted a remedy. But when
are others "in a similar position"? If the holder of a deed to
Blackacre can sue a trespasser, is an adverse possessor in the
same position? If one is not in possession, under what kind of
deed must he claim? In answering questions of this sort we find
ourselves inevitably led back across the dividing line of the antinomy, and we are once again involved in the reasons underlying
the institution of private property. Our prediction of judicial
action turns out to be meaningless unless we examine the reasons
upon which judicial action is predicated, because it is only in this
way that we can predict the scope of the anticipated action.

The same antinomy that lies in concepts like "right," "duty"
and "ownership" can be shown to inhere in all the familiar concepts of legal technique: "contract," "tort," "title," "voidable
obligation," "vested interest"—the list could be expanded indefinitely. It is not accurate to say that these terms are ambiguous, in the sense that they have two distinct meanings. Rather,
each of them stands for a relationship that can be viewed from

[8] *The Path of the Law* (1897), printed in COLLECTED LEGAL PAPERS (1920)
167, 169.

two sides. When we view it from the "under" side, we are attempting to find compelling reasons for the things that are done by courts in cases where these words are used. When we view it from the "upper" side, we are attempting to present the action of the court as a brute fact divorced from the reasons that gave rise to it. Neither of these attempts is, or can be, successful. In terms of a physical analogy both are like trying to produce a magnet with only one pole, or an electric battery that produces only a positive current.

It may be said of concepts like "right" and "ownership" that they are merely ways of describing the impact of general rules of law on particular situations of fact. Accordingly, all that I have just said about such concepts is equally applicable when we deal with the law in terms of rules, rather than in terms of rights and remedies.

The favorite method of refuting the natural law school is to demand of it a rule, even a single rule, that rests on reason alone. This is a test that the natural law school is fated ever to fail. If, for example, the advocate of the law of nature gives as an illustration of the kind of rule demanded by his theory: "Men should perform their agreements," his skeptical interlocutor will be able to point out that there are many agreements which the law does not enforce, and that those regarded as most essential in one system of law are often left without legal sanction in another. The alleged principle of natural law demanding the enforcement of agreements will turn out to read, when properly qualified, something as follows: "*If* a society wishes to achieve the prosperity and efficiency that comes from a division of functions or labor, and *if* no other means for achieving that division (such as a caste system) is available, then at least *some* agreements will have to be enforced by the law, *provided* it is demonstrated that unorganized moral pressures tending toward contract observance require the reinforcement of the law in order to make them effective." This does not sound very impressive, yet in a given social context all these ifs and provisos may receive an answer so clear as to leave no real room for argument. Certainly the principle demanding contract observance has been acted on by thousands of judges in the justified belief that they were respecting a human need broader than any particular system of law. The fact remains, however, that though there are certain human needs that are relatively constant, the concrete expression that shall be given these needs is always conditioned by the social context in which they operate, so that the natural law school is never able to attain its ideal of a system of legal rules categorically demanded by the order of nature and applicable to all kinds of societies.

But if the natural law school is incapable of giving a rule that is pure reason, the opposing school is equally incapable of giving a rule that is pure fiat. It is now nearly half a century since Holmes penned his famous dictum: "The prophecies of what the courts will do in fact, and nothing more pretentious, are what I mean by the law."[9] Since its first enunciation this view has been taken up by dozens of writers, it has become identified with a whole school of jurisprudence, and literally volumes have been written about it. Yet in all this time no one has ever stated a rule of law that was merely a prediction of judicial action excluding all reference to the reasons motivating the action. I am willing to prophesy that no one ever will. The undertaking is impossible of accomplishment for the reason that judicial action cannot be predicted, or even talked about meaningfully, except in terms of the reasons that give rise to it. One may, of course, predict that the Supreme Court of State A will decide in favor of Brown in the case of *Smith v. Brown* that is now before it, just as one might, without assigning reasons, predict that a certain bridge will collapse within a year. But the value of such a prediction would rest entirely on the judgment and insight of the person expressing it. Before a prediction of judicial action can have a less contingent significance it has to be couched in general terms so as to include not only the case of *Brown v. Smith*, but other "similar" cases as well, or— and this amounts to the same thing—it will have to be accompanied by a statement of the reasons on the basis of which, it is assumed, the court will act. But so soon as we attempt either of these things we find ourselves again examining the ethical foundations of the rule, and we have abandoned the basic purpose of the "predictive" theory, which is that of stating law purely in terms of power relations without reference to its ethical bases.

[9] *The Path of the Law* (1897), printed in COLLECTED LEGAL PAPERS (1920) 167, 173.

Every rule of law that has enough meaning in it to be useful to lawyers and judges will inevitably contain within it the antinomy of reason and fiat that runs throughout the law. There are, of course, certain rules that seem to be intended as the expression of self-evident propositions of morality: "No man should profit by his own wrong"; "Where one of two innocent persons must suffer a loss, it should be borne by him whose action made it possible"; etc. But even if we assume that the moral principles expressed in such rules are really self-evident, in their actual application these rules receive concrete meaning only when tied in with an existing system of property and duty relationships that contains many elements that are obviously arbitrary. At the other extreme, even the most arbitrary rule of law, if it issues from the proper authority, such as a duly constituted legislature, has that minimum of reason back of it that justifies a respect for established and authoritative sources of law.

The last remark leads naturally to those basic principles that are assumed to underlie the whole legal order, including the theory of sovereignty. Every attempt to convert the whole of law into state fiat has to rest on some notion of a sovereign lawgiver, or, as with Kelsen, on some depersonified equivalent of such a notion. The law is what the sovereign commands, say Hobbes and Austin and all the positivists who have followed them in the intervening centuries. But what is the sovereign? The sovereign is that authority which is accepted by the people as the lawgiving power. What is the basis of that acceptance? It rests on a conception of law, upon a natural law of the social order which declares that life in society is impossible without a central authority to regulate men's relations with one another. The sovereign determines what is law, but is itself determined by law.

That the whole view of sovereignty, the view that rejects neither branch of the antinomy of reason and fiat, can be stated without mysticism or obfuscation has been brilliantly proved in Guglielmo Ferrero's book *The Principles of Power*.[10] Power or sovereignty there must be, because no ideology or system of natural law can supplant the need for authority, for a deciding power. But power in turn must be "legitimated"; because, unclothed by any principle of legitimacy, power is itself ineffective

[10] (1942).

and eventually frightens into a frustrated impotence both those subject to it and those who try to exercise it. Governmental power supplies the defects of reason, but is in turn powerless unless supported by some rational principle. The positivists who have said that the test of sovereign power is efficacy have failed to see that "efficacy" is an abstraction that cannot be understood in isolation from its roots in morality.

It should be noted that the brief survey just concluded touches on most of the elements of the legal order and runs from rights and remedies, at one end, to the theory of sovereignty at the other. The natural law school, it should be observed, encounters its greatest difficulty in dealing with the law at the point of impact, that is, in the field of rights and remedies, because in this field an arbitrary element is too obvious to be successfully denied. On the other hand, the positivist school encounters its chief embarrassment in dealing with those general notions, like sovereignty, that underlie the whole legal system. If law is defined as being what the sovereign commands, it is impossible to blink the problem of explaining why this lawgiving power should be attributed to one source and not to another. Hobbes was very explicit on this point, and he devoted many pages to showing the social necessity for an arbiter over men's relations with one another, and to showing that the power of the sovereign rests on a contract with his subjects. Since Hobbes' time the legal positivists have sought some means of effecting a more complete severance of the legal system from its ethical bases. Probably the most successful of these attempts is that of Kelsen. Yet even Kelsen admits that his theory of the basic norm rests on natural law—that is, on the social need for peace and order. He claims, however, as a merit of his system, that it admits only that irreducible minimum of natural law without which any notion of a legal order is impossible. As I have suggested elsewhere,[11] this is reminiscent of Pascal's remark about Descartes, that he would have preferred to eliminate God altogether from his system, but needed Him to give his universe a little push to start it going, after which he had no further use for Him.

---

[11] THE LAW IN QUEST OF ITSELF (1940) 85, n.35.

PART III

LEGAL REALISM AND SOCIOLOGICAL JURISPRUDENCE

PART II

Background Statements

O. W. HOLMES, JR.

The Law as Predictions of What Courts Will Do

Oliver Wendell Holmes, Jr. (1841–1935), the "great dissenter," was an Associate Justice of the Supreme Court of the United States from 1902 to 1932. His book, The Common Law (1881), is a classic work of Anglo-American jurisprudence. With his emphasis on the role of the courts, Holmes greatly influenced the development of legal realism in the United States. The following selection is from an address given to law students.

მ

When we study law we are not studying a mystery but a well-known profession. We are studying what we shall want in order to appear before judges, or to advise people in such a way as to keep them out of court. The reason why it is a profession, why people will pay lawyers to argue for them or to advise them, is that in societies like ours the command of the public force is intrusted to the judges in certain cases, and the whole power of the state will be put forth, if necessary, to carry out their judgments and decrees. People want to know under what circumstances and how far they will run the risk of coming against what is so much stronger than themselves, and hence it becomes a business to find out when this

Reprinted from O. W. Holmes, Jr., "The Path of the Law," *Harvard Law Review*, Vol. 10 (1897), pp. 457–68.

danger is to be feared. The object of our study, then, is prediction, the prediction of the incidence of the public force through the instrumentality of the courts.

The means of the study are a body of reports, of treatises, and of statutes, in this country and in England, extending back for six hundred years, and now increasing annually by hundreds. In these sibylline leaves are gathered the scattered prophecies of the past upon the cases in which the axe will fall. These are what properly have been called the oracles of the law. Far the most important and pretty nearly the whole meaning of every new effort of legal thought is to make these prophecies more precise, and to generalize them into a thoroughly connected system. The process is one, from a lawyer's statement of a case, eliminating as it does all the dramatic elements with which his client's story has clothed it, and retaining only the facts of legal import, up to the final analyses and abstract universals of theoretic jurisprudence. The reason why a lawyer does not mention that his client wore a white hat when he made a contract, while Mrs. Quickly would be sure to dwell upon it along with the parcel gilt goblet and the sea-coal fire, is that he foresees that the public force will act in the same way whatever his client had upon his head. It is to make the prophecies easier to be remembered and to be understood that the teachings of the decisions of the past are put into general propositions and gathered into text-books, or that statutes are passed in a general form. The primary rights and duties with which jurisprudence busies itself again are nothing but prophecies. One of the many evil effects of the confusion between legal and moral ideas, about which I shall have something to say in a moment, is that theory is apt to get the cart before the horse, and to consider the right or the duty as something existing apart from and independent of the consequences of its breach, to which certain sanctions are added afterward. But, as I shall try to show, a legal duty so called is nothing but a prediction that if a man does or omits certain things he will be made to suffer in this or that way by judgment of the court—and so of a legal right.

The number of our predictions when generalized and reduced to a system is not unmanageably large. They present themselves as a finite body of dogma which may be mastered within a reasonable time. It is a great mistake to be frightened by the ever increasing number of reports. The reports of a given jurisdiction in the course of a generation take up pretty much the whole body of the law, and restate it from the present point of view. We could reconstruct the corpus from them if all that went before were burned. The use of the earlier reports is mainly historical, a use about which I shall have something to say before I have finished.

I wish, if I can, to lay down some first principles for the study of this body of dogma or systematized prediction which we call the law, for men who want to use it as the instrument of their business to enable them to prophesy in their turn, and, as bearing upon the study, I wish to point out an ideal which as yet our law has not attained.

The first thing for a businesslike understanding of the matter is to understand its limits, and therefore I think it desirable at once to point out and dispel a confusion between morality and law, which sometimes rises to the height of conscious theory, and more often and indeed constantly is making trouble in detail without reaching the point of consciousness. You can see very plainly that a bad man has as much reason as a good one for wishing to avoid an encounter with the public force, and therefore you can see the practical importance of the distinction between morality and law. A man who cares nothing for an ethical rule which is believed and practised by his neighbors is likely nevertheless to care a good deal to avoid being made to pay money, and will want to keep out of jail if he can.

I take it for granted that no hearer of mine will misinterpret what I have to say as the language of cynicism. The law is the witness and external deposit of our moral life. Its history is the history of the moral development of the race. The practice of it, in spite of popular jests, tends to make good citizens and good men. When I emphasize the difference between law and morals I do so with reference to a single end, that of learning and understanding the law. For that purpose you must definitely master its specific marks, and it is for that that I ask you for the moment to imagine yourselves indifferent to other and greater things.

I do not say that there is not a wider point of view from which the distinction between law and morals becomes of secondary or

no importance, as all mathematical distinctions vanish in presence
of the infinite. But I do say that that distinction is of the first importance for the object which we are here to consider—a right study
and mastery of the law as a business with well understood limits,
a body of dogma enclosed within definite lines. I have just shown
the practical reason for saying so. If you want to know the law
and nothing else, you must look at it as a bad man, who cares only
for the material consequences which such knowledge enables him
to predict, not as a good one, who finds his reasons for conduct,
whether inside the law or outside of it, in the vaguer sanctions of
conscience. The theoretical importance of the distinction is no less,
if you would reason on your subject aright. The law is full of
phraseology drawn from morals, and by the mere force of language
continually invites us to pass from one domain to the other without
perceiving it, as we are sure to do unless we have the boundary
constantly before our minds. The law talks about rights, and duties,
and malice, and intent, and negligence, and so forth, and nothing
is easier, or, I may say, more common in legal reasoning, than to
take these words in their moral sense, at some stage of the argument, and so to drop into fallacy. For instance, when we speak of
the rights of man in a moral sense, we mean to mark the limits
of interference with individual freedom which we think are prescribed by conscience, or by our ideal, however reached. Yet it is
certain that many laws have been enforced in the past, and it is
likely that some are enforced now, which are condemned by the
most enlightened opinion of the time, or which at all events pass
the limit of interference as many consciences would draw it.
Manifestly, therefore, nothing but confusion of thought can result
from assuming that the rights of man in a moral sense are equally
rights in the sense of the Constitution and the law. No doubt
simple and extreme cases can be put of imaginable laws which
the statute-making power would not dare to enact, even in the
absence of written constitutional prohibitions, because the community would rise in rebellion and fight; and this gives some plausibility to the proposition that the law, if not a part of morality, is
limited by it. But this limit of power is not coextensive with any
systems of morals. For the most part it falls far within the lines of
any such system, and in some cases may extend beyond them, for

reasons drawn from the habits of a particular people at a particular time. I once heard the late Professor Agassiz say that a German population would rise if you added two cents to the price of a glass of beer. A statute in such a case would be empty words, not because it was wrong, but because it could not be enforced. No one will deny that wrong statutes can be and are enforced, and we should not all agree as to which were the wrong ones.

The confusion with which I am dealing besets confessedly legal conceptions. Take the fundamental question, What constitutes the law? You will find some text writers telling you that it is something different from what is decided by the courts of Massachusetts or England, that it is a system of reason, that it is a deduction from principles of ethics or admitted axioms or what not, which may or may not coincide with the decisions. But if we take the view of our friend the bad man we shall find that he does not care two straws for the axioms or deductions, but that he does want to know what the Massachusetts or English courts are likely to do in fact. I am much of his mind. The prophecies of what the courts will do in fact, and nothing more pretentious, are what I mean by the law.

Take again a notion which as popularly understood is the widest conception which the law contains—the notion of legal duty, to which already I have referred. We fill the word with all the content which we draw from morals. But what does it mean to a bad man? Mainly, and in the first place, a prophecy that if he does certain things he will be subjected to disagreeable consequences by way of imprisonment or compulsory payment of money. But from his point of view, what is the difference between being fined and being taxed a certain sum for doing a certain thing? That his point of view is the test of legal principles is shown by the many discussions which have arisen in the courts on the very question whether a given statutory liability is a penalty or a tax. On the answer to this question depends the decision whether conduct is legally wrong or right, and also whether a man is under compulsion or free. Leaving the criminal law on one side, what is the difference between the liability under the mill acts or statutes authorizing a taking by eminent domain and the liability for what we call a wrongful conversion of property where restoration is out of the question? In both cases the party taking another man's property has to pay its fair value as assessed by a jury, and no more. What significance is there in calling one taking right and another wrong from the point of view of the law? It does not matter, so far as the given consequence, the compulsory payment, is concerned, whether the act to which it is attached is described in terms of praise or in terms of blame, or whether the law purports to prohibit it or to allow it. If it matters at all, still speaking from the bad man's point of view, it must be because in one case and not in the other some further disadvantages, or at least some further consequences, are attached to the act by the law. The only other disadvantages thus attached to it which I ever have been able to think of are to be found in two somewhat insignificant legal doctrines, both of which might be abolished without much disturbance. One is, that a contract to do a prohibited act is unlawful, and the other, that, if one of two or more joint wrongdoers has to pay all the damages, he cannot recover contribution from his fellows. And that I believe is all. You see how the vague circumference of the notion of duty shrinks and at the same time grows more precise when we wash it with cynical acid and expel everything except the object of our study, the operations of the law.

Nowhere is the confusion between legal and moral ideas more manifest than in the law of contract. Among other things, here again the so called primary rights and duties are invested with a mystic significance beyond what can be assigned and explained. The duty to keep a contract at common law means a prediction that you must pay damages if you do not keep it—and nothing else. If you commit a tort, you are liable to pay a compensatory sum. If you commit a contract, you are liable to pay a compensatory sum unless the promised event comes to pass, and that is all the difference. But such a mode of looking at the matter stinks in the nostrils of those who think it advantageous to get as much ethics into the law as they can. It was good enough for Lord Coke, however, and here, as in many other cases, I am content to abide with him. In Bromage *v.* Genning, a prohibition was sought in the King's Bench against a suit in the marches of Wales for the specific performance of a covenant to grant a lease, and Coke said that it would subvert the intention of the covenantor, since he intends it to be at his election either to lose the damages or to make the lease. Sergeant Harris for the plaintiff confessed that he moved the matter against his conscience, and a prohibition was granted. This goes further than we should go now, but it shows what I venture to say has been the common law point of view from the beginning, although Mr. Harriman, in his very able little book upon Contracts has been misled, as I humbly think, to a different conclusion.

I have spoken only of the common law, because there are some cases in which a logical justification can be found for speaking of civil liabilities as imposing duties in an intelligible sense. These are the relatively few in which equity will grant an injunction, and will enforce it by putting the defendant in prison or otherwise punishing him unless he complies with the order of the court. But I hardly think it advisable to shape general theory from the exception, and I think it would be better to cease troubling ourselves about primary rights and sanctions altogether, than to describe our prophecies concerning the liabilities commonly imposed by the law in those inappropriate terms.

I mentioned, as other examples of the use by the law of words drawn from morals, malice, intent, and negligence. It is enough to take malice as it is used in the law of civil liability for wrongs— what we lawyers call the law of torts—to show you that it means something different in law from what it means in morals, and also to show how the difference has been obscured by giving to principles which have little or nothing to do with each other the same name. Three hundred years ago a parson preached a sermon and told a story out of Fox's Book of Martyrs of a man who had assisted at the torture of one of the saints, and afterward died, suffering compensatory inward torment. It happened that Fox was wrong. The man was alive and chanced to hear the sermon, and thereupon he sued the parson. Chief Justice Wray instructed the jury that the defendant was not liable, because the story was told innocently, without malice. He took malice in the moral sense, as importing a malevolent motive. But nowadays no one doubts that a man may be liable, without any malevolent motive at all, for false statements manifestly calculated to inflict temporal damage. In stating the case in pleading, we still should call the defendant's conduct malicious; but, in my opinion at least, the word means nothing about motives, or even about the defendant's attitude toward the future, but only signifies that the tendency of his conduct under the known circumstances was very plainly to cause the plaintiff temporal harm.

In the law of contract the use of moral phraseology has led to equal confusion, as I have shown in part already, but only in part. Morals deal with the actual internal state of the individual's mind, what he actually intends. From the time of the Romans down to now, this mode of dealing has affected the language of the law as to contract, and the language used has reacted upon the thought. We talk about a contract as a meeting of the minds of the parties, and thence it is inferred in various cases that there is no contract because their minds have not met; that is, because they have intended different things or because one party has not known of the assent of the other. Yet nothing is more certain than that parties may be bound by a contract to things which neither of them intended, and when one does not know of the other's assent. Suppose a contract is executed in due form and in writing to deliver a lecture, mentioning no time. One of the parties thinks that the promise will be construed to mean at once, within a week. The other thinks that it means when he is ready. The court says that it means within a reasonable time. The parties are bound by the contract as it is interpreted by the court, yet neither of them meant what the court declares that they have said. In my opinion no one will understand the true theory of contract or be able even to discuss some fundamental questions intelligently until he has understood that all contracts are formal, that the making of a contract depends not on the agreement of two minds in one intention, but on the agreement of two sets of external signs—not on the parties' having *meant* the same thing but on their having *said* the same thing. Furthermore, as the signs may be addressed to one sense or another —to sight or to hearing—on the nature of the sign will depend the moment when the contract is made. If the sign is tangible, for instance, a letter, the contract is made when the letter of acceptance is delivered. If it is necessary that the minds of the parties

meet, there will be no contract until the acceptance can be read
—none, for example, if the acceptance be snatched from the hand
of the offerer by a third person.

This is not the time to work out a theory in detail, or to answer
many obvious doubts and questions which are suggested by these
general views. I know of none which are not easy to answer, but
what I am trying to do now is only by a series of hints to throw
some light on the narrow path of legal doctrine, and upon two
pitfalls which, as it seems to me, lie perilously near to it. Of the
first of these I have said enough. I hope that my illustrations have
shown the danger, both to speculation and to practice, of con-
founding morality with law, and the trap which legal language
lays for us on that side of our way. For my own part, I often doubt
whether it would not be a gain if every word of moral significance
could be banished from the law altogether, and other words adopted
which should convey legal ideas uncolored by anything outside
the law. We should lose the fossil records of a good deal of history
and the majesty got from ethical associations, but by ridding ourselves of an unnecessary confusion we should gain very much in
the clearness of our thought.

So much for the limits of the law. The next thing which I wish
to consider is what are the forces which determine its content
and its growth. You may assume, with Hobbes and Bentham and
Austin, that all law emanates from the sovereign, even when the
first human beings to enunciate it are the judges, or you may
think that law is the voice of the Zeitgeist, or what you like. It is
all one to my present purpose. Even if every decision required
the sanction of an emperor with despotic power and a whimsical
turn of mind, we should be interested none the less, still with a
view to prediction, in discovering some order, some rational explanation, and some principle of growth for the rules which he
laid down. In every system there are such explanations and principles to be found. It is with regard to them that a second fallacy
comes in, which I think it important to expose.

The fallacy to which I refer is the notion that the only force at
work in the development of the law is logic. In the broadest sense,
indeed, that notion would be true. The postulate on which we
think about the universe is that there is a fixed quantitative relation

between every phenomenon and its antecedents and consequents. If there is such a thing as a phenomenon without these fixed quantitative relations, it is a miracle. It is outside the law of cause and effect, and as such transcends our power of thought, or at least is something to or from which we cannot reason. The condition of our thinking about the universe is that it is capable of being thought about rationally, or, in other words, that every part of it is effect and cause in the same sense in which those parts are with which we are most familiar. So in the broadest sense it is true that the law is a logical development, like everything else. The danger of which I speak is not the admission that the principles governing other phenomena also govern the law, but the notion that a given system, ours, for instance, can be worked out like mathematics from some general axioms of conduct. This is the natural error of the schools, but it is not confined to them. I once heard a very eminent judge say that he never let a decision go until he was absolutely sure that it was right. So judicial dissent often is blamed, as if it meant simply that one side or the other were not doing their sums right, and, if they woud take more trouble, agreement inevitably would come.

This mode of thinking is entirely natural. The training of lawyers is a training in logic. The processes of analogy, discrimination, and deduction are those in which they are most at home. The language of judicial decision is mainly the language of logic. And the logical method and form flatter that longing for certainty and for repose which is in every human mind. But certainty generally is illusion, and repose is not the destiny of man. Behind the logical form lies a judgment as to the relative worth and importance of competing legislative grounds, often an inarticulate and unconscious judgment, it is true, and yet the very root and nerve of the whole proceeding. You can give any conclusion a logical form. You always can imply a condition in a contract. But why do you imply it? It is because of some belief as to the practice of the community or of a class, or because of some opinion as to policy, or, in short, because of some attitude of yours upon a matter not capable of exact quantitative measurement, and therefore not capable of founding exact logical conclusions. Such matters really are battle grounds where the means do not exist for determinations that shall be good for all time, and where the decision can do no more than embody the preference of a given body in a given time and place. We do not realize how large a part of our law is open to reconsideration upon a slight change in the habit of the public mind. No concrete proposition is self-evident, no matter how ready we may be to accept it, not even Mr. Herbert Spencer's. Every man has a right to do what he wills, provided he interferes not with a like right on the part of his neighbors.

Why is a false and injurious statement privileged, if it is made honestly in giving information about a servant? It is because it has been thought more important that information should be given freely, than that a man should be protected from what under other circumstances would be an actionable wrong. Why is a man at liberty to set up a business which he knows will ruin his neighbor? It is because the public good is supposed to be best subserved by free competition. Obviously such judgments of relative importance may vary in different times and places. Why does a judge instruct a jury that an employer is not liable to an employee for an injury received in the course of his employment unless he is negligent, and why do the jury generally find for the plaintiff if the case is allowed to go to them? It is because the traditional policy of our law is to confine liability to cases where a prudent man might have foreseen the injury, or at least the danger, while the inclination of a very large part of the community is to make certain classes of persons insure the safety of those with whom they deal. Since the last words were written, I have seen the requirement of such insurance put forth as part of the programme of one of the best known labor organizations. There is a concealed, half conscious battle on the question of legislative policy, and if anyone thinks that it can be settled deductively, or once for all, I only can say that I think he is theoretically wrong, and that I am certain that his conclusion will not be accepted in practice *semper ubique et ab omnibus.*

Indeed, I think that even now our theory upon this matter is open to reconsideration, although I am not prepared to say how I should decide if a reconsideration were proposed. Our law of torts comes from the old days of isolated, ungeneralized wrongs, assaults, slanders, and the like, where the damages might be taken to lie where they fell by legal judgment. But the torts with which our courts are kept busy to-day are mainly the incidents of certain well known businesses. They are injuries to person or property by railroads, factories, and the like. The liability for them is estimated, and sooner or later goes into the price paid by the public. The public really pays the damages, and the question of liability, if pressed far enough, is really the question how far it is desirable that the public should insure the safety of those whose work it uses. It might be said that in such cases the chance of a jury finding for the defendant is merely a chance, once in a while rather arbitrarily interrupting the regular course of recovery, most likely in the case of an unusually conscientious plaintiff, and therefore better done away with. On the other hand, the economic value even of a life to the community can be estimated, and no recovery, it may be said, ought to go beyond that amount. It is conceivable that some day in certain cases we may find ourselves imitating, on a higher plane, the tariff for life and limb which we see in the Leges Barbarorum.

I think that the judges themselves have failed adequately to recognize their duty of weighing considerations of social advantage. The duty is inevitable, and the result of the often proclaimed judicial aversion to deal with such considerations is simply to leave the very ground and foundation of judgments inarticulate, and often unconscious, as I have said. When socialism first began to be talked about, the comfortable classes of the community were a good deal frightened. I suspect that this fear has influenced judicial action both here and in England, yet it is certain that it is not a conscious factor in the decisions to which I refer. I think that something similar has led people who no longer hope to control the legislatures to look to the courts as expounders of the Constitutions, and that in some courts new principles have been discovered outside the bodies of those instruments, which may be generalized into acceptance of the economic doctrines which prevailed about fifty years ago, and a wholesale prohibition of what a tribunal of lawyers does not think about right. I cannot but believe that if the training of lawyers led them habitually to consider more definitely and explicitly the social advantage on which the rule they lay down must be justified, they sometimes would hesitate where

now they are confident, and see that really they were taking sides
upon debatable and often burning questions.

JOHN CHIPMAN GRAY

The Judge as Law-Giver

*John Chipman Gray (1839–1915), one of America's great
analytical jurists, taught law at Harvard. His own thinking was
influenced by John Austin, although Gray rejects Austin's
definition of "law." In focusing attention on the law-making
role of the judge, Gray had an important influence on the
development of legal realism in the United States.*

The Law of the State or of any organized body of men is composed
of the rules which the courts, that is, the judicial organs of that
body, lay down for the determination of legal rights and duties. The
difference in this matter between contending schools of Jurisprudence arises largely from not distinguishing between the Law
and the Sources of the Law. On the one hand, to affirm the existence of *nicht positivisches Recht*, that is, of Law which the
courts do not follow, is declared to be an absurdity; and on the
other hand, it is declared to be an absurdity to say that the Law
of a great nation means the opinions of half-a-dozen old gentlemen, some of them, conceivably, of very limited intelligence.

The truth is, each party is looking at but one side of the shield.
If those half-a-dozen old gentlemen form the highest judicial
tribunal of a country, then no rule or principle which they refuse
to follow is Law in that country. However desirable, for instance,

Reprinted from John Chipman Gray, *The Nature and Sources of the Law*,
pp. 84–91, 93–4, 96–100, 102–4, 170–3, 308–9. by permission of Ronald
Gray and Beacon Press. Copyright © 1909 by Columbia University Press,
1921 by Roland Gray. Abridged by the editor.

it may be that a man should be obliged to make gifts which he has promised to make, yet if the courts of a country will not compel him to keep his promise, it is not the Law of that country that promises to make a gift are binding. On the other hand, those six men seek the rules which they follow not in their own whims, but they derive them from sources often of the most general and permanent character, to which they are directed, by the organized body to which they belong, to apply themselves. I believe the definition of Law that I have given to be correct; but let us consider some other definitions of the Law which have prevailed and which still prevail.

Of the many definitions of the Law which have been given at various times and places, some are absolutely meaningless, and in others a spark of truth is distorted by a mist of rhetoric. But there are three theories which have commended themselves to accurate thinkers, which have had and which still have great acceptance, and which deserve examination. In all of them it is denied that the courts are the real authors of the Law, and it is contended that they are merely the mouthpieces which give it expression.

The *first* of these theories is that Law is made up of the commands of the sovereign. This is Austin's view. "Every Positive Law," he says, "obtaining in any community, is a creature of the Sovereign or State; having been established immediately by the monarch or supreme body, as exercising legislative or judicial functions; or having been established immediately by a subject individual or body, as exercising rights or powers of direct or judicial legislation, which the monarch or supreme body has expressly or tacitly conferred."

In a sense, this is true; the State can restrain its courts from following this or that rule; but it often leaves them free to follow what they think right; and it is certainly a forced expression to say that one commands things to be done, because he has power (which he does not exercise) to forbid their being done.

Mr. A. B., who wants a house, employs an architect, Mr. Y. Z., to build it for him. Mr. Y. Z. puts up a staircase in a certain way; in such a case, nine times out of ten, he puts it up in that way, because he always puts up staircases in that way, or because the books on construction say they ought to be so put up, or because his professional brethren put up their staircases in that fashion, or because he thinks to put it up so would be good building, or in good taste, or because it costs him less trouble than to put it up in some other way; he seldom thinks whether Mr. A. B. would like it in that way or not; and probably Mr. A. B. never thinks whether it could have been put up in any other fashion. Here it certainly seems strained to speak, as Austin would do, of the staircase as being the "creature" of Mr. A. B.; and yet Mr. A. B. need not have had his staircase put up in that way, and indeed need never have had any staircase or any house at all.

Austin's statement that the Law is entirely made up of commands directly or indirectly imposed by the State is correct, therefore, only on the theory that everything which the State does not forbid its judges to do, and which they in fact do, the State commands, although the judges are not animated by a direct desire to carry out the State's wishes, but by entirely different ones.

In this connection, the meaning of "Law," when preceded by the indefinite, is to be distinguished from that which it bears when preceded by the definite, article. Austin, indeed, defines the Law as being the aggregate of the rules established by political superiors; and Bentham says, "*Law,* or *the Law,* taken indefinitely, is an abstract and collective term; which, when it means anything, can mean neither more nor less than the sum total of a number of individual laws taken together." But this is not, I think, the ordinary meaning given to "the Law." A law ordinarily means a statute passed by the legislature of a State. "*The* Law" is the whole system of rules applied by the courts. The resemblance of the terms suggest the inference that the body of rules applied by the courts is composed wholly of the commands of the State; but to erect this suggestion into a demonstration, and say:—The system administered by the courts is "the Law," "the Law" consists of nothing but an aggregate of single laws, and all single laws are commands of the State,—is not justifiable.

Austin's theory was a natural reaction against the views which he found in possession of the field. Law had been defined as "the art of what is good and equitable"; "that which reason in such sort defines to be good that it must be done"; "the abstract expression of the general will existing in and for itself"; "the organic whole of the external conditions of the intellectual life."[1] If Austin went too far in considering the Law as always proceeding from the State, he conferred a great benefit on Jurisprudence by bringing out clearly that the Law is at the mercy of the State.

The *second* theory on the nature of Law is that the courts, in deciding cases, are, in truth, applying what has previously existed in the common consciousness of the people. Savigny is the ablest expounder of this theory. At the beginning of the *System des heutigen römischen Rechts*, he has set it forth thus: "It is in the common consciousness of the people that the positive law lives, and hence we have to call it *Volksrecht*. . . . It is the *Volksgeist*, living and working in all the individuals in common, which begets the positive law, so that for the consciousness of each individual there is, not by chance but necessarily, one and the same law. . . . The form, in which the Law lives in the common consciousness of the people, is not that of abstract rule, but the living intuition of the institute of the Law in its organic connection. . . . When I say that the exercise of the *Volksrecht* in single cases must be considered as a means to become acquainted with it, an indirect acquaintance must be understood, necessary for those who look at it from the outside, without being themselves members of the community in which the *Volksrecht* has arisen and leads its continuous life. For the members of the community, no such inference from single cases of exercise is necessary, since their knowledge of it is direct and based on intuition."

Savigny is careful to discriminate between the common consciousness of the people and custom: "The foundation of the Law," he says, "has its existence, its reality, in the common consciousness of the people. This existence is invisible. How can we become acquainted with it? We become acquainted with it as it manifests itself in external acts, as it appears in practice, manners, and custom: by the uniformity of a continuous and continuing mode of action, we recognize that the belief of the people is its common root, and not mere chance. Thus, custom is the sign of positive law, not its foundation."

Savigny is confronted by a difficulty of the same kind as confronted Austin. The great bulk of the Law as it exists in any

[1] Celsus; Hooker; Hegel, Krause.

community is unknown to its rulers, and it is only by aid of the
doctrine that what the sovereign permits he commands, that
the Law can be considered as emanating from him; but equally, the
great bulk of the Law is unknown to the people; how, then, can
it be the product of their "common consciousness"? How can it
be that of which they "feel the necessity as law"?

Take a simple instance, one out of thousands. By the law of
Massachusetts, a contract by letter is not complete until the
answer of acceptance is received.[2] By the law of New York, it is
complete when the answer is mailed. Is the common consciousness of the people of Massachusetts different on this point from
that of the people of New York? Do the people of Massachusetts
feel the necessity of one thing as law, and the people of New York
feel the necessity of the precise opposite? In truth, not one in a
hundred of the people of either State has the dimmest notion on
the matter. If one of them has a notion, it is as likely as not to be
contrary to the law of his State.

A *third* theory of the Law remains to consider. That theory is
to this effect: The rules followed by the courts in deciding questions
are not the expression of the State's commands, nor are they the
expression of the common consciousness of the people, but, although what the judges rule is the Law, it is putting the cart
before the horse to say that the Law is what the judges rule. The
Law, indeed, is identical with the rules laid down by the judges,
but those rules are laid down by the judges because they are the
law, they are not the Law because they are laid down by the judges;
or, as the late Mr. James C. Carter puts it, the judges are the discoverers, not the creators, of the Law. And this is the way that
judges themselves are apt to speak of their functions.

This theory concedes that the rules laid down by the judges
correctly state the Law, but it denies that it is Law because they
state it. Before considering the denial, let us look a moment at the
concession. It is a proposition with which I think most Common-
Law lawyers would agree. But we ought to be sure that our ideas
are not colored by the theories or practice of the particular system
of law with which we are familiar. In the Common Law, it is

---

[2] This used to be the Law in Massachusetts. I am not so sure that it is
now.

now generally recognized that the judges have had a main part in erecting the Law; that, as it now stands, it is largely based on the opinions of past generations of judges; but in the Civil Law, as we shall see hereafter, this has been true to a very limited extent. In other words, judicial precedents have been the chief material for building up the Common Law, but this has been far otherwise in the systems of the Continent of Europe. But granting all that is said by the Continental writers on the lack of influence of judicial precedents in their countries to be true, yet, although a past decision may not be a source of Law, a present decision is certainly an expression of what the Law now is. The courts of France to-day may, on the question whether a blank indorsement of a bill of exchange passes title, care little or nothing for the opinions formerly expressed by French judges on the point, but, nevertheless, the opinion of those courts to-day upon the question is the expression of the present Law of France, for it is in accordance with such opinion that the State will compel the inhabitants of France to regulate their conduct. To say that any doctrine which the courts of a country refuse to adopt is Law in that country, is to set up the idol of *nicht positivisches Recht*, and, therefore, it is true, in the Civil as well as in the Common Law, that the rules laid down by the courts of a country state the present Law correctly.

To come, then, to the question whether the judges discover preëxisting Law, or whether the body of rules that they lay down is not the expression of preëxisting Law, but the Law itself. Let us take a concrete instance: On many matters which have come in question in various jurisdictions, there is no doctrine received *semper, ubique, et ab omnibus*. For instance, Henry Pitt has built a reservoir on his land, and has filled it with water; and, without any negligence on his part, either in the care or construction of his reservoir, it bursts, and the water, pouring forth, floods and damages the land of Pitt's neighbor, Thomas Underhill. Has Underhill a right to recover compensation from Pitt? In England, in the leading case of *Rylands* v. *Fletcher*, it was held that he could recover, and this decision has been followed in some of the United States—for instance, in Massachusetts; but in others, as, I believe, in New Jersey, the contrary is held.

Now, suppose that Pitt's reservoir is in one of the newer States, say Utah, and suppose, further, that the question has never arisen there before; that there is no statute, no decision, no custom on the subject; the court has to decide the case somehow; suppose it should follow *Rylands* v. *Fletcher* and should rule that in such cases the party injured can recover. The State, then, through its judicial organ, backed by the executive power of the State, would be recognizing the rights of persons injured by such accidents, and, therefore, the doctrine of *Rylands* v. *Fletcher* would be undoubtedly the present Law in Utah.

Suppose, again, that a similar state of facts arises in the adjoining State of Nevada, and that there also the question is presented for the first time, and that there is no statute, decision, or custom on the point; the Nevada court has to decide the case somehow; suppose it should decline to follow *Rylands* v. *Fletcher*, and should rule that in such cases the party injured is without remedy. Here the State of Nevada would refuse to recognize any right in the injured party and, therefore, it would unquestionably be the present Law in Nevada that persons injured by such an accident would have no right to compensation.

Let us now assume that the conditions and habits of life are the same in these two adjoining States; that being so, these contradictory doctrines cannot both conform to an ideal rule of Law, and let us, therefore, assume that an all-wise and all-good intelligence, considering the question, would think that one of these doctrines was right and the other wrong, according to the true standard of morality, whatever that may be. It matters not, for the purposes of the discussion, which of the two doctrines it is, but let us suppose that the intelligence aforesaid would approve *Rylands* v. *Fletcher*; that is, it would think the Law as established in Nevada by the decision of its court did not conform to the eternal principles of right.

The fact that the ideal theory of Law disapproved the Law as established in Nevada would not affect the present existence of that Law. However wrong intellectually or morally it might be, it would be the Law of that State to-day. But what was the Law in Nevada a week before a rule for decision of such questions as adopted by the courts of that State? Three views seem possible:

first, that the Law was then ideally right, and contrary to the rule now declared and practised on; *second*, that the Law was then the same as is now declared practised; *third*, that there was then no Law on the matter.

The first theory seems untenable on any notion of discovery. A discoverer is a discoverer of that which is,—not of that which is not. The result of such a theory would be that when Underhill received the injury and brought his suit, he had an interest which would be protected by the State, and that it now turns out that he did not have it,—a contradiction in terms.

We have thus to choose between the theory that the Law was at that time what it now is, and the theory that there was then no law at all on the subject. The latter is certainly the view of reason and common sense alike. There was, at the time in question, *ex hypothesi*, no statute, no precedent, no custom on the subject; of the inhabitants of the State not one out of a hundred had an opinion on the matter or had ever thought of it; of the few, if any, to whom the question had ever occurred, the opinions were, as likely as not, conflicting. To say that on this subject there was really Law existing in Nevada, seems only to show how strong a root legal fictions can strike into our mental processes.

When the element of long time is introduced, the absurdity of the view of Law preëxistent to its declaration is obvious. What was the Law in the time of Richard Cœur de Lion on the liability of a telegraph company to the persons to whom a message was sent?

The difficulty of believing in preëxisting Law is still greater when there is a change in the decision of the courts. In Massachusetts it was held in 1849, by the Supreme Judicial Court, that if a man hired a horse in Boston on a Sunday to drive to Nahant, and drove instead to Nantasket, the keeper of the livery stable had no right to sue him in trover for the conversion of the horse. But in 1871 this decision was overruled, and the right was given to the stable-keeper. Now, did stable-keepers have such rights, say, in 1845? If they did, then the court in 1849 did not discover the Law. If they did not, then the court in 1871 did not discover the Law.

And this brings us to the reason why courts and jurists have so struggled to maintain the preëxistence of the Law, why the common run of writers speak of the judges as merely stating the Law, and why Mr. Carter, in an advance towards the truth, says of the judges that they are discoverers of the Law. That reason is the unwillingness to recognize the fact that the courts, with the consent of the State, have been constantly in the practice of applying in the decision of controversies, rules which were not in existence and were, therefore, not knowable by the parties when the causes of controversy occurred. It is the unwillingness to face the certain fact that courts are constantly making *ex post facto* Law.[3]

Rules of conduct laid down and applied by the courts of a country are coterminous with the Law of that country, and as the first change, so does the latter along with them. Bishop Hoadly has said: "Whoever hath an *absolute authority* to *interpret* any written or spoken laws, it is *he* who is truly the *Law-giver* to all intents and purposes, and not the person who first wrote or spoke them";[4] *a fortiori,* whoever hath an absolute authority not only to interpret the Law, but to say what the Law is, is truly the Law-giver. *Entia non multiplicanda.* There seems to be nothing gained by seeking to discover the sources, purposes, and relations of a mysterious entity called "The Law," and then to say this Law is exactly expressed in the rules by which the courts decide cases. It is better to consider directly the sources, purposes, and relations of the rules themselves, and to call the rules "The Law."

There is a feeling that makes one hesitate to accept the theory that the rules followed by the courts constitute the Law, in that it seems to be approaching the Law from the clinical or therapeutic side; that it is as if one were to define medicine as the science of the rules by which physicians diagnose and treat diseases; but the difference lies in this, that the physicians have not received from the ruler of the world any commission to decide what diseases are, to kill or to cure according to their opinion whether a sickness is mortal; whereas, this is exactly what the judges do with

[3] Technically the term *"ex post facto* Law" is confined with us to statutes creating crimes or punishments. I use the term here in its broader sense of retroactive Law.

[4] Benjamin Hoadly, Bishop of Bangor, Sermon preached before the King, 1717, p. 12.

regard to the cases brought before them. If the judges of a country decide that it is Law that a man whose reservoir bursts must pay the damage, Law it is; but all the doctors in town may declare that a man has the yellow fever, and yet he may have only the German measles. If when a board of physicians pronounced that Titius had the colic, *ipso facto* Titius did have the colic, then I conceive the suggested definition of medicine would be unobjectionable.

To sum up. The State exists for the protection and forwarding of human interests, mainly through the medium of rights and duties. If every member of the State knew perfectly his own rights and duties, and the rights and duties of everybody else, the State would need no judicial organs; administrative organs would suffice. But there is no such universal knowledge. To determine, in actual life, what are the rights and duties of the State and of its citizens, the State needs and establishes judicial organs, the judges. To determine rights and duties, the judges settle what facts exist, and also lay down rules according to which they deduce legal consequences from facts. These rules are the Law.

It may be urged that if the Law of a society be the body of rules applied by its courts, then statutes should be considered as being part of the Law itself, and not merely as being a source of the Law; that they are rules to be applied by the courts directly, and should not be regarded merely as fountains from which the courts derive their own rules. Such a view is very common in the books. And if statutes interpreted themselves, this would be true; but statutes do not interpret themselves; their meaning is declared by the courts, and *it is with the meaning declared by the courts, and with no other meaning, that they are imposed upon the community as Law.* True though it be, that, of all the sources from which the courts draw the Law, statutes are the most stringent and precise, yet the power of the judges over the statutes is very great; and this not only in countries of the Common Law, but also on the Continent of Europe, where the office of judge is less highly esteemed.

A statute is the expressed will of the legislative organ of a society; but until the dealers in psychic forces succeed in making of thought transference a working controllable force (and the psychic transference of the thought of an artificial body must stagger the most advanced of the ghost hunters), the will of the legislature has to be expressed by words, spoken or written; that is, by causing sounds to be made, or by causing black marks to be impressed on white paper. "Only in an improper sense can we speak of a communication or transfer of thought; the thought itself is not transferred, but the word gives only the impulse and the possibility of a *like process of thought*, the reproduction of a like spiritual movement in the mind of the hearer, as in that of the speaker. . . . The principle of communication by words is wholly the same as of that by signs; one means is complete, the other incomplete, but they *work* in the same way; neither gives the thought itself, however exact the expression of it may be; it gives only the invitation and the point of departure for it to *reconstruct* itself."[5]

A judge puts before himself the printed page of the statute book; it is mirrored on the retina of his eye and from this impression he has to reproduce the thought of the law-giving body. The process is far from being merely mechanical; it is obvious how the character of the judge and the cast of his mind must affect the operation, and what a different shape the thought when reproduced in the mind of the judge may have from that which it bore in the mind of the law-giver. This is true even if the function of the judge be deemed only that of attempting to reproduce in his own mind the thought of the law-giver; but as we shall see in a moment, a judge, starting from the words of a statute, is often led to results which he applies as if they had been the thought of the legislature, while yet he does not believe, and has no reason to believe, that his present thought is the same as any thought which the legislature really had.

As between the legislative and judicial organs of a society, it is the judicial which has the last say as to what is and what is not Law in a community. To quote a third time the words of Bishop Hoadly: "Whoever hath an *absolute authority* to *interpret* any written or spoken laws, it is *he* who is truly the *Law-giver* to all intents and purposes, and not the person who first wrote or spoke them." And this is now recognized even in Germany: "A ju-

[5] 2 Ihering, Geist des röm. Rechts (4th ed.). § 44, pp. 445, 446.

dicial decree is as much as a statute the act of the law-making power of the State. Like the legislative determination of the Law, so the judicial determinations are filled with the power and compulsive force of the State. A judgment of a court has the force of Law; it carries the whole force of the Law with it. A judicial determination of Law has, in the region belonging to it, the power of a fixed, legally binding order, more fully, with stronger, more direct working, than the statutory, merely abstract statements of the Law. The power of Law is stronger than the power of Legislation, a legal judgment maintains itself if it contradicts a statute. Not by its legislative, but by its judicial determinations, the law-regulating power of the State speaks its last word."[6]

But the matter does not rest here. A fundamental misconception prevails, and pervades all the books as to the dealing of the courts with statutes. Interpretation is generally spoken of as if its chief function was to discover what the meaning of the Legislature really was. But when a Legislature has had a real intention, one way or another, on a point, it is not once in a hundred times that any doubt arises as to what its intention was. If that were all that a judge had to do with a statute, interpretation of statutes, instead of being one of the most difficult of a judge's duties, would be extremely easy. The fact is that the difficulties of so-called interpretation arise when the Legislature has had no meaning at all; when the question which is raised on the statute never occurred to it; when what the judges have to do is, not to determine what the Legislature did mean on a point which was present to its mind, but to guess what it would have intended on a point not present to its mind, if the point had been present. If there are any lawyers among those who honor me with their attention, let them consider any dozen cases of the interpretation of statutes, as they have occurred consecutively in their reading or practice, and they will, I venture to say, find that in almost all of them it is probable, and that in most of them it is perfectly evident, that the makers of the statutes had no real intention, one way or another, on the point in question; that if they had, they would have made their meaning clear; and that when the judges are professing to declare

---

[6] Bülow, Gesetz und Richteramt, 6, 7.

what the Legislature meant, they are in truth, themselves legislating to fill up *casus omissi*.

A chief object in these lectures has been an attempt to show that one of the main difficulties and causes of confusion in Jurisprudence has been the failure to distinguish between Law and the sources of Law. The Law of a country or other organized body of men is composed of the rules for conduct that its courts follow and that it holds itself out as ready to enforce; no ideas, however just, that its courts refuse to follow are Law, and all rules which they follow and to which it enforces obedience are Law; and to introduce any notion of the Law of Nature or of *nicht positivisches Recht* into the conception of the Law is to take a step backward in Jurisprudence.

On the other hand, it is the failing of many advocates of codification to regard the Law too much as a fixed product of statutes, precedents, and customs, and not to take into sufficient account the growth and change of the Law. This growth and change is not a mere weaving of spider webs out of the bowels of the present rules of Law; a source of the Law, not the only source, but a source and a main source, is found in the principles of ethics. These principles, therefore, are legitimately a part of Jurisprudence, and the more the bounds of Comparative Jurisprudence are extended, the greater part will they play.

Formulations

EUGEN EHRLICH

Law and the Inner Order of Associations

Eugen Ehrlich (1862–1922) is recognized as one of the founders of the sociology of law, and pioneered in the study of the actual social effects of legal institutions and legal doctrines. He was professor of law at the University of Czernowitz in Bukovina. His Fundamental Principles of the Sociology of Law, *from which this selection is taken, was first published in German in 1913 and was translated by Walter L. Moll.*

It is often said that a book must be written in a manner that permits of summing up its content in a single sentence. If the present volume were to be subjected to this test, the sentence might be the following: At the present as well as at any other time, the center of gravity of legal development lies not in legislation, nor in juristic science, nor in judicial decision, but in society itself. This sentence, perhaps, contains the substance of every attempt to state the fundamental principles of the sociology of law.

Reprinted by permission of the publishers from Eugen Ehrlich, *Fundamental Principles of the Sociology of Law* (Cambridge, Mass.: Harvard University Press), pp. xiv, 26–9, 32–9, 159, 388–90, 504–5. Copyright, 1936, by the President and Fellows of Harvard College. Abridged by the editor.

It is axiomatic that all study in the field of social science is based on the concept of human society. Society is the sum total of the human associations that have mutual relations with one another. And these associations that constitute human society are very heterogeneous. The state, the nation, the community of states which are bound together by the ties of international law, i.e. the political, economic, intellectual, and social association of the civilized nations of the earth extending far beyond the bounds of the individual state and nation, the religious communions and the individual churches, the various sects and religious groups, the corporations, the classes, the professions, the political parties within the state, the families in the narrowest and in the widest sense, the social groups and cliques—this universe of interlacing rings and intersecting circles—constitute a society to the extent that acting and reacting upon one another is at all perceptible among them.

From these various kinds of groups of human beings, we must select, first of all, a certain kind of organized association, which we shall hereafter designate as the primitive (genetic) association. We meet with it in primitive times in various forms as clan (*Geschlecht, gens, Sippe*), family, house community. The clan and the family are its original forms. It cannot as yet be determined which of these two must be considered the true original form (*Urform*); whether the clan is nothing more than a full-grown, enlarged family, or whether the family developed at a much later time than, and within, the clan. It is self-evident that, from the moment in which men begin to form associations, increased capacity for association with others becomes a weapon in the struggle for existence. It effects the gradual exclusion and extinction of those in whom self-seeking and predatory instincts predominate, and the survival of those that have capacity for socialization, who henceforth are the stronger because they can avail themselves of the strength of the whole association. Accordingly natural selection and heredity produce a race of human beings which is increasingly capable of socialization. This feeling of solidarity which has its roots in the dim consciousness of mutual interdependence begets the clan, and, strengthened by the consciousness of common ancestry, the (cognatic, based on blood relationship) family. Among breeders of cattle and tillers of the soil, whose common toil leads them to dwell together, the family develops into the house community, which is usually also called family. Out of the union of genetic associations, clans, families, house communities, grows the tribe, and, in course of time, the nation.

In lower stages of development, the social order of mankind rests exclusively upon the genetic associations and their union into tribe and nation. These associations therefore fulfil a number of functions. The clan, the house community, the family, is an association economic, religious, military, and legal; it is a community of language, ethical custom, and social life. But in more advanced societies, these functions are gradually severing from the genetic associations; groups of a different kind arise, which add to their new functions by taking over the original functions of the genetic associations. These are: the commune, the state, the religious communion, the society, the political party, the social coterie, the social club, the economic association in agriculture, shop, and factory, the cooperative society, the association of the members of a calling, all the associations connected with the transportation of persons or goods. Among the peoples of the highest degree of civilization, a man becomes a member of an almost incalculable number of associations of the most diverse kinds; his life becomes richer, more varied, more complex. And in consequence, the once powerful genetic associations languish and, in part, fall into decay. Only the house community of the nearest blood relatives, who dwell under the same roof, the family in the narrowest sense of the word, has been able to maintain itself in full vigor down to our day; the wider family has largely faded out, and of the clan only a few scarcely perceptible traces remain, and these are to be found exclusively among the higher nobility and among the peasantry.

Though we know very little of the law of the early times of the peoples from whom the civilized nations of Europe have sprung, there can be no doubt that of what today is mostly, and sometimes even exclusively, called law, i.e. of the fixed rule of law, formulated in words, which issues from a power superior to the individual, and which is imposed upon the latter from without, only a few negligible traces can be found among them. Their law is chiefly the order of the clans, families, houses. It determines the prerequisites and the consequences of a valid marriage, the mutual relation of the spouses, of parents and children, and the mutual relations of the other members of the clan, family, and household. Each association creates this order for itself quite independently. It is not bound by the order which exists in other associations for the same relations. And if the orders in associations of the same kind differ very little from each other, this must be attributed to the similarity of the conditions of life; often to borrowing; but by no means to a uniform order in some manner prescribed for them from without. In the language of German scholarship, there may possibly be a general law (*allgemeines Recht*) in these associations, but not a common law (*gemeines Recht*).

As soon as ownership of land becomes established, law arises concerning it, but without any general rules of law. Each settlement creates its own land law; each landlord imposes it independently upon his villeins; each royal grant, quite independently of all others, makes provision for the legal status of the estate it grants. There are concrete legal relations in the various communes, settlements, and manors, but no law of ownership in land such as is found in the *corpus iuris* or in modern statute books.

The same holds true for the contract. The law of contracts is based solely upon the content of the contracts that are being entered into. There are no general legal propositions governing contracts. There is an utter absence of all those rules of compulsion, of eking out, and of interpretation with which the *corpus iuris* and modern statute books abound. Where the contract is silent, there is no law; and the literal, narrow interpretation of contracts, which is so characteristic of the older law, is not based upon formalism, which is usually imputed to primitive times, but which in reality is quite foreign to them, but upon the fact that, outside of the language of the contract, there is nothing to stand on.

In the primitive stage, the whole legal order consists in the inner order of the human associations, of which, indeed, the state is one. Each association creates this order for itself, even though it is true that an association often copies an order existing in other associations, or in case of a splitting up of an association, takes over an order and continues it. Because of these facts, to which must be added the similarities caused by the similarity of the relations, common features will not be lacking. To an observer from the outside these common features might appear to constitute a common law of the nation. But this is only a generalization made by the observer himself on the basis of what he has seen and heard. Tacitus makes a number of statements about the legal relations of the ancient Germans, but a cursory glance at his account suffices to show that it contains no legal propositions, but only statements about what the Germans customarily did and left undone. Society, if one may use the term with reference to those times, maintained its balance not by means of rules of law, but by means of the inner order of its associations.

Passing over a great number of generations of men, we reach the feudal state. It has been extremely difficult for the modern man to understand the feudal state, for the reason that, for a long time, he had been trying to find a constitution of the feudal state; whereas the chief characteristic of the feudal state is the fact that it has no constitution, but only agreements. The relation between the king and the great lords to whom he has granted fiefs is a contractual one. Likewise the relation between the great lords and those whom they have enfeoffed; likewise the relation between the latter and those whom they, in turn, have enfeoffed. On the lowest rung of the ladder are the serfs. Of course, one or more rungs may be omitted, and the feudal lords may have serfs at any level in this scale. In order to write an exhaustive description of the feudal state, one must be able to state the content of all the agreements entered into between the lords and their liege-men and of the relation between the lords and the villeins, which often is merely contractual. The agreements and the relation between the lord and the villeins may be very much alike in a certain district and among a certain people. But this similarity also is based upon the similarity of the attendant circumstances, upon direct imitation or borrowing, not upon a general rule. What is called "feudal law" is primarily a scientific elaboration of the common element in the individual agreements, which at a later period is transformed into a general rule of law which ekes out the content of the agreements.

It is true, in the more developed feudal law, assemblies of the feudal tenants of the individual feudal lords are not unknown. Occasionally these are assemblies not only of the immediate tenants of the feudal lord, but also of the tenants of the intermediate feudatories. Sometimes there are assemblies of villeins. These assemblies adopt common resolutions. But before the idea of law had made its way, these resolutions did not contain legal propositions in the modern sense of the term. They are merely expressions of the common will, and their legal significance is based upon the fact that they are being accepted by the feudal lord, and thereby become collective agreements with the feudal lord. Collective agreements in this sense of the term were: the most ancient resolutions of the German Imperial Diet, the Magna Charta Libertatum, which to the present day has remained the foundation of the English constitution, and on the whole, the law of the German manorial rights and of the corresponding services.

But the feudal constitution was far from being the whole content of the social order of the feudal state. Within the feudal state, the clan, the family, the house continued; but the clan was weakened considerably. Side by side with it, new local associations arose, which took over a considerable number of social functions. Among the local associations, the city soon became very important, and achieved a considerable measure of independence, which in effect placed it outside of the feudal constitution. The feudal constitution, in fact, has always remained a constitution of the open country. Within the walls of the city, a vast number of social associations, which were unknown elsewhere, and an active legal life developed. Here for the first time fully developed legal institutions were expressed in a number of legal propositions: the law of real property, of pledge, of contract, of inheritance.

But these legal propositions constitute an infinitesimal part of the legal order. In the feudal state as well as elsewhere, the great bulk of the legal order is not based upon the legal propositions, but upon the inner order of the social associations, of the older ones (the clan, the family, the house community), as well as of those of more recent origin—the feudal association, the manor, the mark community, the urban community, the guilds and trade unions, the corporations and foundations. If one would obtain a knowledge of the law of mediaeval society, one must not confine oneself to a study of the legal propositions, but must study it in the deeds of grant, the charters, the land registers, the records of the guilds, the city books, the regulations of the guilds. Even at this period, the center of gravity of the law lies in the inner order of the human associations.

If one compares the law of the present with that of past centuries, one cannot but be struck at the first glance by the great importance which in the course of centuries has attached to the legal proposition, authoritatively pronounced and formulated. With the sole exception of Great Britain, the *Staatsrecht* (public law in the narrow sense) of all European states has been put into this form, as well as the law of the state magistracies, administrative law, procedural law, and, apparently, the whole body of private law and of penal law. For this reason the idea that the law is nothing but a body of legal propositions dominates legal thinking today.

This idea, however, contains so many contradictory elements that it refutes itself. This inner inconsistency is least apparent in *Staatsrecht* (public law in the narrow sense), in administrative law, and in the law of procedure. But modern investigation of the normative significance of the factual, of the *Konventional-regel*,[1] and of the practice of administrative boards has shown that this branch of the law too does not consist exclusively of legal propositions. On the other hand, the legal rules barely touch the surface of the modern order of the family. The law of corporations and of foundations is based in the main upon the articles of association. In spite of the detailed provisions of the law of contracts, the content of the contract is of greater importance in the individual case than the rules of law governing contracts. Testamentary declarations of will, nuptial agreements, contracts of inheritance, agreements among heirs, are of much greater importance in the law of inheritance than the rules of law concern-

[1] The *Konventionalregel*, i.e. conventional rule or law, is a rule or law (to which a person is subject only so long as he chooses) created by agreement between the parties. The agreement may either be express or arise from the conduct of the parties.

ing it. Every judge, every administrative official, knows that, comparatively speaking, he rarely renders a decision based solely on legal propositions. By far the greatest number of decisions are based upon documents, testimony of witnesses or experts, contracts, articles of association, last wills and testaments, and other declarations. In other words, in the language of jurists, in a much greater number of instances judgment is being rendered upon questions of fact than upon questions of law. And the fact is a matter of the inner order of the human associations, as to which the judge obtains information from the testimony of witnesses and experts, from contracts, agreements among heirs, declarations by last will and testament. Even today, just as in primitive times, the fate of man is determined to a much greater extent by the inner order of the associations than by legal propositions.

This truth is hidden from the eye of the jurist by the fact that to him an adjudication upon a question of fact merely amounts to a subsumption of the ascertained facts under a legal proposition. But this is due solely to a juristic habit of thought. The state existed before the constitution; the family is older than the order of the family; possession antedates ownership; there were contracts before there was a law of contracts; and even the testament, where it is of native origin, is much older than the law of last wills and testaments. If the jurists think that before a binding contract was entered into, before a valid testament was made, there must have been in existence a legal proposition according to which agreements or testaments are binding, they are placing the abstract before the concrete. Perhaps it seems more readily understandable to a jurist that a legal proposition concerning the law of contracts or the law of wills might be binding than that a contract or a will might be binding without a legal proposition. But the mental processes of nations and of men, excepting the jurists among them, do not function in this fashion. It can be shown that the idea that prevailed among men in the past was that their right had arisen from a contract or from a grant; the idea that it had arisen from a legal proposition was altogether foreign to them. And at the present time, unless legal theory exerts its influence, men generally assume that their rights arise not from legal propositions but from the relations of man to man, from marriage, contract, last will and testament. That anyone might owe his rights to a legal proposition, is a notion that even today is current only among jurists. Social phenomena, however, can be explained not by construing them juristically but by inferring from facts the modes of thought that underlie them.

Up to this point, I have been confining this presentation intentionally to the nations of Europe; but its application is not limited to these. Among primitive races, the law is generally identical with the inner order of their associations. At this stage of development there are no legal propositions at all. At a somewhat higher stage, they appear in the form of religious commands. And it seems that until man has reached a very high stage of development, he cannot fully conceive the idea that the abstract rules of law can force their will upon life. It is true, the German folk laws of the early Middle Ages contain very detailed legal propositions, but probably they were applied only in those parts of the country in which there was a Roman population sufficiently large to bring about the continuation of Roman modes of thought even in a Germanic society. How small the influence of legislation was, even in the Middle Ages, is sufficiently well known. Travelers in backward countries, in the Orient, in parts of eastern and southern Europe, are struck by the general disorder. This disorder is caused by the fact that general legal propositions, even if there are such; are not being followed. There is a strange contrast between this lack of order in public life and the strictness with which the traditional order of the small association, of the household, of the family, of the clan, is followed.

The inner order of the associations of human beings is not only the original, but also, down to the present time, the basic form of law. The legal proposition not only comes into being at a much later time, but is largely derived from the inner order of the associations. In order to explain the beginnings, the development, and the nature of law, one must first of all inquire into the order of the associations. All attempts that have been made until now to comprehend the nature of law have failed because the investigation was not based on the order of the associations but on the legal propositions.

The inner order of the associations is determined by legal norms. Legal norms must not be confused with legal propositions. The legal proposition is the precise, universally binding formulation of the legal precept in a book of statutes or in a law book. The legal norm is the legal command, reduced to practice, as it obtains in a definite association, perhaps of very small size, even without any formulation in words. As soon as there are legal propositions within an association that have actually become effective, they give rise to legal norms. But in every society there is a much greater number of legal norms than of legal propositions; for there always is much more law that is applicable to individual cases than is applicable to all relations of a similar kind; much more law than the contemporary jurists who have attempted to formulate it in words have realized. Every modern legal historian knows how small a portion of the law that was valid at the time is contained in the Twelve Tables or in the *Lex Salica*. Modern codes are in the same case. In the past centuries, all legal norms that were determinative of the inner order of the associations were based upon custom, upon contracts, and upon articles of association of corporations. In the main, this is the situation today.

A social association is a plurality of human beings who, in their relations with one another, recognize certain rules of conduct as binding, and, generally at least, actually regulate their conduct according to them. These rules are of various kinds, and have various names: rules of law, of morals, of religion, of ethical custom, of honor, of decorum, of tact, of etiquette, of fashion. To these may be added some of lesser importance, e.g. rules of games, the rule that one must wait one's turn, for instance at the ticket window or in the waiting room of a busy physician. These rules are social facts, the resultants of the forces that are operative in society, and can no more be considered separate and apart from society, in which they are operative, than the motion of the waves can be computed without considering the element in which they move. As to form and content, they are norms, abstract commands and prohibitions, concerning the social life within the association and directed to the members of the association. In addition to rules of conduct of this kind, there are rules that are not norms because they do not refer to the social life of human beings: e.g. the rules of language, of taste, or of hygiene.

The legal norm, therefore, is merely one of the rules of conduct, of the same nature as all other rules of conduct.

. . . the prevailing concept of the nature of law . . . is, in the main, that a norm is a legal norm only if it has been posited by the state as a legal norm. This view has, I think, been refuted by our present discussion, for we have seen that only a small part of the law, i.e. state law, is, in actual fact, created by the state. As a rule, however, when writers attribute the creation of all law to the state, they mean only that a norm, whatsoever may have been its origin, becomes a legal norm only when the state recognizes it as a legal norm, and surrounds it with norms of the second rank, penal provisions, procedure, administrative regulations. If this is really a constituent element of the concept "legal norm," the formations which we have discussed hitherto, i.e. the order of the Roman household, of the mediaeval manor, of the primitive community (unless one looks upon the latter as states) are not parts of the law.

Summarizing the influence of state law upon the state of the law in the course of its historical development down to the present day, we may say the following: By creating constitutional and administrative law, the state has created its own law for its own needs. It has fused the various groups that are occupying its territory into a unified people of the state (*Staatsvolk*) and by doing so has prepared the way for a unitary development of law. Through its courts and administrative tribunals, with the aid of its secondary norms, penal law, police law, procedural law, it has brought about for the state and social institutions an increased measure of security. It has established ownership as distinguished from possession, and made possible the right of succession in the collateral relatives. It has created *rentes* and monopolies. By its prohibitions and limitations it has exerted a powerful influence upon social institutions, upon communal life, relations of domination, ownership, possession, contract, succession.

Thereafter society keeps on building on the foundation laid by the state. Communities, relations of domination and of possession, contracts, articles of association, declarations by last will and testament establish their inner order, in part at least, according to the directions of the authorities, according to the kind and measure of protection which they can expect to receive from the courts, or they make special arrangements to avoid the hindrances and traps put in their way by the latter, So in the last analysis the state of the law is a resultant of the cooperation, the interaction, and the antagonism of state and society. And in this way state law, too, can become juristic law.

As soon as state law has actually become part and parcel of everyday life, and has exerted a moulding influence upon it, jurists will no longer confine their attention to the words of the statute but will be concerned with the forms of life that have come into being under its influence. The universalizations which they arrive at in doing this, the norms which they find, will, of course, be juristic law. This happened in Rome in the case of the *Lex Falcidia* and of the *senatusconsultum Velleianum*, and has happened again and again since that time. English commerce is regulated by the Statute of Frauds to such an extent that the English were unwilling to change it although it is quite antiquated, but took it over in part almost verbatim into the Sales of Goods Act of the year 1893. Inasmuch as the German testament is derived from the Roman testament, the *Lex Falcidia* was received into German law together with the latter, and has become a part of the living German law no less than the testament. It is well known and generally understood that the canon law prohibition against usury is in exactly the same case. It has all the hall-marks of state-made law. The church, which promulgated it, was an association partaking of the nature of a state, and was, in this case, as the state is in other cases, an agency of society for the purpose of creating law. Through its own courts and through its influence upon the courts of the state, the church was enabled to give effect to its law as readily as a state.

Accordingly we shall have to call the part played by the state in the creation of law a very limited one. Nevertheless we are all under the influence of the notion of the omnipotence of the state; and this conception has undoubtedly given rise to a series of social thought sequences which, though they are conditioned historically, and therefore destined to perish at some time in the future which cannot be determined in advance, nevertheless dominate the thinking of the whole civilized human race at this time. Chief of these is the thought that the power to legislate is the highest power in modern society, and that resistance to it is to be condemned under all circumstances; that there cannot be any law within the territory of the state that is in conflict with statute law; and that a judge who in the administration of law disregards a statute is guilty of gross violation of duty. Since it is the function of the sociological science of law, like that of every other science, to record facts, not to evaluate them, it cannot possibly, as some have believed, tend to establish, at the present stage of human development, a doctrine which might lead the judge to violate his judicial oath. And even though it cannot but state that the judge in the performance of the duties of his office is frequently quite unconsciously, albeit sometimes consciously, guided by non-legal considerations, in making this statement it is merely recording facts, not evaluating them.

But the basic social institutions, the various legal associations, especially marriage, the family, the clan, the commune, the guild, the relations of domination and of possession, inheritance, and legal transactions, have come into being either altogether or to a great extent independently of the state. The center of gravity of legal development therefore from time immemorial has not lain in the activity of the state but in society itself, and must be sought there at the present time. This may be said not only of the legal institutions but also of the norms for decision. From time immemorial the great mass of norms for decision has been abstracted from the social institutions by [juristic] science and by the administration of justice, or has been freely invented by them; and legislation by the state, too, can generally find them only by following the social institutions and by imitating scientific or judicial methods.

In order to understand the actual state of the law we must institute an investigation as to the contribution that is being made by society itself as well as by state law, and also as to the actual influence of the state upon social law. We must know what kinds of marriages and families exist in a country, what kinds of contracts are being entered into, what their content is as a general rule, what kinds of declarations by last will and testament are being drawn up, how all of these things ought to be adjudged according to the law that is in force in the courts and other tribunals, how they are actually being adjudged, and to what extent these judgments and other decisions are actually effective. An investigation of this sort will reveal that although the legislation of two different countries may be identical, e.g. of France and Roumania, the law of one country may differ from that of the other; that in spite of the fact that the courts and other tribunals of Bohemia, Dalmatia, and Galicia apply the same code, the law of these countries is by no means the same; and that because of the differences in the actual state of the law, there is no uniform law even in the various parts of Germany in spite of the Civil Code, quite apart from the particular divergencies of legislation.

JOSEPH W. BINGHAM

Are There Legal Rules?

Joseph W. Bingham, a professor of law at Stanford University for many years, was one of the early champions of legal realism.

Many attempts have been made to define the field of law. Perhaps the most familiar sort of result is typified by Blackstone's dictum: "Municipal law * * * is properly defined to be a rule of civil conduct, prescribed by the supreme power in a state, commanding what is right and prohibiting what is wrong." John Austin simi-

Reprinted by permission from Joseph W. Bingham, "What is the Law?," *Michigan Law Review*, Vol. 11 (1912), pp. 2–15, 22–3. Abridged by the editor.

larly defined "the matter of jurisprudence" as "positive law; law, simply and strictly so called: or law set by political superiors to political inferiors" and "a law" as a "rule laid down for the guidance of an intelligent being by an intelligent being having power over him." In the explanation and elaboration of this definition Austin, with his superior independence of mind and analytical power and the advantage of a more enlightened environment of thought, attacked Blackstone's exposition at various points; but criticised and critic and all who have followed similar lines display a common fault. They start with the idea of defining the *word "law"* as the proper avenue to the determination of the field of jurisprudence and they assume that its ordinary general meaning, "a rule," is an essential pervasive element of its technical meaning. There is nothing which will tend to pervert critical investigation of a field of study or exposition of the results from its proper purpose more radically than the very common habit of entangling it at the outset in a mesh of carefully interwoven and finely distinguished technical terms. In any such work, the more we can keep language to its proper subordinate function of assisting thought and communication with efficiency and dispatch, the greater are our chances for success. It is always best to realize external facts and distinctions and to make others see them with as little stress upon technical verbal definition as possible. Then the independent and subordinate matter of verbal labels may be discussed with less mental strain. We are not interested primarily in knowing the various discriminated uses of the word "law," but the various elements in the field of law and their interrelations.[1]

All the ambitious attempts to define this field which the student ordinarily will run across, agree that it consists of a system of rules and principles enforced by political authority. I believe that this idea is fundamentally erroneous and that it is a bar to a scientific understanding of our law and its particular problems. Therefore my first task will be to attempt to make clear its error. In order to establish my points efficiently, it is necessary that I recall to my readers some facts concerning knowledge and

[1] The law is essentially a practical matter. No theory or effort concerning it can command much attention and respect unless it is directed by an intelligent recognition of this fact.

particularly concerning the nature and use of generalizations. The digression will be made as brief as is consistent with its purpose and will justify itself, I hope, by preventing doubt and misunderstanding later in the article.

In the development of any science, phenomena of certain sorts are studied to ascertain their causes and effects. A purpose common to all intelligent students of a science not purely historical, is the acquisition of an ability to predict that described effects will or will not follow from definite concrete conditions and forces. This is the practical end of their scientific inquiries.

I imagine that some of my readers may dispute the soundness of this last statement. "Science," they may say, "is organized, generalized knowledge. It does not consist of knowing the results which may be expected from a given concrete condition and operating forces. Often this sort of knowledge is merely empiric. The essence of scientific work is the extraction of the principles which govern sequences within the scope of a particular field and the utilization and systematization of such principles as already have been ascertained. Therefore any science consists of an organized mass of definitions, principles, rules, and formulae."

As a natural step to indicating my objections to the views outlined in the preceding paragraph I desire to combat especially the vague current idea that the purpose of scientific investigation is the extraction from their hiding places and the domestication of certain wild beasts of the jungle of ignorance known as principles and rules. We unconsciously are led by common speech to think of principles and rules as integral things existing outside of the human mind, which may be perceived by a gifted or trained intelligence and communicated to others. We speak of "grasping" a principle or a rule and of "transmitting" it to others. We speak of a principle as having been "discovered" at a certain time in history and used by men of succeeding generations. Regarded in any other than a metaphorical light, the conceptions of principles and rules indicated by such language are erroneous.

That which we label an idea is a concept or a group or combination of concepts. A rule or a principle is a connected series of concepts or associations or combinations of concepts. A concept is a psychological phenomenon. It does not exist outside of the mind entertaining it. Without discussing the possible physiological causes and processes of its occurrence, we may postulate as an axiom upon the basis of common knowledge that the idea of X cannot be literally the idea of Y. Figuratively speaking, X can transmit his idea to Y. What occurs, however, is not the passage of the idea to Y, but the formation of a similar one in Y's mind because of the expression which X uses as his means of communication. Principles and rules cannot exist outside of the mind. The external expression of them does; and, in the case of writing, it may endure from generation to generation; but the external expression consists only of signs and symbols, and the meaning thereof exists only in the mind of the speaker or writer as he makes it and in the mind of the interpreter when he interprets. A generation derives ideas from preceding ones, but they are the several ideas of the members of the later generation who entertain them, similar to those entertained at various times by the members of preceding generations. The principle that one man should not forcibly attack another is old in the common law. By that I mean that from generation to generation judges have entertained such a principle in deciding cases to which it is applicable; but the principle entertained to that effect by a certain judge in the 15th century is not the same principle as that similar one entertained by another judge in the same century or by any particular judge today. When we say that the principle is old, we are speaking figuratively. To conceive of these many similar strings of mental concepts as one enduring thing existing outside of the minds which have used them is a convenient and time-saving metaphor and is so much a part of our everyday mental equipment that we lose sight of the fact of its lack of literal truth. When we come to analyze the law, however, it is necessary to see naked realities if we are to escape being led into false theories.[2]

If we would think clearly, we must distinguish carefully three sorts of things. First, there are objective facts external to our

[2] I have dealt with this in some detail, because it is essential to comprehension of my argument that my readers see the nature of rules and principles. Now that I have made these points, however, I shall return to the use of that common time-saving metaphor which treats similar mental ideas, rules, and principles of the same or different persons as identical and continuously enduring.

thought, with which our thinking may be concerned; for instance we may think about a bit of scenery, or a picture, or the expression of the thought of another person, or a series of events constituting, perhaps, an experiment. Secondly, there are our mental processes concerning these facts. Thirdly, there is the expression of our consciousness.

Now I am ready to state my objections to the theory that any science consists of a system of definitions, rules, principles, and formulae. Every science has a practical bearing, either direct or indirect, immediate or more remote. It deals with sequences of concrete phenomena. The object of scientific inquiry is to obtain thorough knowledge of sequential causes and effects of sorts within a circumscribed field of study and to communicate this knowledge to others. The knowledge is obtained by observation, experiment, comparison, induction, deduction and other elements of learning and reasoning. Abstract concepts are used and principles and rules are formulated. They are mental processes and are not external things discovered and abstracted by the mind. Definitions are made of words, phrases, and other labels. Formulae are devised. Orderliness and systematization are aimed at throughout. All of these mental processes, however, are inspired by the purpose of acquiring, retaining, and communicating knowledge concerning concrete objective phenomena. For instance the purpose of the study of chemistry is the acquisition of ability to determine the potential causes and results of any of the possible concrete chemical combinations and disintegrations within its scope. Principles, rules, definitions and formulae are only tools for the acquisition, retention, and communication of such knowledge. I do not deny that these tools are necessities of a perfected science nor that they tend to assume a stereotyped form; but I insist that science is substantially thorough and efficient knowledge and that these mental tools are necessary only because such knowledge cannot be acquired, retained, used, and imparted without them. We should not confuse the content of knowledge with its form or with the mode of its expression, nor blur the proper relation between these things to such an extent as to think of science as in essence merely formally organized knowledge rather than broad and deep knowledge which is systematized and for-

---

mulated as a means to effectuating economically the practical scientific ends.

In view of the very common mental haziness covering the points which I have been discussing, it is not logically a cause of wonderment that a theory of law should have been evolved which makes the essential subject matter of legal study a mass or system of principles and rules conceived as existing independently of the comprehension of any individual observer. If there were, as some of these theorists apparently would have us imagine, a system of co-ordinated rules and principles, developed by the experience of the race or evolved by inspired human reasoning from an enmeshment in the nature of things, which might be devoured and digested in all its ready made symmetry, and which infallibly and clearly would indicate through deductive processes all the concrete legal consequences that are being produced day after day by regular governmental action, and if none of these generalizations or sets of generalizations would fail correctly to indicate legal consequences within its scope until another had been substituted in its place by authoritative promulgation, there would be less cause to condemn this doctrine. Prudence and practical wisdom might satisfy themselves with mastering the import of the system. I venture to say, however, that no one who is not entangled in the mazes of a theory would assert that we have such a system. If the law consists only of rules and principles, it does not exist outside of the minds which for the moment are using those rules and principles. For instance, a common law principle demanding consideration as a prerequisite to the validity of a simple contract does not exist literally at the present moment unless it is part of the active comprehension of some person, although we may say figuratively that it exists because of the potentiality of its use when a problem shall arise to which it is applicable. The field of any science consists of sequences of concrete phenomena which are studied to determine their causes and effects, and, if the science is not purely historical, to predict concerning similar future sequences. The generalizations and definitions used are only mental implements manufactured by the mind and senses to aid in acquiring, retaining, and communicating knowledge of the objective phenomena within the scope of the science. I assume that no one will contradict that the field of law is part of the field of the science of government. What are the proper objects of comprehension within this field? Only or primarily rules, principles and definitions? No. The lawyer, as does the scientist, studies sequences of external phenomena and he studies them with a similar purpose—to determine their causes and effects and to acquire an ability to forecast sequences of the same sort.

I have stated that the field of law is part of the field of the science of government.[3] I delimit it further by saying that it includes only the organization of the institutions and agencies of authoritative government, their concrete operations and effects, and the causal facts which bring about those operations. These things constitute external sequences of phenomena which correspond to the working field of the scientist. Knowledge of such concrete governmental phenomena obtained by observation, report, inductive and deductive reasoning, and the other implements of scientific investigation, may be generalized into rules and principles. A technical vocabulary and stereotyped methods of phrasing may be developed with accompanying definitions. When thorough knowledge so obtained has been fully organized we shall have that which may with propriety be called a science of law.

Though the entire range of the operations of authoritative government come within the scope of the lawyer's profession, he is usually concerned particularly with one sort of these operations—those of the law-determining bodies and their complementary and supplementary agencies. Of these, the courts are the most prominent in the view of the student of law, for in the great majority of cases where stubborn disputes over questions of law are fought out, those questions are ultimately determined by the courts. It will facilitate our discussion and not prejudice its soundness, I think, to confine it to law which has been or may be so determined.

To obviate as much as possible certain confusing facts which

[3] The existence of the law as we know it is dependent on the existence of authoritative government. In a state of anarchy there is nothing closely analogous to the field of our profession because there is no continuity of authority and therefore no certainty concerning the governmental sequences of events.

might prevent a clear perception of the argument which I am making, let us pause here a moment to determine the attitude from which we are to view the field of law. The judge, presiding over and deciding litigation, is engaged in the art of government. He is making law. The lawyer, who argues a case before judge, jury, or other law determining agency, is assisting in the law-making process. The legislator also indirectly influences similar future processes by the part which he plays in determining the existence and form of legislative expression, which authoritatively indicates what shall or shall not be done in concrete instances. These processes lie in the field of legal study. They are some of its objective phenomena. Therefore to view the field from the attitude of the judge at his official work, or of the lawyer in court, or of the legislator performing his function is, metaphorically, to attempt to see the field from a small spot inside it instead of from above and outside of it. If we are to view the law as a field of study analogous to that of any science, we must look at it from the posi-tion of the law teacher, the law student, the legal investigator, or the lawyer who is engaged in searching the authorities to determine "what the law is." These men are not directly acting as part of the machinery of government. Their study is not part of the ex-ternal phenomena which compose the field of law. They are studying that field from without and therefore from the position which will give a wholly objective and the least confusing view. Let us continue our discussion from this external attitude.

To clarify the expression "external governmental (or legal) phenomena" which I shall use occasionally, imagine any case which passes through our courts of law to final judgment. The actual concrete facts on which the action is or might be based and defended are external and generally non-legal phenomena. When the suit is initiated, however, the string of legal conse-quences commences and continues until it finally is disposed of, by full execution of judgment or otherwise, and completion of the records. Such strings or combinations of interwoven strings of causal external facts and legal external consequences[4] consti-

---

[4] Including the facts of pertinent legislation, of course, and all other sorts of facts that produce strings of consequences which finally enter into the determination of litigation.

tute the laboratory material of the lawyer and jurist. In using such material, their purposes are, first, to learn by mental processes similar to those employed in scientific investigation, essential causal elements in the strings of occurrences producing certain of the legal consequences in those strings and, secondly, to base upon knowledge so obtained and other pertinent knowledge a forecast of the potential legal consequences of similar or analogous causal facts. Concrete occurrences to the lawyer are pregnant with potential sequences which threaten governmental action. His essential business is to predict these future sequences accurately and to induce the desired and guard against the undesired. The generalizations expressed in text-books, on the statute books, or in judicial opinions have no value to him—have no practical value to any man—except insofar as they affect such problems or aid in their solution. They are but means to an end.

What of it? The field of law is far wider and more complex than an imaginary system of promulgated or developed stereotyped rules and principles. It is a field for scientific study analogous to the field of any other science. Concrete sequences of facts and their legal consequences are the external phenomena for investigation and prediction. Knowledge of the causative interrelations of such sequences and of the causes, organization, and operation of the governmental machinery entering into them constitutes knowledge of law in one of the legal senses of the word. Rules and principles have been developed for use in this field and technical terms with definitions more or less stereotyped have been adopted. They are only mental tools which are used to classify, carry, and communicate economically the accumulated knowledge of the law similarly to the use of generalizations and definitions in other sciences.

Although I have said that it is not my purpose to define the word "law," it may contribute to my argument to point out some of its different legal senses. Therefore I shall pause occasionally in the course of my discussion to do so. At this place I call attention to the use of the word to indicate the field of the lawyer's study or, often, a part of that field. When it is used in this sense, the speaker or writer consciously or unconsciously indicates by it causal relations of occurrences external to the mind of the observer and their governmental consequences, past or potential.[5] The fact that the use is unconscious in the sense that the speaker or writer does not realize the nature of the thing he designates, and the fact that if he were asked to define his use he might repeat a variation of the Blackstonian definition of law, do not affect the usage. A man may be mistaken both in his assumption of knowledge of the nature of things concerning which he converses and in the analysis of his thinking. In such cases his definitions are not likely to indicate the actual application of his terms.

Our field of law does not consist of rules and principles only. Similar fields existed before adequate rules and principles were developed to aid in comprehending them, just as the field of geology existed before the science of geology was developed. It would not be true, however, to say that the field of law exists independently of rules and principles as does that of geology. The objective phenomena of law include principally human actions and the legal sequences are brought about through voluntary action. The intelligent direction of human action necessarily involves the use of generalizations. Generalizations therefore have a causative force in producing legal effects, and that force must be estimated as carefully as any other operating within the field; but they are not the whole field. In order that we may appreciate the function of generalizations in producing legal sequences, let us spend a little time discussing judical reasoning, judicial opinions, and especially the authoritative effect of judicial generalizations.

In the course of my studies in particular parts of the field of law, I have become convinced that there exists widespread a vague theory that the "unwritten" or "common" law finds its only authoritative expression in abstract pronouncements in judicial opinions and that the concrete determinations of cases do not constitute law, but normally are made "according to law" and "illustrate" law. That is to say, they are deduced from its application. In its older phase this theory denies that judges legislate

---

[5] This use occurs when one speaks of studying "law," or "the law of property" or labels a described sequence of facts and their predicated legal consequences "law" or "the law."

in expressing legal rules and principles, and asserts that they only discover, announce, and apply them. In a newer phase, it admits that judges make the law, but still insists upon generality as an essential characteristic of law. It has even been contended that nothing which can be called law legitimately exists concerning a class of legal questions until a generalization which covers them has been announced judicially or by legislation. I consider these ideas to be erroneous fundamentally, and prejudicial not only to understanding of our system of law, but also to progress towards the perfection of our administration of justice. An elemental error in the theory lies in the idea that the statement of a rule or a principle of law by the judges of a court as a material part of their reasoning in explanation of the decision of a case is normally a fundamental and essentially authoritative thing.

How do judges reason towards a determination of the cases before them? Insofar as valid legislative expression is deemed applicable, it is controlling. The validity, effective purport, and applicability of such expression is determined by the court. Concerning the causative potency of legislation in producing legal consequences, I shall make a few remarks later in this article. For the present we may facilitate understanding by excluding consideration of legislation entirely.* Precedents are also given a weight in judicial reasoning which we shall discuss when we have finished the present theme. Within the bounds of the established jurisdiction and procedure of their courts, and excepting insofar as they are guided by legislative expression, precedents, and a tradition that any but the most gradual and conservative innovation is not a proper product of judicial functions, judges are free to give weight in their deliberations to all considerations of justice or

* [Legislation is a collateral causal phenomenon which affects the sequences of facts and their legal consequences within its interpreted scope. It affects them because courts adjudge that legislation and its expression is binding on them in deciding cases, and interpret and "apply" it accordingly. The fact of ultimate and direct practical importance is not the literal meaning of the words and phrases, but the causal effects on governmental sequences of external phenomena which it may have. Legislative expression affects such sequences in the same general manner as other external facts which may enter into the deliberations of a court; but it differs from other such facts in the compelling authoritative force which it normally possesses. (Taken from original article in *Michigan Law Review*, p. 25.)]

policy logically applicable to their legal problems. Ordinarily they
exercise this freedom to the varying degrees which might be expected from men who vary widely in intellectual ability, independence, and initiative. Cases are not decided by reference to
some mysteriously and anciently evolved system of rules and principles of inherent authority and potency, nor do the mental
processes of the judges commonly consist of using stereotyped
generalities. The processes of decision are processes of intelligent
reasoning, such as are operative in other fields of mental activity.
Generalizations are used, but they are only the mental implements
of those who use them. Impressions, beliefs, and conclusions concerning the facts of the case, concrete precedents, applicable customs, habits, common ideas, moral blameworthiness, and other
logically pertinent considerations are consolidated and welded in
generalizations. Some of these generalizations are constructed by
a judge on the basis of data obtained by his investigation of preceding cases. Some are based on knowledge obtained from the
evidence or from his general experience. Some, metaphorically,
are adopted from the works of text writers or from the opinions
in previous cases. These last, however, are used, as are the others,
only because the judge accepts them as correct indications of facts
and as considerations pertinent to the decision of his problem.
The mental forms which considerations took in the judicial mind
in previous cases and the language in which they were expressed
are not abstractly of fundamental importance, but knowledge concerning all external facts which logically are relevant to a present
legal problem, including knowledge of the relative weight given
to each sort of fact in former adjudications, is important. This
last knowledge is of peculiar pertinency because in our system of
law precedents are potent arguments and the precedential facts
considered include not only the concrete question and adjudication in a former case, but also, with lesser stress, the reasoning
through which the adjudication was reached. I wish to discuss
briefly the effect which precedents have in determining judicial
decisions and its reasons a few pages further on.* At present I
insist only that the statements of rules and principles by judges
in their opinions of previous cases are not commonly given an

* [Omitted.]

authoritative force analogous to that of valid legislative expression and that neither their language nor the particular mental forms which it communicates are binding logically on subsequent judicial reasoning.

Are there then no such things as rules and principles of law? I have had this question put to me in protest against my analysis. Certainly there are rules and principles of law, as there are rules and principles of biology or of architecture or of any other science or art. They occur whenever legal problems are under process of solution. We find statements of them in text-books and in judicial opinions and elsewhere. They are mental things. A rule of law is a generalized abstract comprehension of how courts would decide concrete questions within its scope. A principle of law is an abstract comprehension of considerations which would weigh with courts in the decision of questions to which it is applicable. Any one with sufficient knowledge and mental ability can construct a principle or a rule of law. Courts and legislatures have not a monopoly in producing them. There is nothing authoritative in the existence of a rule or a principle. Courts produce concrete legal consequences. Legislation guides courts through their construction of it to the decision of cases within its range. Anyone of sufficient intelligence may investigate the authorities, predict concerning potential legal consequences within selected limits, and make his own generalizations to carry his knowledge. If these generalizations accurately indicate potential legal effects within their scope, or comprehend accurately considerations which would be given weight by courts in the decision of cases, they are valid rules or principles of law.

The mental forms in which the same sort of potent facts have been grasped and considered in previous judicial opinions need not be copied. Abstractly they are not of essential importance to the investigator. Nor is the maner of statement of rules and principles in judicial opinions logically of any binding force. Such generalizations, however they are evolved, may be stated in any language the speaker chooses without impairing their validity. The usual purpose of statement is facilitation of thinking, memory, and exposition. Accomplishment of this purpose justifies any particular statement. These matters of mental processes and of

language are matters for free intelligent choice. The building and
statement of legal rules and principles is not a prerogative of the
judge or of the legislator, and such statements as are made in
judicial opinions are as subject to criticism for inaccuracy and
other defects as are those of other lawyers. Substantially the same
considerations or other facts may be stated in various ways. Although the statement of a rule of law may differ from any ever
made in court, its validity is not thereby affected. Its validity is
to be tested by ascertaining whether it accurately indicates potential concrete decisions within its scope. Likewise the validity
of a statement of a principle of law is to be tested only by ascertaining whether the substance of the considerations which it includes would weigh with the courts, not necesarily in the form
which the statement communicates, but in any form.[6]

[6] The common view that the law is something general doubtlessly is colored
by the facts that "laws" of any sort are general rules, that order, which the law
connotes, is ordinarily associated with system and therefore abstract and general
ideas, that legislative expression, to which modern minds independently of legal
training instinctively turn as a familiar and normal type of "a law," is usually
general in terms, and that it is natural to jump to the conclusion that "the law"
is simply a name for the totality of a mass of "laws." If we had had two
different terms to denote "the law" and "a law" or rule of law, such as "jus"
and "lex" of Roman jurisprudence, the misleading influence of language
might have been obviated; but there are other co-operating causes of the common confusion which probably suffice to produce it. These causes are familiar to
intelligent students of the history of law, government, and philosophy.
[Author's note in original article, p. 115.]

K. N. LLEWELLYN

Law and the "Behavior Analysis"

Karl N. Llewellyn (1893–1962) was a prolific writer on legal topics, and had great influence as a law professor at Columbia University and the University of Chicago.

The Problem of Defining Law; Focus versus Confines

The difficulty in framing any concept of "law" is that there are so many things to be included, and the things to be included are so unbelievably different from each other. Perhaps it is possible to get them all under one verbal roof. But I do not see what you have accomplished if you do. For a concept, as I understand it, is built for a purpose. It is a thinking tool. It is to make your data more manageable in doing something, in getting somewhere with them. And I have not yet met the job, or heard of it, to which all the data that associate themselves with this loosest of suggestive symbols, "law," are relevant at once. We do and have too many disparate things and thinkings to which we like to attach that name. For instance, legislators pass "a law," by which we mean that they officially put a new form of words on the statute books. That calls up associations with regard to attorneys and judges, and to suits being brought "under the statute." But it also calls up associations with regard to those sets of practices and expectations and people which we call political parties and machines and lobbies. The former we should want, in some way, to include under the head "law," I suspect. If we did not, we ought to stop defining and

Reprinted by permission from Karl N. Llewellyn, "A Realistic Jurisprudence—the Next Step," *Columbia Law Review*, Vol. 30 (1930), pp. 431–8, 441–50, 455–7, 459–60, 462–4. Abridged by the editor.

think a little further. The latter—the parties and lobbies—we might have more doubt about, even if we did stop and think. Again, it seems fairly clear that there has been something we could not well dissociate from our symbol "law" in places and times when there was no legislature and even no state—indeed when there was no organization we can call "political" that was distinct from any other organization. You cannot study the simpler forms of society nor "the law" of such forms without looking into the mechanisms of organized control at such times and places; but today you will be likely to distinguish such types of control as *non-legal.* Of course, you would not disregard them, if you wanted to know anything about "law" that was worth knowing. But you would regard them as background, or foreground, or underground, to your center of interest. They would be something that you would compare and contrast with "law," I suspect, in the present order of society. And yet I also suspect you would have your hands full if you set about to draw the line between "the two." Or again, there are gentlemen who spend a good deal of time discussing "the ends of law," or "what law ought to be." Are they talking about "law"? Certainly their postulates and conclusions, in gross and in detail, have no need to look like anything any judge ever did; and at times some of those gentlemen seem to avail themselves of that freedom; but it would be a case-hardened person who denied that what they are dealing with is closely connected with this same loose suggestive symbol. What interests me is that when a judge is working in a "well-settled field" he is likely to pay no attention to what such gentlemen say, and to call it irrelevant speculation; whereas when he is working in an "unsettled field" he seems to pay a lot of attention to their ideas, or to ideas of much the same order. This I take to mean that *for some purposes* they are talking something very close to "law," under any defini-tion; and for *other* purposes, they are talking something whose connection with "law" as just used is fairly remote. And this prob-lem of the word calling up wide-scattered and disparate references, *according to the circumstance,* seems to me vital.

I shall not attempt a definition. I shall not describe a periphery, a stopping place, a barrier. I shall instead devote my attention to the *focus* of matters legal. I shall try to discuss a *point of refer-*

ence; a point of reference to which I believe all matters legal can most usefully be referred, if they are to be seen with intelligence and with appreciation of their bearings. I am, therefore, going to talk about substituting a somewhat unfamiliar, but more exciting and more useful focus for the focus that most thinking about law in the past has had.

Two references to the course that thought has taken will help to set the perspective: one, to the tenets of the nineteenth-century schools of jurisprudence; one, to the development of the concepts of rights and of interests.

For the nineteenth-century schools I am content to accept one of Pound's summaries.[1] It fits with what reading in the field I have done; it is based upon vastly more reading in the field than I shall ever do. With regard to the analytical jurists, Pound stresses their interest in a body of established precepts whereby a definite legal result is supposed to be fitted to a definite set of facts; he stresses the centering of their definition upon the "aggregate of authoritative legal precepts applied by tribunals as such in a given time and place," and their presupposition of a state which makes those precepts and tribunals authoritative. The historical jurists, on the other hand, he finds making little distinction between law and other forms of social control; with them customary precepts, irrespective of whether they originate in the organs of politically organized societies, come in for heavy attention; central in their picture of law are the traditional techniques of decision and the traditional or customary notions of rightness. (All this, it may be added, without any too close analysis as to what is meant by "custom.") For the philosophical jurists, finally, Pound finds that "philosophical, political and ethical ideas as to the end of law and as to what legal precepts should be in view thereof" occupy the center of the stage.

Precepts as the Heart and Core of Most Thinking About Law

You will have noted running through his summary of their views the word "precepts." This is traditional. When men talk or think

[1] LAW AND MORALS, 25 *et seq.* (1924).

about law, they talk and think about *rules*. . . . But the use made in Pound's writings of the idea, brings out vigorously the limitations of rules, or precepts, of *words*, when made the focus, the *center of reference*, in thinking about law.

Indeed, those limitations appear throughout the current analysis of law in terms of interests, rights, and remedies. The growth of that analysis requires a short digression, but one that I believe worth making. It has to do with the *subject matter* of the rules and precepts of which men regarded the legal system as made up. Both with us and in the Roman system that subject matter has in the course of time undergone striking changes.

In the earlier stages the rules were thought of almost exclusively as rules of remedies. Remedies were few and specific. There were a few certain ways to lug a man into court and a few certain things that you or the court could do with him when you got him there. We are concerned here not with why that was (why "can" a court of law give no injunctive relief today?) but only with *that* it was. The question for the man of that day took this shape: on what facts could one man make use of any specific one of the specific ways of making the court bother another man? And the rules of law were rules about that. They clustered around each remedy. In those terms people thought. They thought about what they could see and do. Their crude minds dealt only with what they could observe. What they observed, they described.

To later writers this seemed primitive. The later thinkers find a different kind of order in the field of law. Remedies seem to them to have a *purpose*, to be protections of something else. They could imagine these somethings and give them a name: *rights*, substantive rights. Thus the important, the substantial rules of law become rules defining rights. Remedies are relegated to the periphery of attention. They are "adjective law" merely—devices more or less imperfect for giving effect to the important things, the substantive rights which make up the substance of the law. The relation of rights to rules is fairly clear: the two are aspects of the same thing. When a rule runs in favor of a person, he has a right, as measured by the rule. Or, if he has a right, that can be phrased by setting out a rule ascribing to him and persons in like situation with him the benefits connoted by the rights. Rights are thus precise counterparts of rules, when the rights are ascribed generally to all persons in a class in given circumstances; and this is the typical postmortemizer's line of discourse. Or rights, when ascribed to particular individuals in specific circumstances, are deductions which presuppose the rule; the major premise is the general rule on rights; the minor is the proposition hooking up this individual and these circumstances with that general rule. Rights and rules are therefore for present purposes pretty much interchangeable; the right is a shorthand symbol for the rule.

Far be it from me to dispute that the concepts of substantive rights and of rules of substantive law have had great value. They moved definitely and sharply toward fixing the attention of thinkers on the idea that procedure, remedies, existed not merely because they existed, nor because they had value in themselves, but because they had a purpose. From which follows immediate inquiry into what the purpose is, and criticism, if the means to its accomplishment be poor. They moved, moreover, to some extent, toward sizing up the law by significant life-situations, instead of under the categories of historically conditioned, often archaic remedy-law: a new base for a new synthesis; a base for law reform.

The term *interests*, on the other hand, comes in to focus attention on the presence of social factors, and to urge that substantive rights themselves, like remedies, exist only for a purpose. Their purpose is now perceived to be the protection of the interests. To be sure, we do not know what interests are. Hence, behind substantive rights (which we need not check against anything courts *do*) we now have interests (which we need not check against anything at all, and about whose presence, extent, nature, and importance, whether the interests be taken absolutely or taken relatively one to another, no two of us seem to be able to agree). The scientific advance should again be obvious. Complete subjectivity has been achieved.

The use of precepts, or rules, or of rights which are logical counterparts of rules—of *words*, in a word—as the *center* of reference in thinking about law, is a block to clear thinking about matters legal. I want again to make sure that I am not misunderstood. (1) I am not arguing that "rules of substantive law" are without importance. (2) I am not arguing that it is not humanly *possible* to use the interests-rights and rules-remedies analysis and still think clearly and usefully about law. (3) Least of all am I attempting to urge the exclusion of substantive rights and rules from the field of "law." Instead of these things, I am arguing (1) that rules of substantive law are of far less importance than most legal theorizers have assumed in most of their thinking and writing, and that they are *not* the most useful center of reference for discussion of law; (2) that the presence of the term "rights and rules" in the interest set-up (a) has a persistent tendency to misfocus attention onto that term; (b) that the avoidance of that tendency is a great gain in clarity; and (c) that to both attempt such avoidance and retain the term is to cumber all discussion with embarrassing and quite unnecessary baggage; (3) that substantive rights and rules should be removed from their present position at the *focal point* of legal discussion, in favor of the *area of contact* between judicial (or official) *behavior* and the *behavior* of laymen; that the substantive rights and rules should be studied not as self-existent, nor as a major point of reference, but themselves with constant reference to that area of behavior-contacts.

Do I suggest that (to cut in at one crucial point) the "accepted rules," the rules the judges say that they apply, are without influence upon their actual behavior? I do not. I do not even say that, *sometimes*, these "accepted rules" may not be a very accurate description of the judges' actual behavior. What I say is that such accuracy of description is rare. The question is how, and how much, and in what direction, do the accepted rule and the practice of decision diverge? More: how, and how much, *in each case?* You cannot generalize on this, *without investigation.* Your guesses may be worth something, in the large. *They are worth nothing at all, in the particular.* The one thing we know now for certain is, that different rules have totally different relations to the behavior of judges, of other officials, and of the particular persons "governed" (optimistic word!) by those different rules. The approach here argued for admits, then, out of hand, *some* relation between *any* accepted rule and judicial behavior; and then proceeds to deny that that admission involves anything but a problem for investigation in the case in hand; and to argue that the significance of the particular rule will appear only *after* the investigation of the vital, focal, phenomenon: the behavior. And if an empirical *science* of law is to have any realistic basis, any responsibility to the facts, I see no escape from moving to this position. Thus, and only thus, is the real gain sought by the interests-rights and rules-remedies analysis to be made tangible.

Meaning of Rules and Rights Under the Behavior Analysis

What now, is the place of rules and rights, under such an approach? To attempt their excision from the field of law would be to fly in the face of fact. I should like to begin by distinguishing real "rules" and rights from paper rules and rights. The former are conceived in terms of behavior; they are but other names, convenient shorthand symbols, for the remedies, the actions of the courts. They are descriptive, not prescriptive, except insofar as there may commonly be implied that courts *ought* to continue in their practices. "Real rules," then, if I had my way with words, would *by legal scientists* be called the practices of the courts, and not "rules" at all. And for such scientists statements of "rights" would be statements of likelihood that in a given situation a certain type of court action loomed in the offing. Factual terms. No more. This use of "rights," at least, has already considerable standing among the followers of Hohfeld. This concept of "real rule" has been gaining favor since it was first put into clarity by Holmes. "Paper rules" are what have been treated, traditionally, as rules of law: the accepted *doctrine* of the time and place—what the books there say "the law" is. The "real rules" and rights— "what the courts will do in a given case, and nothing more pretentious"—are then predictions. They are, I repeat, on the level of isness and not of oughtness; they seek earnestly to go no whit, in their suggestions, beyond the remedy actually available. Like all shorthand symbols, they are dangerous in connotation, when applied to situations which are not all quite alike. But their intent and effort is to describe. And one can adapt for them Max Weber's magnificent formulation in terms of probability: a right (or practice, or "real rule") exists *to the extent that* a likelihood exists that A can induce a court to squeeze, out of B, A's damages;

more: *to the extent that* the likely collections will cover A's damage. In this aspect *substantive* rights and "rules," as distinct from adjective, simply disappear—on the descriptive level. The measure of a "rule," the measure of a right, becomes what can be done about the situation. *Accurate* statement of a "real rule" or of a right includes all procedural limitations on what can be done about the situation. What is left, in the realm of *description*, are at the one end the facts, the groupings of conduct (and demonstrable expectation [and/or needs]) which may be claimed to constitute an interest; and on the other the practices of courts in their effects upon the conduct and expectations of the laymen in question. Facts, in the world of isness, to be compared directly with other facts, also in the world of isness.

The Place and Treatment of Paper Rules

Are "rules of law" in the accepted sense eliminated in such a course of thought? Somewhat obviously not. Whether they be pure paper rules, or are the accepted patter of the law officials, they remain present, and their presence remains an actuality— an actuality of importance—but an actuality whose *precise* importance, whose bearing and influence become clear. First of all they appear as what they are: rules of authoritative ought, addressed *to* officials, telling *officials* what the *officials* ought to do. To which telling the officials either pay no heed at all (the pure paper rule; the dead-letter statute; the obsolete case) or listen partly (the rule "construed" out of recognition; the rule to which lip-service chiefly is paid, while practice runs another course) or listen with all care (the rule with which the official practice pretty accurately coincides). I think that every such official precept-on-the-books (statute, doctrine laid down in the decision of a court, administrative regulation) tacitly contains an element of pseudo-description along with its statement of what officials ought to do; a tacit statement that officials do act according to the tenor of the rule; a tacit prediction that officials will act according to its tenor. Neither statement nor prediction is often true *in toto*.

Administrative Action as Law

I should like to glance at a few further implications of the [behavior] approach. Three of them appear together. First, to focus on the area of contact between judicial behavior and the behavior of the "governed" is to stress *interactions*. Second, central as are the judges' actions in disputed cases, there is a vast body of other officials whose actions are of no less importance; quantitatively their actions are of vastly greater importance, though it may well be that the judge's position gives him a leverage of peculiar power. In what has preceded I have somewhat lightly argued as if judge and court were the be-all and end-all of the legal focus. It is time to reformulate, to grow at once more accurate and more inclusive. The actions of these other officials touch the interested layman more often than do those of the judge; increasingly so, and apparently increasing at a rising rate of increase as the administrative machine gains in function and in force. More often than not, administrative action is, *to the layman affected*, the last expression of the law on the case. In such a situation, I think it highly useful to regard it, for him, as being the law of the case. I see no gain whatever, and much loss, from setting up a fictitious unity in the law, when some officials do one thing, some another, and the courts now and again a third. Realistically, the law is then not one, but at least three, and by no means three-in-one.

Hence I argue that the focus, the center of law, is not merely what the judge does, in the impact of that doing on the interested layman, but what *any* state official does, officially.

Laymen's Behavior as a Part of Law

Interactions between official behavior and laymen's behavior, first; and second, the recognition of official behavior of all officials as part of the core of law. Third, and an immediate part of both, the recognition of what Nicholas Spykman so strongly and properly stresses: that the word "official" tacitly presupposes, connotes, reaches out to include, all those patterns of action (ordering, initiative) and obedience (including passivity) on the part both of the official and of all laymen affected which *make up* the official's position and authority as such. Something of this sort is the idea underlying "consent of the governed," "ultimate dependence upon public opinion," and the like; but these older phrasings have no neatness of outline; they do not even suggest the need of sharp-edged drawing, which I take to be the reason why they act as a soporific, while the Spykman formulation acts as a stimulant to the curiosity and imagination. In a passing it is well to note that here, too, Max Weber's method of formulation becomes classic: the official exists as such precisely *insofar* as such patterns of action and obedience prevail.[2] I agree whole-heartedly that these patterns are an essential part of any phenomena we call law. The more whole-heartedly because Spykman's formulation brings out with fresh emphasis the difference between paper rules and resultant behavior, and the extent to which the behavior which results (if any) from the official formulation of a rule depends on the patterns of thought and action of the persons whose behavior is in question.

The Narrow Applicability of Most Rules

Most pieces of law affect only a *relatively* small number of persons ever or at all, with any directness—or are intended to. Where that is the case, the *organization, attitude, present and probable behavior of the persons sought to be affected* is what needs major consideration, from the angle of getting results (or of understanding results). Indeed, the very *identification* of those persons may be a precondition calling for much study. Which is a somewhat absurdly roundabout way of saying that unless those matters are studied, the rules drawn, and the administrative behavior adapted to the persons in question, results will be largely accident. "*To the persons in question*," and, indeed, "to those persons *under the*

[2] In the same way (borrowing Spykman again) *to the extent* that the official's behavior plays into these interlocking patterns of action it becomes "official" rather than personal behavior, and so of direct interest here. "Purely" personal behavior of an official approaches inconceivability; but substantially personal behavior may take up a great bulk of a given official's time.

conditions in question." It cannot be too strongly insisted that our attitude toward "rules" of law, treating them as universal in *application,* involves a persistent twisting of observation. "Rules" in the realm of action *mean* what rules *do;* "rules" in the realm of action *are* what they do. The *possible* application and applicability are not without importance, but the *actual* application and applicability are of controlling importance. To think of rules as universals—especially, to think of them as being applicable to "all persons who bring themselves within their terms"—is to muffle one's eyes in a constitutional fiction before beginning a survey of the scene. To be sure, constitutions purport to require rules of law to be "equal and general." But most rules, however general as to the few they cover, are highly special, when viewed from the angle of how many citizens there are. And most rules "applying" to "all who come within their terms" (all those who set up barber shops, or are tempted to commit murder, or to bribe officials, or to embezzle from banks or certify checks without the drawer having funds, or to adopt a child, or to run a manufacturing establishment employing five or more persons) do not and will not, realistically considered, ever be "applicable" in any meaningful sense of the term, to *most* people in the community. Such rules are indeed open. Persons do move in and out of the sphere of their applicability. But that sphere is much more clearly seen when viewed (as compared with the commmunity) as narrow, as special, as peculiar. Obviously even more special is the sphere of *real* application: of official *behavior* with reference to application.

What Law Is Thought to Be: Folk-Law

In all the emphasis placed upon behavior I may have created the impression that a "realistic" approach would make itself unrealistic by disregarding what people *think* law is. Not so. But a realistic approach would cut at once into analysis and subdivision of the terms "people," "think," and "law" in such a phrase. For the great mass of persons not particularly concerned, I suspect that "law" in this aspect, *so far as* it concerns themselves, means "what I ought to do" and is not much distinguished from those

selective slight idealizations of current practice we think of as
morals. At times the issue certainly gets closer: "I want this contract to stick"—and doubtless I will then think of putting it in
writing, and will meditate on reciting a formula I saw somewhere
(in a deed, was it?) : "for one dollar and other good and valuable
considerations"; I may get a witness to the signing, too. In the field
of private law we know singularly little of this folk-law-in-action.
In that of the older criminal law we can suspect a very rough
coincidence of folk-law-in-action with folk-morality-in-action, except that here and there the thought of cop and jail will work
deterrently when plain external and internal non-official social
sanctions might not wholly click; we can suspect further that over
considerable fields criminal law is too new and too specialized to
have much background or counterpart in folk-morality; and, finally,
that some fairly wide bodies of non-moral (or not yet moral)
criminal law aspects will have percolated into folk-law: I think
of traffic law (as known to the traffickers) as distinctly in advance
in most places of traffic morality, and of similar discrepancies
in regard to liquor, gambling, and sex matters, as to some portions
of a population with variant morals. Now clearly what people
think law to be, as regards themselves, has some effect at times
upon their action. My guess is, however, that the effect on the
side of forbidding is much slighter than the lawyer is likely to
imagine, whenever any important pressure of self-interest is present, except for a relatively small minority, or over relatively small
areas of action for any particular person. On the other hand, my
guess is that in the field in which law provides "helpful devices"
—the attempt to use which presupposes concurrent self-interest—
folk-law has very considerable influence in shaping conduct.

Ideals as to What Law Ought to Be

No less important than what people think law is, is what people
conceive that law should be. Any change in law is in good part a
reflection of someone's desire to produce a difference. And just as
attitudes and expectations must be taken into account along with
overt behaavior, so must purposes and the ideal pictures toward

which purposes drive. Thus far, even from the angle of a purely descriptive science.

Into another aspect of ideals as to what law ought to be this present paper does not attempt to go. I make no effort *here* to indicate either the proper rule or the proper action of any legal subject. I do, however, argue, and with some vigor, that as soon as one turns from the *formulation* of ideals to their *realization*, the approach here indicated is vital to his making headway. It is only in terms of a sound descriptive science of law (or of what is roughly equivalent, a soundly built working art, which takes equal account of conditions) that ideals move beyond the stage of dreams. Moreover, as has so often been pointed out, both the feasibility of accomplishing a policy and the cost of its accomplishment are in a world of limited possibilities vital elements in arriving at a judgment of the worthwhileness of the policy itself.

Comment

M. R. COHEN

Nominalism and the Reality of Rules

Morris R. Cohen (1880–1947) was a professor of philosophy at the College of the City of New York for many years. He was, until recently, one of the few professional philosophers in the United States to deal seriously with legal philosophy. In this selection, he discusses Bingham and Holmes.

ह्र

The decisive rôle of judicial decisions in modern law leads some behaviourists to substitute the behaviour of the judge for that of the people, as the substance of the law. The most direct expression of this is the view of Professor Bingham that the law consists of the actual individual decisions and that rules are no part of the law, but are mere subjective ideas in the minds of those who think about the law.

If we are to have a rational science of law, we must realize the untenability of this position, which is not at all involved in Holmes's dictum that "the prophecies of what the courts will do in fact and nothing more pretentious are what I mean by law."

Bingham's position is explicitly based on a dualistic metaphysics that assumes a mind and a world external to it. Judges, cases, and

Reprinted by permission of the executor of the estate of Morris R. Cohen from Morris Raphael Cohen, *Law and the Social Order* (New York: Harcourt, Brace and Co., 1933), pp. 208–15.

decisions presumably exist in the external world. But "Principles and rules cannot exist outside of the mind. . . . The external expression of them does . . . the meaning then exists only in the mind of the speaker or writer as he makes it." This is an old popular metaphysics going back to medieval times, and still regnant, but quite untenable on reflection.

Let us in the first place distinguish between the meaning of things, and what exists in our minds when we apprehend this meaning. The former belongs to or follows from the nature of the things considered, while the latter depends not only on there being such objective meaning but also on our willingness and ability to apprehend. Consider, for instance, the meaning of entropy or of the chemical law of multiple proportion. It consists, as Peirce has shown, of all the possible conseqences that follow from it. We may, by study, learn more or less of this meaning, and it may then in a metaphorical sense be said to have entered into, and to be in, our mind. But the condition of this happening is that there should be such meanings in the nature of the things studied. If the law of entropy or that of multiple proportion is true, its objective meaning or set of consequences held true before they entered the mind of any speaker or writer—indeed before our planetary system was formed. The meanings of things do not, then, depend on the mind of the individual thinker, speaker, or writer. Rather does the fate of the individual depend on his seeing what there is to be seen of the principles or rules which enter into these meanings.

Far from its being absurd, as Bingham asserts, to suppose that principles and rules can exist independently of the comprehension of the individual observer, that is exactly what we all assume whenever we undertake to teach any science or systematic truth. And the law is no exception. Certainly when the lawyer argues any case or tries to expound any legal doctrine, he tries to make his hearer or reader comprehend the meaning of certain rules or general principles previously not in the mind of the hearer or reader. And it is a sheer fallacy to suppose that because meanings may in a sense be said to enter into or exist in our minds when we apprehend them, they cannot therefore be genuine parts or features of the objective world apprehended.

Back, however, of the subjectivist's failure to realize the objectivity of meaning is the nominalist's difficulty in seeing the reality of the universals that enter into all meaning. This difficulty, as has been intimated before, arises from the fallacy of reification, that is, of regarding universals as if they were additional particular things, so that it seems reasonable to ask, Where are they? But the question shows a confusion, since everything localized in time and space is by definition particular. As all, however, that we can ever say about anything involves abstract traits, relations, or universals, no one can well dismiss them as mere meaningless sounds or words on paper, and the nominalist tries to meet the difficulty by locating all universals or abstractions in the mind. But if there is any difficulty about conceiving them in objective nature, that difficulty is not cured by putting them in the mind. For if the nominalistic logic is good it should lead us, as it led Berkeley, to deny that there can be any universal ideas in the mind. My idea of a triangle (in the sense of an image existing in the mind) must be of a particular size, scalene or isosceles, etc. Indeed, Professor Bingham does argue that there is no real identity between a rule in the mind of A and a rule in the mind of B that in common speech would be called the same rule.

But why stop here? If the same rule cannot exist in two different minds, can it exist in the same mind at different times? Indeed, how can any existing mind or anything whatsoever be the same if there is no identity in nature? And if there is no identity in nature, all references to any object as the same are false or meaningless. If, per contra, abstract identity and diversity are real traits of things in nature, there is no difficulty in recognizing them as universal principles that are part of the objective meaning of things. Things and their meanings do not exist in absolutely separate worlds "external" to each other, if these meanings follow from or express the nature of things. Rules, we are told, help us to analyze the facts. They could not do so if the facts were unrelated to them and had nothing in common with them.

The root difficulty of the nominalist is that he confuses the existence of particular images in individual minds with the objective meaning of principles or rules in our common world. In considering a rule, such as the rule in Shelley's case, different thinkers may look at it from different points of view and see different phases of it. They will have different images in their minds and will express themselves in different words, perhaps in different languages. Yet it is possible for them to mean or refer to the same object. Otherwise, there could be no possibility of argument or communication. Communication presupposes a common world.

If the reader finds the foregoing paragraphs too abstruse, he may consider the reality of rules and principles independently of the metaphysical quagmire on which Bingham chooses to rest it. The gist of the question is, Do or do not legal decisions that form the law necessarily involve rules and principles? The issue may perhaps be made somewhat clearer if we ask whether a given judge is acting in an official or a purely personal capacity. Obviously, if we make any such distinction it is because there are rules that give legal effect to the judge's decision only when he acts in conformity with them. Moreover, within the scope of the judge's legal power we may distinguish between the rulings that are taken as precedents in similar cases and the exercise of discretionary power that issues binding orders which do not serve as rules for the future. Thus a judge may legally deny the plea of counsel for an adjournment; but so long as it does not serve as a precedent the denial cannot be said to make law, though it is within the law. The same is true of any discretionary administrative act, e.g., when a postmaster refuses to listen to my suggestions as to the improvement of the service.

The *mediatore* in the Spanish market who terminates the haggling by making the two parties close the bargain can hardly be called a judge. Neither is an arbitrator a judge, unless his decisions are supposed to follow or embody some rule or principle of social authority. Consider on the other hand a court of appeal deciding that the trial judge erred in admitting certain evidence, that replacement value rather than original cost is the proper basis on which to compute railway rates, or that the law of the domicile should govern the validity of a divorce. In these cases, the decisions are clearly meaningless apart from the rule that they explicitly embody. But every decision of a court is nowadays taken by the community as a norm or rule for all similar cases because of the community's faith that the courts will consistently enforce that rule. Mr. X sues Bank Y for a specific amount of money computed on the basis of the value of the Russian rouble at a specific time. We can say that the court decides only the case before it. But in fact all who deal in foreign exchange are affected and adjust their practices accordingly. For they expect that the courts will rule similarly in all similar cases. The element of identity that makes different cases similar is what we formulate as the rule of the case.

Bingham admits that courts are and should be governed by constitutional provisions and statutes enacted by legislatures. Are not these formulated in general rules? And are not parts of the common law as definite as that?

The present wave of nominalism in juristic science is a reaction by younger men against the *abuse* of abstract principles by an older generation that neglected the adequate factual analysis necessary to make principles properly applicable. It is natural, therefore, for the rebels to claim as their own one who for more than the time of one generation has valiantly stood for the need of more factual knowledge in the law. But no group can claim Justice Holmes as its own unless it shares his respect for the complexity of the legal situation and exercises the same caution against hastily jumping from one extreme error to the opposite. Holmes's position is, I judge, in perfect agreement with that of a logical pragmatist like Peirce: Legal principles have no meaning apart from the judicial decisions in concrete cases that can be deduced from them, and principles alone (i.e., without knowledge or assumption as to the facts) cannot logically decide cases. But Holmes has always insisted that the man of science in the law must not only possess an eye for detail but also "insight which tells him what details are significant." And significance involves general principles that determine which facts are relevant and which may be neglected as irrelevant. The law consists of prophecies as to how the public force (as directed by courts) will act. But the judge whom Holmes most respects is the one who, like Shaw, not only has technical knowledge, but also understands "the ground of public policy to which all laws must ultimately be referred." Indeed, no modern state appoints judges at random or backs up their arbitrary whims. Judges are generally required to have some legal knowledge, so that their decisions, despite the element of discretion,[1] should conform to the general pattern of the legal system. Such conformity would be impossible if the judicial decisions were entirely capricious. If the decision of each case were independent of any principle explicitly stated by some authority or implicitly contained in previous cases, there could be no point in judge, counsel, or any one else studying or knowing any law. No case can serve as a clue to any other except to the extent that they both contain some common elements to which a common principle is applicable.

The fact that the judge has a large element of discretion need not prevent us from expecting of him, as of any other official—perhaps even more than of others—conformity to the law. "Sittest thou to judge me after the law and commandest me to be smitten contrary to the law?" Justice involves conformity to some rule, not anarchy.

The difficulty of seeing what rule a given case involves is partly due to the traditional way of talking about the *ratio decidendi* as if a single case by itself could logically determine a rule. Since every individual case can be subsumed under any number of rules of varying generality, it clearly cannot establish any of them. It is only because every case is related more or less to previous cases —no human situation can be altogether unrelated to all previous situations—that a decision on it tends to fix the immediate direction of the stream of legal decision. The relation between decisions and rules may thus be viewed as analogous to that between points and a line. No single point nor, in strict accuracy, any finite number of points can by themselves completely determine the nature of the line or curve that passes through them. For every curve is the locus of an infinite number of points that conform to its rule or formula. We have to know the nature of the curve before we can determine whether any given point is on it or not. The

[1] The regimental commander or the classroom teacher also has a large element of discretion. But if there is any difference between wise and unwise, loyal or disloyal use of discretion, it must ultimately be expressible in some formula or rule that gives the rational ground of the distinction. The rule need not be always explicitly formulated. But the gift of acting in accordance with it goes more often with trained than with untrained intuition. And training must consist in seeking to grasp a rule so that we may recognize old elements in new situations.

practice of physicists in drawing continuous curves through a number of points that are near to each other (the latter representing accurate observations or measurements), and then using this curve for purposes of interpolation and extrapolation, suggests that a number of points may determine a line. This has led inductively minded jurists to view particular decisions as the primary realities and to look on rules as secondary and entirely derivative. But this is an inadequate view. In the physical as in the legal field, neither specific observations or decisions nor the law or rule is absolutely certain. Error may enter all of these, and to banish the inquiry whether any particular observation or decision is in any way erroneous is to rule out the possibility of rational or scientific inquiry.

Actual scientific procedure uses what are regarded as established laws or rules to determine the correctness of particular observations or decisions, and uses large numbers of reliable observations or decisions to test the correctness of proposed laws or rules. The logical circularity of this procedure shows that in this way we cannot attain absolute material truth. But we can by ever enlarging our circle obtain the best that is available. Thus Kepler tests the proposed Ptolemaic, Tychonian, and Copernican lines or laws of planetary motion by their relative accuracy in meeting the well authenticated tables of astronomical observations. But the question, which observations are the best and most reliable, can be answered only on theoretic grounds. So in the law we test rules by the closeness with which they fit what we regard as the right decisions in particular cases; but if the question is raised as to whether any particular decision is right or not, we test it by rules that we regard as operating in analogous cases, i.e., in cases that embody the same principle.

HERMANN KANTOROWICZ

Some Rationalism About Realism

*Hermann Kantorowicz (1877–1940), was an eminent historian
of law and legal theory. He was dismissed by the Nazis from
his professorship at Kiel University in 1933, and thereafter
taught in the United States and England.*

It should be stressed from the outset that this article is meant as
a criticism and is therefore directed exclusively against those sides
of the realist movement in American jurisprudence which are open
to criticism. I do not intend to give a comprehensive picture of
the whole movement, nor do I minimize the admirable achieve-
ments of the realists, especially in the field of research. Moreover,
I do not deny that my remarks can be criticized on the ground
that the realists teach the contrary of what I say they teach. It is
indeed one of their weak points that it is possible to find in their
writings contradictions of many of their assertions. It will therefore be necessary to give a number of literal quotations in order
to prove my criticism, but I know and admit that I could give
other quotations to the contrary. These contradictions are to be
found in the same author, often even in the same article, still more
often in different authors. For the realist movement—and this is
another difficulty for the critic—does not form a school or a party;
it has no caucus, no boss, no platform, no slogans. It suffices to
name some of the adherents in order to realize that one can not
expect them to agree. Their senior is the "great dissenter," Oliver
Wendell Holmes, and among his followers there are such different

personalities as Bingham, Clark, Cook, Frank, Llewellyn, Oliphant, Moore, Patterson, Radin and Yntema. But nevertheless they agree in two fundamental postulates, one, a substantive postulate regarding the nature of the law, the other, a formal postulate regarding the nature of legal science. It is these fundamental theories alone which I wish to discuss here.

The substantive theory is that the law is not a body of rules but of facts; the formal theory, that legal science is not a rational but an empirical science. I do not assert that these theories are simply untrue; I shall try to show that they are exaggerations of the truth. But the truth is not original. The nucleus of the substantive theory was developed by a Franco-German movement which produced the free law doctrine; the nucleus of the formal theory, by a German-American movement known as the sociological school of law.

The free law doctrine teaches (if we may sum up an elaborate system in a few words): The traditional sources of the law, the "formal" law, statutes and precedents, have gaps which must be filled up, must be filled up with law if the decision is to be a judicial decision, and this law must have a general character if equality before the law is to be maintained; the gap-filling material must therefore consist of rules, rules of law. These are "free" law in the sense that they are not formal law: they have not been formalized but are still in a state of transition like bills, principles of policy, business customs, inarticulate convictions, emotional preferences. Many of them are formulated for the purpose of a concrete judicial decision by the courts, acting within their discretion, through acts of will and value-judgments, and constitute therefore judge-made law. Their validity is far less than that of the formal law and sometimes nil, but their practical importance is even greater, because, where the formal law is clear and complete, litigation is not likely to occur. This free law thesis has been exaggerated by those realists who teach that law consists of judicial decisions alone, and therefore of facts.

The sociological school of law teaches that the law must be interpreted according to its aims, that these aims are to be found in its (desirable) effects on social (including economic) life, and that therefore the law cannot be understood nor applied without the aid of a sociological (including economic) study of social reality. This sociological thesis has been exaggerated by those realists who teach that legal science is itself a sociological, and therefore an empirical science.

The writer has himself had a certain share in both movements. But for the realist exaggerations he is not responsible, although he has sometimes been praised for them. It is disagreeable enough for a man to have to pay alimony for his own illegitimate issue; but he cannot be expected to pay for other men's bastards, and like it.

The Nature of the Law According to the Realists

In setting forth the realists' concept of the nature of law, let us adduce a number of typical quotations:

"I use the phrase 'the law' in the sense of sequences of external facts and their concrete legal consequences through the concrete operation of governmental machinery."[1]

"This past behavior of the judges can be described in terms of certain generalizations which we call rules and principles of law."[2]

"Rules, whether stated by judges or others, whether in statutes, opinions or text-books by learned authors, are not the Law, but are only some among many of the sources to which judges go in making the law of the cases tried before them . . . The law, therefore, consists of decisions, not of rules. If so, then, whenever a judge decides a case he is making law."[3]

"*What these officials* [the officials of the law] *do about disputes is, to my mind, the law itself.*"[4]

". . . the theory that rules decide cases seems for a century to have fooled not only library-ridden recluses, but judges."[5]

"To say that a legal institution,—private property, the federal government of the United States, Columbia University,—exists is to say that a group of persons is doing something, is acting in some way."[6]

[1] Bingham, *What is the Law?* (1912) 11 MICH. L. REV. 109, n. 29. Obviously Bingham defines "the law" by the concept of "legal."

[2] Cook, *Scientific Method and the Law* (1927) 13 A. B. A. J. 303, 308.

[3] FRANK, LAW AND THE MODERN MIND (1930) 127–128.

[4] LLEWELLYN, THE BRAMBLE BUSH (1930) 3. Italics are those of the author quoted.

[5] Llewellyn, *The Constitution as an Institution* (1933) 33 COL. L. REV. 1, 7.

[6] Moore, *The Rational Basis of Legal Institutions* (1923) 23 COL. L. REV. 609.

The realists' conception of the Law, their substantive thesis, is therefore: the Law is not a body of rules, not an Ought, but a factual reality. It is the real behavior of certain people, especially of the officials of the Law, more especially of the judges who make the Law through their decisions, which, therefore, constitutes the Law.

Before we criticize this theory, one logical observation may be permitted. The discussion, by all means, must not degenerate into a fruitless logomachy—one man understanding by law, this, and another desirous of understanding something else. This question is far more than a terminological dispute. It has momentous consequences. Whatever we define as "law" must be the chief subject among those which the "law" schools teach, or ought to teach; whatever we define as "law" must be the topic, or the chief topic, of the science of "law"; and whatever, in an American discussion, is defined as "law" must be in harmony with positive American Law insofar as it uses the expression "law." Now, for instance, the judge charges a jury on questions of law, not of fact; the error in fact sometimes excuses, the error in law does not; appellate jurisdiction is not the same over law as it is over fact. This alone should suffice to show that in the interpretation of American law, and for that matter of European law also, we must distinguish between law and facts. For this reason alone a theory which ignores this distinction by calling only factual behavior "law" breaks down at the outset. But then, how can we explain the commission of such an elementary mistake by distinguished jurists?

The explanation is that it is based on extrajural dogmas, on erroneous assumptions, not about the law but about the philosophy of law. It is, therefore, based mostly on unconscious *prejudices*, six of which may be pointed out. Fortunately, we can illustrate this connection between the theory and the underlying prejudices by means of literal quotations from Llewellyn, who is as outspoken in his premises as we have seen him to be in his conclusions. The illustrations are confined to the writings of a single author, in view of the indubitable fact that Mr. Llewellyn is considered the most representative among American realists. It ought, however, to be pointed out, that the same views could be traced in the writings of other realists, especially in those of Joseph W. Bingham, Jerome Frank, and Max Radin.

1.

"If rules decided cases, one judge would be as good as another, provided only the rules had been adduced before him."[7]

This displays the formalistic prejudice, which, by the way, is common also to many critics of realism. It is a prejudice to believe that the Law consists of nothing but formal law handed down by tradition, and it is fatal to overlook those rules which a judge must form whenever the formal law has a gap. Of course, only the best judges, only lawyers who know more than law, who have thoroughly studied, not only experienced, real economic and social life, its effects and its needs, are capable of conceiving and formulating the proper rules for the concrete cases. One should not object that this would be a task solely for the judge's discretion. Discretion is not opposed to rules, as is usually said; it is an intuitive way of finding rules: those "inarticulate major premises," which must be general if they are to be *major* premises, and which must be rules of law if they are to serve as major premises for *judicial* decisions.

2.

"An inch from the eye is a portion of the Text; the whole living world behind is 'covered' by it . . . It is institutions which validate the Words, not the Words which validate the institutions . . . To study the Words of a Document . . . is to invite inattention to either [governmental] effects or needs."[8]

Here we are faced by the verbalistic prejudice: it is erroneous to believe that the law is the wording of the Law, still more erroneous to believe that it is the printed document. This prejudice overlooks the fact that only the *meaning* of the Law counts in the decision. But every interpretation, however free and audacious, must be at least compatible with the text, with one of its possible meanings. Here lies the great significance of the language technique as a means of interpreting the wording of statutes and decisions. The frequent attacks on words are therefore unjustified. Whatever the

[7] Llewellyn, *supra* note 5, at 7.
[8] Llewellyn, *supra* note 5, at 17, 35.

relation of thought to language may be, words are indispensable tools for fixing and communicating legal ideas; even an attack on words must be couched in words. If I myself have rejected the old conception of legal science as that of a *Wortwissenschaft,* I have meant that the words of the Law must not be considered in the way the professional word scholar, the philologist, considers them. The philologist interprets them as they were subjectively meant, the lawyer as carrying an objective meaning which must be construed by highly technical means. This meaning can remain unaltered even if the words are changed—many rules of English law have been translated from law-French without essential alterations of their meanings and vice versa—and this shows that the subject-matter with which the lawyer deals is not words but their meanings.

3.

"If rules decided cases, law stood still . . . whereas growth and change of law were as striking in nineteenth—and twentieth—century America as they have ever been. . . . At the beginning of a code experiment, intent of the language has a clear and proper bearing on men's actions. . . . The words are thus—at the beginning—best read in terms of the legislative history. . . . But even here, intent cannot rule purely. Some cases have *not* been put in the debate. Resort must then be had to language and circumstance, to 'obvious' rather than to real intent."[9]

This is what may be called the historical prejudice. To the historian, of course, the Law is an historical act; its meaning is the original, the "real" intent of the makers of the statute or of the drafters of the decision, and therefore unchangeable like everything that is past. To the jurist the Law is the objective meaning of statute or opinion, that which the legislator or the judge would have meant if he had been able to fit his meaning into the whole body of the Law. As Mr. Justice Holmes has said: "We do not inquire what the legislator meant; we ask only what the statute means." That which we call the "life" of the Law, its constant adaptation to constantly changing social conditions, is due to this objective method more than to anything else.

[9] Llewellyn, *supra* note 5, at 7, 12–13. *Cf.* HOLMES, COLLECTED LEGAL PAPERS (1921) 207.

4.

"Let us assume a case not involving any doubt, but a case nevertheless which would never have occurred to anyone at the time the rule
in question was established. . . . The legislator could not have *intended*
the inclusion of this case *in concreto;* the case was by hypothesis not
yet thought of."[10]

This introduces the nominalistic prejudice (in the philosophical
meaning of the term). The nominalist overlooks the fact that the
language of the legislator, like most language, is chiefly related to
classes of things, not to individual objects. With the same right,
one could oppose the application of any statute because it speaks
of persons, and the litigating persons were not yet born when the
statute was enacted.

5.

"The existence of an institution lies first of all and last of all in the
fact that people do behave in certain patterns a, b and c. . . . Every
living constitution is an institution; it *lives* only so far as that is true."[11]

Here we have the sociological prejudice. It is not true that social
phenomena can be studied by themselves without regard for the
rules that govern them. Gray has given a brilliant example: "Suppose King, Lords and Commons should meet in one chamber and
vote together, an order passed by them would not be obeyed by
the English people." The pure sociologist could not explain this
phenomenon. In the same way we may ask: Which is the institution with which Llewellyn identifies the Constitution of the
United States? Is it Columbia University? Or some speakeasy?
Certainly not, but the Congress is one of them. Why? Only
because it acts more or less according to the rules of the Constitution. No constitutional institution can be singled out among
all other institutions except against the background of the rules
of the Constitution.

The sociological bias is particularly prevalent among constitu-
tionalists who are obviously dazzled by the frequent contrast

[10] Translated from 1 LLEWELLYN, PRAEJUDIZIENRECHT UND RECHT-
SPRECHUNG IN AMERIKA (Leipzig, 1933), 72, 74.

[11] Llewellyn, *supra* note 5, at 17. *Cf.* GRAY, THE NATURE AND SOURCES
OF THE LAW (2d ed. 1921) 76.

between the legal and the factual aspect of the state and the immensely greater interest attached to the latter. But I challenge any sociologist to describe, for instance, the difference between sovereign and non-sovereign states and between states and municipalities in terms of power, size, population or other factual elements. The first attempt would evince the futility of any such effort.

6.

Of the last prejudice, the professional one, examples have already been given. The realists constantly speak of the Law as the behaviour chiefly of the judges. Why chiefly of these? Because the judges are the persons whom the attorney has professionally—directly or indirectly—to handle; and the realists are attorneys, or have been attorneys, or else they are trainers of attorneys. But if we are to speak as real realists, not as mere legalists, the behavior of every normal layman, of everybody standing in any normal jural relation to anybody else, is infinitely more important; for the great majority of these jural relations never come before the courts. We now understand why the realists, instead of focusing their attention upon the invisible certainty of the law in the normal cases, are obsessed by the obvious uncertainty of the law in the few contested cases. If they were more conscious of the logical distinctions between the legal and the sociological approach they would give full credit to the latter method and would accordingly be more interested in those phenomena which influence and shape the whole body of society, not only the functions of one important organ of it, the courts of law.

The Nature of Legal Science According to the Realists

As shedding light upon the realists' conception of the nature of legal science, the following quotations are significant:

"The prophecies of what the courts will do in fact, and nothing more pretentious, are what I mean by the law."[12]

[12] Holmes, *The Path of the Law* (1897) 10 HARV. L. REV. 457, 461. *Cf.* also, Bingham, *supra* note 1, at 11, 12: "His [the lawyer's] essential business is to predict these future sequences accurately . . . it is a field for scientific study analogous to the field of any other science. . . . [When the word law

". . . lawyers, like the physical scientists, are engaged in the study of objective physical phenomena. . . . As lawyers we are interested in knowing how certain officials of society—judges, legislators, and others—have behaved in the past, in order that we may make a prediction of their probable behavior in the future."[13]

The realists "want law to deal, they themselves want to deal, with things, with people, with tangibles, with *definite* tangibles, and *observable* relations between tangibles—not with words alone; when law deals with words, they want the words to represent tangibles which can be got at beneath the words, and observable relations between those tangibles."[14]

"The 'normative' conception of legal science . . . precludes the objective narration of conventional legal principles by confusing law and ethics . . ."[15]

According to these quotations, then, legal science is not a rational and normative science which tries to transform the given law into a more or less consistent system of rules. To the realists, legal science is empirical, the method of which is observation; the purpose, foretelling effects; the model, natural science. This naturalistic thesis clashes with the oldest teachings of logic as well as with modern conceptions of methodology. It is based upon confusion of categories. It will suffice to point out six of these confusions.

First of all, the realists confuse *natural* and *cultural* science. Natural science deals only with real events governed by laws of nature. Even if it should prove to be true that these laws were nothing but statistical averages, they would always remain inviolable in the sense that facts can never contradict them, since they would then cease to be laws of "nature." At the same time the harmony of observed facts with the laws of nature provides a test for the reality of the facts. But cultural sciences deal with

is used in the sense of 'studying law' or 'the law of property'] the speaker or writer consciously or unconsciously indicates by it causal relations of occurrences external to the mind of the observer and their governmental consequences, past or potential."

[13] Cook, *The Logical and Legal Basis of the Conflict of Laws* (1924) 33 YALE L. J. 475. *Cf.* also, Oliphant. *A Return to Stare Decisis* (1928) 14 A. B. A. J. 159: "Not the judges' opinions, but which way they decide cases will be the dominant subject matter of any truly scientific study of law."

[14] Llewellyn, *Some Realism about Realism* (1933) 44 HARV. L. REV. 1922, 1223.

[15] Yntema, *The Rational Basis of Legal Science* (1931) 31 COL. L. REV. 925, 945.

human actions and are governed by laws of men, and these actions can be either lawful or unlawful. Indeed, they are very often unlawful, and it is precisely the existence of unlawful acts which makes legal science necessary; it alone allows us to judge unlawful acts and this presupposes the knowledge of how they *ought* to have been. But these unlawful acts are quite as real as the lawful acts. For this reason a natural science which knows nothing of "unlawful" and, therefore, of unreal acts, nor of unreal and, therefore, of "unlawful" acts, can teach us nothing decisive. Ours is a science which must learn to distinguish between lawful and unlawful acts, which must be able to judge the unlawful ones and therefore must previously know the unreal acts which *ought* to have been real. The natural science which a realist should study is that part of astronomy which might teach us how the stars ought to move, and how they move and whenever they choose to violate the laws of celestial mechanics. Unfortunately, such a branch of astronomy has not been developed, and if a person actually developed it, he would probably look to legal science for guidance, not vice versa.

Secondly, the realists confuse *explanation* and *justification*. If legal science were an empirical science, its chief method would be explanation through cause and effect. If it were a rational and normative science, its chief category would be justification through reason and consequence. Now let us approach the courts in a realistic attitude and ask which of these methods they in fact apply, for the actions of courts must be an application of legal science to a concrete question. Must a court refuse to apply a clearly worded statute if it fails to understand its historical causes or the intentions of the legislators, on the ground that a judgment based on such a statute cannot be scientifically explained? Not at all. The question chiefly interesting the judge is whether the decision he wants to give can be justified as a consequence of the particular statue, or at least as being compatible with its consequences. And what about an appellate court which has to pass on an absurd decision of the trial judge, explainable, and only explainable, by the fact that the judge was intoxicated or insane? Must his decision be upheld on the ground that it has been explained and therefore satisfies legal science? On the contrary, it will be reversed because it cannot be reasonably justified by law, and this is the only question which interests the appellate court. Genetic explanation and normative justification must be kept apart —this is one of the most important lessons of modern epistomology. It may be sense or nonsense to explain with Jerome Frank that the "childish" desire to attribute inviolable certainty to the law is caused by a "father complex"—in any case the truth or untruth of that alleged attribution is quite independent of its psycho-analytic or any other genetic explanation. Of course, the genetic method may be used as a tool in the service of the normative method and vice versa.

The third confusion is between *law* and *ethics*. This is the reproach which the realists make to the classical, normative conception. But their misgivings are entirely due to their own mistake, their confusion of legal with moral norms. The former demand some external behavior and can be complied with whatever may be the motives. The latter always take into account the motive— for instance, a selfish or altruistic aim.

Fourthly, the realists fail to distinguish between *realities* and their *meaning*. Llewellyn wishes to restrict legal science to "observable" and even "tangible" facts. Now the essential relations in law are never observable; for instance, at the same moment that a man dies in an accident without having made his will, his new born child may have become a rich man by having inherited the deceased's property without anybody knowing it. Nothing in this important legal change is in any way observable—and so it is everywhere in law. It is the *meaning* of observable realities with which the lawyer is concerned, but meanings are not observable, still less tangible. It is the *history* of law which is interested in observable and unobservable facts, and much of the research work of the Realists is indeed nothing but contemporary American legal history. This is one of the legal sciences and a very respectable science at that, especially if it is approached in a true sociological spirit, so that not only contemporary American facts, but also the general problem of law as conditioned by its social background is taken into consideration. But this is not the legal science of which we are speaking, the legal science which the law schools teach and which the future lawyer must learn—if for no other purpose than to influence the judge.

The fifth confusion is between the *concept* and one of the *elements* which compose the concept. If, as Mr. Justice Holmes says and all the realists repeat (as if they wished to advertise the one theory of the great judge and jurist which one would prefer not to find in his work), the law is what courts of law do, one could also say: religion is what the churches preach; science is what the universities teach; medicine is what the doctor prescribes; art is what the artist produces; and shoes are what the shoemaker makes. All this is placing the cart before the horse. One cannot define church without religion, university without science, doctor without medicine, artist without art, shoemaker without shoe, and courts of law without law. The law is not what the courts administer but the courts are the institutions which administer the law. For this reason alone can it be foretold what the courts will do. In so far as the lawyer knows the law, and in so far as the judge will follow the law, the lawyer will be able to foretell what the judge will do. The other sources of the judge's decision are in great part unknown and always will be unknown.

The last confusion is that between *cases* and *case law*. The realist movement could start and progress only in a case law country because there indeed the law seems to be a heap of decisions, and therefore a body of facts. But the cases themselves are not binding; they are not the case law; only the rationes decidendi are binding. These are—according to the controversal theory which here, of course, cannot be discussed—not the factual reasons adduced by the judge, which are only psychological facts, often based on self deception, or otherwise subject to suspicion. They are the principles from which the decisions ought to have flowed, the principles by which alone the decisions could be justified. These rationes decidendi therefore cannot simply be arrived at by an inductive process; they must be construed through purposive interpretation, they must be generalized and fitted into the whole body of the Law, which is more or less a system.[16] The

---

[16] If the Realists object to the idea of a "system" they are thinking of a "rational" system in the strict sense of the term, and in this, of course, the

system into which these rationes decidendi are assimilated is the case law, and therefore something very different from a mere fact that could be the object of an empirical research. But even if it were nothing else, it would lose its meaning if there were not behind it the rule of stare decisis, whatever its limits and authority may be. Accordingly, the whole temple of case law is founded upon a rule and not upon a fact. Those who deny that rules are binding can hardly admit the binding force of precedents, which they profess to worship. Thus they destroy the Law itself.

Reductio ad Absurdum

Let us finally endeavor to know the realists by their fruits. We may first consider the startling consequences of the substantive thesis: that there is no law outside the decisions. Undecided cases could not be decided, since the respective human actions would be outside the range of the law. But every case was at one time undecided. To violate a new statute would not mean breaking the "law," nor could new statutes be interpreted, since there would be no science of law to interpret them if this science dealt with decision alone. But every statute was once a new statute. The same holds true of such parts of an old statute concerning which there are contradictory decisions. Here the decision cannot be foretold and therefore, where scientific treatment would be most necessary, it would be impossible. Certain rules which have never come before the courts, nor ever could come, would cease to be law. For instance, the rule of the Constitution that the President must be 35 years of age could not be law, and it would, therefore, not be unconstitutional to make Colonel Lindbergh President. It is futile to answer that such rules are merely sources of law. They are not "sources" in the factual sense because no decisions have flowed from them. And if one means by calling them "sources" that decisions *ought* to be drawn from them, one does nothing else but recognize them as rules of law.

---

writer concurs. The whole free-law movement has always emphasized that the "system" which legal science tries to erect is permeated with many emotional and volitional elements.

Establishment of rules by legislation would be practically useless; it would not change the jurisprudence of the courts since they are not determined by rules, or are so determined only to a small extent. The legislator, if he is not to be considered a "ruler," would be a liar: "murder is punishable by death" would mean that it is in truth punished by death. But we know that many murderers are not, because the murderers have not been caught or convicted. Why should we have learned men to decide the cases? Whatever the courts decide is the law. This may be tolerable today, because the judges have learned how they ought to decide; but a realist should not insist on their legal training. Why not staff the Supreme Court with nine generals? Surely they would know how to enforce their decisions, such a Court would "work," and that is all a realist ought to demand.

Equally startling are the consequences of the formal theory: that the objective of legal science must be to foretell future behavior. Dissenting opinions would always be contrary to legal science, and consciously so since the dissenting judge himself knows beforehand that the prevailing opinion will be different. True, sometimes he foresees that in the future his opinion will be adopted by the Court, and then according to the formal theory both opinions would be in harmony with legal science, the dissenting as well as the prevailing. Charging a jury would involve telling it what it is about to do. This seems rather superfluous. The proper study of the law student would be the behavior of individual judges; such a study would be not only farcical but also useless. Every new generation of students would have to be taught the psychology of a new batch of judges. An essential feature of this law study of the future would be the art of bribing judges. In such a case the appellate court would be in a strange position. It would be compelled to say: it was foreseeable that the judge of the first instance would be bribed; his decision therefore corresponds to realistic legal science, and accordingly must be upheld. The most important task of the law schools would be to teach which citizens are going to abide by the law and which of them are going to break it. But the law schools cannot compete with inquiry offices and detective bureaus. It is their task to turn out men like Mr. Justice Holmes, not like Mr. Sherlock Holmes.

HARRY W. JONES

Legal Realism and Natural Law

Harry W. Jones is a professor of law at Columbia University. The view presented here is somewhat modified in his later article, "Law and Morality in the Perspective of Legal Realism," Columbia Law Review, vol. 61 (1961), pp. 799–809.

ঽঌ

. . . I have spoken of Natural Law philosophy in its aspect as a basis for profound moral criticism of the positive law. Natural Law literature is most meaningful when it is addressed to doctrinal questions: "Is this statute, this rule—taken in the large as a generalization—just or unjust?" But the problems of law in action center less often on the ethical merits of general propositions, considered as such, than on the application of such general propositions to the rich and limitless variety of concrete situations that occur in society. The moral problem of the judge, the prosecutor or the practicing lawyer is only rarely, "Is this a just general rule?" Far more commonly the painful question is "What is justice in this concrete situation?" No law, no generalization, ever fully reaches the singularity and uniqueness of the individual case that must be decided. A theory of justice is incomplete unless it takes equal account of the demand of the general principle and the appeal of the particular situation.

I propose, therefore, that we seek the moral dimension of law not in precepts and rules but in the process of responsible decision which pervades the whole of law in life. And in this quest, we must include in our synthesis the essential insights of the

Reprinted by permission of the author from The Riverside Lectures, delivered in 1956.

approach that has become known as American legal realism. If I have a hortatory mission in these lectures, it is to help free legal realism from the loose indictment, voiced during the years since World War II by Catholic, Protestant and Jewish legal thinkers alike, that realism is an unmoral and unworthy approach to law, subversive of basic human values and somehow allied to the perversities of Hitler and Stalin.

What then is legal realism? It is not a systematic philosophy of law to which all the so-called realists subscribe, but rather a way of looking at legal rules and legal processes. In points of stress and details of belief, the members of this loose federation differ widely—often passionately—one from another. The common feature that justifies bringing them all under one tent is a shared sceptical temper towards legal generalizations, a shared conviction that the processes of law administration involve operations far more complex than the search for and logical application of pre-existing doctrines. Mr. Justice Holmes is, of course, the hero figure of the clan. "The prophesies of what the courts will do in fact, and nothing more pretentious, are what I mean by the law." "The life of the law has not been logic; it has been experience." "General propositions do not decide concrete cases." Thus the realist appraisal of law stresses not a critique of rules—a weighing of the content of generalizations in law books—but a testing of law as an institutional process. The constant realist inquiry is not, "What do the rules of law have to say as to this problem" but, rather, "What happens in life—in courtrooms, law offices and prosecutors' conferences? What is the cut and texture of the materials with which the judge and the practicing lawyer work? Where is the power, the discretion, the responsibility for decision?"

As would be expected, there is not *a* legal realism but rather a range of views, all starting from the core conception that the administration of law is something far less orderly than a dispassionate, mathematically precise application of established principles to particular fact-situations falling logically within them. Beyond this, there is a complete lack of doctrinal conformity among the realists. But this is certainly nothing new in philosophy. Without straining too much, we manage to apply the term

LEGAL REALISM AND NATURAL LAW (263

"existentialist" to Marcel as well as Sartre, to Jaspars as well as Heidegger, to Casserly as well as Madame Beauvoir. They are all "existentialists," we say, because they share at least a minimum legacy from Kierkegaard, a common conviction that existence is prior to essence and that man struggles endlessly for his own authentication. Similarly, I shall be using the tent term, "legal realist" in a sense broad enough to accommodate the behavioral focus of Karl Llewellyn, the fact-scepticism of Jerome Frank, the institutional empiricism of Underhill Moore and the logical pragmatism of Edwin Patterson. What they, and many more, have in common is an attitude—in this sense, a shared legacy from Holmes—that judges, prosecutors, and practicing lawyers do not really think in syllogisms, that substantive doctrine is not the essence of law, and that one who would know the ways of legal action must dig beneath the doctrines formally announced in judicial opinions down into the substrata of personal preference, empirical fact, and conflicting social interests.

One might have thought, at first impression, that the Natural Law philosophers would not have been entirely unsympathetic to this realist thesis that there is more to legal processes than the more-or-less automatic application of the generalizations of the positive law. I will suggest later that there are, to my mind, far closer affinities between the approach of legal realism and that of Natural Law than exist between conventional analytical jurisprudence and the Natural Law tradition. Actually, however, there was at once an uncompromising attack on the legal realists—and particularly on their founding father, Holmes—from the Natural Law camp. Thus, the profound and usually moderate Father Lucey of Georgetown: "This much must be said for Realism. If man is only an animal, Realism is correct, Holmes was correct, Hitler is correct." This is guilt by association with a vengeance, however provocative may have been the excesses of some of the realist extremists.

The reasons for this Natural Law–legal realist antagonism are, I would say, three in number. To begin with, much of the Natural Law criticism of the realists was merely a returning of blow for blow. Early realist writings, particularly, contain a good deal of hit-and-run cynicism directed not only at the method but at the

aspiration of Natural Law thinking. Second, and more important,
the realists were answering different questions, attempting a long-
needed analysis of the decisional *process*, without always making
it clear that this was what they were about. There was underbrush
to be cleared away—particularly the old slot-machine theory of
judicial decision—and realist commitment to this limited mission
was such as to create a widespread impression that the realists,
as a group, were not at all interested in the problem of justice.
This concentration on the decisional process as it is in fact, and
consequent under-playing of the legal ought-to-be, was bound to
draw fire from the members of a philosophical tradition that had
focussed its attention for seven hundred years on justice and
righteousness in law. Third, and I think this the fundamental
source of antagonism, one basic realist attack was on what Holmes
called "the fallacy of logical form" in law, the adequacy of the
syllogism as an explanation of the process of judicial decision.
The historic association of Scholastic thought—including Scholastic Natural Law—with the method of formal logic is such that
sharp dissent from the Natural Law quarter was inevitable.

The difference in approach can be suggested in another way.
A recurring theme in the literature of Natural Law is the problem
of obligation—the obligation of the subject and the obligation of
the judge—when the positive law clearly directs one course of
conduct and the ideal precept of the natural law clearly commands a different and irreconcilable course. What, for instance,
is the Christian subject to do when the positive law commands
commission of murder, or desecration of holy places, or the bearing
of false witness? But this is rarely the way a moral question arises
in a decent legal system like our own. We have very little affirmatively unjust law in our statute books—none, that I can think of,
that actually commands conduct contrary to Divine good. The
real moral issue, in the context of professional decision, is more
likely to be something like this: "What does the Natural Law—
or, shall we say, Justice—command of me *above and beyond* the
bare minimum of orderly behavior which the positive law prescribes?" Paul Tillich has said that "Law is externalized conscience;
conscience is internalized law" and that "Rules of justice are created by the interplay of law and conscience." Mere conformity

with legal requirements is no answer in the higher court of conscience.

This interplay of law and conscience is better seen in the decisional process than in abstract disputations about general rules. Let us consider then, as briefly as manageable, how choice and decision are inevitable in the life of the law and so inescapable in the life of the lawyer. And this, unavoidably, compels us to accompany the realists in their analysis of what lawyers *do* in their manifold tasks as judges, prosecutors, counsellors, law-makers and advocates.

Positivist insistence on the separation of the legal *is* and the legal *ought to be* is entirely inacceptable—one might almost say "abhorrent"—to those who see legal precepts and institutions from the perspective of the Natural Law tradition. Lon Fuller has defined Natural Law as "the view which denies the possibility of a rigid separation of the *is* and the *ought* and which tolerates a confusion of them in legal discussion." A legal philosopher wholly within the Natural Law Tradition, as Fuller is not, would state the matter much more forcefully. A Natural Law thinker finds both his *is* and his *ought to be* in the final and immutable precepts of the Natural Law. For in Natural Law theory any asserted statutory or case-law rule that fails to conform to the *ought to be* of the Natural Law is not law at all. Such an enactment, such a case-law principle is, as the Natural Lawyers say, "a law only in appearance."

The full reach of the classic Natural Law position on the relation in law of the *is* and *ought to be* is stated with characteristic forthrightness in *The American Philosophy of Law* (5th Ed., 1953) by Francis P. Le Buffe, S.J. and James V. Hayes:

"Austin brought confusion into this question by saying that a law may be morally unjust and yet legally binding, and it is quite common now . . . to assert that when a law is formally valid, i.e. when it is enacted by a genuine ruler, then even though the contents of the law are evil, the law is genuinely a valid law. Such writers might have known, both from reason and from history, that refusal to obey would here be legitimate, even obligatory. For the law is a law only seemingly.

Its 'legally binding' is nothing more than a specious bond, since there is no obligation imposed by such a law, however great may be the penalty for disobedience.

"Here we may note succinctly a distinction which is important. Moral right and wrong is that which is allowed or forbidden by God either through natural reason or by revelation. Legal right and wrong is that which the state has allowed or forbidden. If by law moral wrong becomes legal right, or moral right becomes legal wrong, the law is invalid."

This is no mere semantic dispute between the Natural Law tradition and the school of legal positivism. More than terminology is at issue. In law as in other fields of human art, we live by symbols, and the words we choose for an expression of our key ideas reflect deeply-held convictions and preferences. When our deepest feelings are offended, the positivist statement, "This is law, but unjust" seems cool and thin-blooded when measured against the robust Natural Law declaration: "This is unjust and hence no law at all!" And yet there is a nagging question that will not be put down. Would we want our judges to accept the full implications of the Natural Law theory that a legislative enactment or established case-law rule is *invalid*—and so to be disregarded—if, by its provisions, "moral wrong" becomes legal right, or moral right becomes legal wrong? Powerful as the Natural Law rhetoric is, there is still embodied in it an assumption that there is little room for honest differences of opinion on the morally right and the morally wrong.

What if the question before the judge concerns an area of practice or belief in which different segments of our diverse national community do not see eye-to-eye on what is "moral wrong" or "moral right"? The legal *is*—the statutes and case-law of the state—reflects what Learned Hand has called a "tolerable compromise" of conflicting interests and convictions. The enacted law of a state on divorce, or on birth control, or on motion picture censorship is likely to embody that kind of adjustment, a legal *is* which satisfies no group entirely but is the best compromise that could be arrived at to accommodate conflicting views in society. Would we have the judge who, after all, is the product of a given background and a given tradition, appraise the validity of the compromise *is* in terms of his personal *ought to be*? Let us assume the best—that the judge's *ought to be* springs from a profound and thoughtful reading by him of the precepts of the Natural Law. But another judge, from another tradition, might read the law of nature differently. The conclusion seems inescapable: if the state-sanctioned law provides a clear and controlling direction, the judge is bound to apply that clear direction to the case before him unless there are specific and definite constitutional grounds justifying a declaration of invalidity.

At this point I want to be absolutely sure not to give the false impression—conveyed in some positivist writings—that contemporary Natural Law theory in the United States requires or even urges that a judge refuse to enforce the clear mandate of state enactments which the judge, by reason or authority, considers contrary to the fundamental precepts of the Natural Law. One of the most interesting analyses I have seen of the contemporary Natural Law position is contained in *The Moral Obligations of Catholic Civil Judges*, written in 1953 by Father John Denis Davis of the Society of Jesus. Father Davis's book is subtle and tightly reasoned, and his complete thesis cannot possibly be examined in an hour's lecture. The best illustration of his general approach is found, perhaps, in his discussion of the role of the Catholic civil judge in divorce cases. He begins with a forthright statement of the essential Natural Law position:

"What judgment can be made of these state divorce laws except to say that they are unjust? They are in direct opposition to the Divine law. In enacting these laws, the state takes to itself a power which it does not possess. As a human agency, it defies the law of God and attempts to rend asunder what God has joined together, attempts to terminate the marriage bond and to permit remarriage contrary to an express Divine command. The state has no right whatsoever to declare a valid marriage no longer existent and to permit entrance into a new contract, and whatever laws it does make in this regard are invalid and totally ineffective in breaking the real marriage bond."

Does it follow that the Natural Law judge is bound in conscience to refuse to act as the "invalid" statute commands him to act? Father Davis continues:

"In the light of Catholic principles is the Catholic judge permitted to handle divorce cases? If so, how does he justify himself? What is to be his mode of action, and what are his obligations in handling the cases. . . .

"In our own United States in our day it may safely be said that Catholic judges have at times sufficiently weighty reasons for granting divorces from marriages valid before God and the Church, even when there is probability or certainty of remarriage. Should a Catholic judge be called upon in his office to grant such a divorce, in accordance with the existing, even though unjust, law, refuse to do so, in all probability he would suffer serious abuse, criticism, loss of prestige and probably the loss of his office. . . . Theologians in the United States consider these reasons sufficiently present and weighty for Catholic judges here to grant such divorces when they must do so in the course of fulfilling the duties of their office."

. . . Let us assume, for the moment at least, that we have rejected the original theory of Natural Law that the individual judge is entitled to appraise the validity of the positive law *is* in terms of his personal, moral or religious *ought to be*. In terms of decisional *result*, at least, contemporary Natural Law theory in the United States is not irreconcilable with this rejection. Does it follow, then, that the positivists are entirely right and the Natural Law theorists entirely wrong on the analytical separateness of the legal *is* and the legal *ought to be*? Why, in other words have I entitled tonight's lecture *"Law's Inseparable Is and Ought to Be"*?

Let us reconsider our ground, for the moment. All we have concluded so far is that *if* the state-sanctioned positive law provides a clear and controlling direction, the judge is bound to apply that clear direction to the controversy before him. But, as I tried to demonstrate in my opening lecture, the task of the law— the day-to-day work of judges, practicing lawyers, prosecutors, and law-makers—involves a process far less orderly and far more difficult than the mechanical application of legal generalizations to fact-situations falling neatly within them. Decisions, uncontrolled by strictly *legal* doctrine, must be made every day in the administration of justice. It is in this area of inescapable leeway—of choice that is responsible in the sense of being uncontrolled by existing legal doctrine—that we have located the moral dimension of the law. And within this area of inescapable choice—where a decision either way can be justified with all traditional legal proprieties—the legal *is* and the legal *ought to be* are, I think, inseparable. The legal *is*, here, is not a command but an authorization of alternative decisions. The choice between or among alternatives—the selection of the path to be pursued—is controlled by the *ought to be*. This is not a matter of theory but of realistic analysis. Legal Realism—with its emphasis on the inevitability of discretion and choice in the life of the law—casts its vote with the tradition of Natural Law and against the school of legal positivism on the centuries old issue of the *complete* analytical separateness of the law that *is* and the law that *ought to be*.

Every principle of the positive law—by which I mean every statute, every constitutional provision, and every case-law rule—creates both zones of legal certainty, in which there is no proper occasion for operation of the personal "ought to be" of the deciding judge, and areas of leeway—inescapable choice among legally permissible alternatives—in which, whatever the judge may say in his opinion, his *ought to be* will inevitably influence his act of decision. Let us take a statutory example, a simple illustration from the same field as the extract earlier quoted from Father Davis's book. A statute of the State of Minnewaska provides that a divorce shall be granted, among other grounds, for "mental cruelty." Two judges, sitting in adjoining rooms of the same Domestic Relations Court, happen to have profoundly different personal views on the morality of divorce. Judge A, by cultural and religious background, is opposed to divorce on principle and so thinks of the "mental cruelty" statute as immorally lenient, perhaps even as violative of an immutable precept of the Natural Law. Judge B, with a different educational and religious orientation, thinks it immoral that the state should interfere at all with the free choice of those who wish to dissolve their marriage status and so looks on the "mental cruelty" statute as unduly restrictive on individual freedom of action and inconsistent with contemporary psychiatric thought.

There are here, I submit, zones of certainty in which the personal views of Judge A and Judge B, as to what the grounds for divorce *ought to be*, are, and under our theory of government must be, entirely irrelevant. If the case is one in which the defendant husband has made it a marriage-long practice to ridicule his wife, undermine her relations with the children, and deprive her by intellectual and emotional tyranny of the opportunity for development as a human being, "mental cruelty," the fixed statutory ground, has been made out by any standard. Judge A, under the obligation of his office, is ethically bound to grant the divorce, whatever he may think of the propriety of mental cruelty as a ground for dissolution of the marriage tie. If he cannot do so in good conscience, he has no alternative but to resign his judicial commission.

The case may be equally clear at the opposite zone of certainty. It may become evident, as another case proceeds before Judge B, that there has been no conduct on the part of either spouse that is remotely within the area of the statutory term "mental cruelty." Judge B, in his personal convictions, may believe profoundly in divorce by mutual consent, but the statute, in its zone of certainty, gives him no leeway, no good faith alternative. Mutual consent is not "mental cruelty"; that was not the "tolerable compromise" arrived at in the legislature.

But the hard cases, the judges' "serious business" as Cardozo called them, will fall outside the zones of certainty. These will be suits for divorce in which the evidence establishes less than a pattern of psychically sadistic tyranny and more than mere mutual eagerness to discard the obligations of the marital status. Here the legal *is* is, at most, arguable, and judge's *ought to be*, as a matter of realist analysis, will be determinative. It is nonsense in this context of leeway to speak of a rigid separation of the *is* and the *ought to be*. Take, for one of a hundred possible illustrations, the problem most commonly arising today under the "mental cruelty" statutes. The husband, let us say, suffers from that most heart-breaking of illnesses, compulsive alcoholism. During his bad times, his conduct is as painful to his wife as any intentional "mental cruelty" could be. But it is not a course of conduct over which the poor devil has the slightest real control. One might talk as sensibly of self-control, of the command of will-power, over the manifestations of cancer or the disabilities of polio. Is the case one of "mental cruelty" within the statute—as it indisputably is if appraised wholly from the perspective of the wife's suffering? Or does "mental cruelty" carry an indispensable connotation of malice, of the *intentional* infliction of pain on another person?

Here is the area of the judge's inescapable choice between two legally permissible alternatives. The law—the statute itself, does not *control* his action. The *is* is quite inseparable from the *ought to be*. Inevitably the judge will be influenced by his own ingrained conception of the morality of the situation, above all by his attitude towards divorce.

The same situation—the legal *is* creating both zones of certainty and zones of inescapable, uncontrolled, decision—arises, time and again, in constitutional law. By the joint impact of the First and Fourteenth Amendments to the Constitution of the United States, the federal government and the states are barred from taking any action that interferes, unreasonably, with "the free exercise of religion." Any one can see the zones of certainty, the issues on which all judges will see alike, the areas we can be sure about. "Free *exercise* of religion" clearly means more than liberty of *worship*, more than the prayer or contemplation of the believer in his closet or his church. "Exercise" includes, manifestly, the social expression of a faith, the evangelical as well as the contemplative. No one would have any real doubt that it would be unconstitutional for a state to create a licensing system for ministers, restricting the ministerial function to those who could satisfy some licensing official of the sincerity and social value of their vocations. At the other extreme of certainty, no one would have much doubt that the constitutional guaranty of "free exercise of religion" does not put all religious, or assertedly religious, practices entirely beyond the reach of regulation in the public interest. Federal law outlawed the practice of polygamy, even by dissident Mormon sects to which it was an honestly entertained tenet of religious faith. And a state education law can compel parents to send their children to school, even though the parents happen to have sincere, though eccentric, views that all secular learning is contrary to the will of God. Nor would we have too much trouble about the power of the state to outlaw the rattle-snake handling rituals of certain Holiness cults, even though the rituals be characterized by good faith believers as a free exercise of their religion.

But, whatever the zones of certainty, they can never cover the entire area of decision. Do you remember the "flag salute" cases of the late 1930s and early 1940s? In the period immediately before

the second World War, many states—in what we now think of
as a misguided and undiscriminating excess of patriotic fervor—
passed statutes and regulations requiring all pupils in public and
private schools to salute the flag of the United States and repeat
the familiar pledge of allegiance. Quite a few children, particularly
children from families belonging to the sect of Jehovah's Witnesses, refused to participate in the ceremony, on religious grounds
reminiscent of the Old Quaker objection to oath-taking, and were
excluded from the schools. In 1940, the Supreme Court of the
United States was called on to determine whether this compulsory
flag-salute was an unjustified interference by the state with the
religious liberty guaranteed by the federal Constitution. The
Court decided, Chief Justice Stone alone dissenting, that the requirement was legitimate and not unreasonable and that children
refusing to take part in the ceremony, even on sincere religious
grounds, might be excluded from school.

We had then an authoritative decision by the highest tribunal
in the country. A resolute positivist, speaking in 1941, would have
said without reservation that the law *is* that a state may require a
flag salute, even over sincerely held religious objection. But the
ought to be would not down. When an identical case came back
to the federal courts after no great lapse of time, three lower federal
judges simply refused to follow an asserted *is* so manifestly inconsistent with their deeply felt views as to what the extent of religious
liberty *ought to be*. Their action was almost unprecedented, a
refusal by a lower court to follow a direct precedent of the highest
court. And yet, when the case reached the Supreme Court, the
rebels were vindicated, and the 1940 precedent overruled by a vote
of 6-3. Chief Justice Stone's solitary *ought to be* of 1940 had
become the *is* of 1943. What better instance of the higher moral
claim of the *ought to be* at work, in a zone of discretion and inescapable choice, as the moulding principle of the legal *is*?

To see where we are now on the asserted analytical separateness
of the legal *is* and the legal *ought to be* let us go back and pay a
short visit to our earlier acquaintance, Justice Holmes' *Bad Man*.
He, you may remember, "does not care two straws" for the *ought
to be*; he *does* want to know "what the courts will do in fact."
He cares only for material consequences, not for the reasons for

conduct that inhere in the "vague sanctions of conscience." And Holmes has said that we must look at the law with his eyes, if we "want to know the law and nothing else." Poor old Bad Man, with a vision so astigmatic he will be bankrupt almost before he knows it! Because an approach to law that is entirely focussed on the positivist *is*—and ignores the constant working of the *ought to be* in the regions of choice and leeway outside the law's zones of certainty—is utterly unrealistic. Our Bad Man may have no *ought to be* of his own, but he had better look out for the *ought to be* of others if he is to predict what courts are likely to do in fact. If his plans are outside the zones of certainty—and Bad Men customarily push their conduct to the limits they think allowable by the law—he may skate into an area of inescapable judicial choice where the judge's *ought to be* inevitably furnishes the moral content of the legal *is.* Or he may find himself before a jury where his claim is so offensive to the deeply-felt *ought* of the 12 men in the jury box that they simply refuse to find the facts that must be found to exist if the Bad Man's version of the legal *is* is to be brought into play. Or our Bad Man's asserted *is* may be so manifestly unjust that a responsible lawyer will refuse to represent him, or accept the case only on condition that a morally defensible line be followed in the litigation. He wanted to know "the law and nothing else." He will find, when he pushes outside the zones of legal certainty, that you cannot know *the law* if you think of it as a body of doctrine principles stripped of the impulses that give it life and direction. Our Bad Man was such a complete positivist that he sacrificed his status as a realist. By ignoring the "vague sanctions of conscience" he has made it impossible for himself to achieve his own limited objective, a prediction of what the courts are likely to do in fact. Oddly enough, in his Bad Man anecdote, Holmes is perhaps less the legal realist than St. Thomas Aquinas.

We see, then, the impossibility of a rigid separation of the *is* and the *ought to be* in the areas of law-in-action which I have described as outside the zones of certainty. And these are the very areas—otherwise described as the areas of inescapable choice, or leeway, or responsible decision—in which we apprehend most clearly the moral dimension of the law. The legal *is* here is a mere authorization, a fixing of outer bounds on the exercise of discretion. The judge here, as contrasted with his situation in a zone of certainty, must choose among legally permissible alternatives. The practicing lawyer here—as we saw on our first evening —is authorized by professional tradition to accept the dubious case; equally authorized by professional tradition to refuse it. The prosecutor may be authorized to file a hundred criminal cases, but the bare positive law does not and cannot tell him which half-dozen of the hundred are to be filed in the criminal court. The sentencing judge is authorized to impose a fine, to sentence to prison for one year or seven, to suspend sentence in appropriate cases. Where the legal *is* does not provide a controlling imperative —as so often in law—direction and consistency must be found in the *ought to be*. It is nonsense in this context to insist on a rigid analytical separation of the *is* and the *ought to be*.

Bibliography

The following is a selected list of books and articles which contain surveys of various theories of the nature of law or which discuss aspects of this topic. Generally, see:

Dias, R. W. M. A *Bibliography of Jurisprudence*; London: 1964.

Cairns, H. *Legal Philosophy from Plato to Hegel*, Baltimore: 1949.
Cogley, J. (*et al.*) *Natural Law and Modern Society*, Cleveland and New York: 1962.
Cohen, M. R. *Law and the Social Order*, New York: 1933.
———— *Reason and Law*, Glencoe: 1950.
d'Entrèves, A. P. *Natural Law*, London: 1951.
———— "Legality and Legitimacy," *Review of Metaphysics*, vol. 16 (1963), 687–702.
Ebenstein, W. *The Pure Theory of Law*, Madison: 1945.
Frank, J. *Law and the Modern Mind*, 6th ed.; New York: 1949.
Friedmann, W. *Legal Theory*, 4th ed.; London: 1960.
Friedrich, C. J. *The Philosophy of Law in Historical Perspective*, 2nd ed.; Chicago: 1963.
Fuller, Lon L. "Positivism and Fidelity to Law—A Reply to Professor Hart," *Harvard Law Review*, vol. 71 (1958), 630–72.
Garlan, E. N. *Legal Realism and Justice*, New York: 1941.
Golding, M. P. "Kelsen and the Concept of 'Legal System,'" *Archiv für Rechts-und Sozialphilosophie*, vol. 47 (1961), 355–86.
Hall, J. *Studies in Jurisprudence and Criminal Theory*, New York: 1958.
Hart, H. L. A. "Kelsen Visited," *UCLA Law Review*, vol. 10 (1963), 709–28.
———— "Positivism and the Separation of Law and Morals," *Harvard Law Review*, vol. 71 (1958), 593–629.
Jennings, W. I., ed. *Modern Theories of Law*, London: 1933.

Jolowicz, H. F. *Lectures on Jurisprudence;* London: 1963.

Kantorowicz, H. *The Definition of Law,* Cambridge: 1958.

Kelsen, H. *What Is Justice?,* Berkeley: 1957.

Llewellyn, K. N. *Jurisprudence,* Chicago: 1962.

MacGuigan, M. R. "St. Thomas and Legal Obligation," *New Scholasticism,* vol. 35 (1961), 281–310.

Morison, W. L. "Some Myth about Positivism," *Yale Law Journal,* vol. 68 (1958), 212–33.

Morris, H. "Verbal Disputes and the Legal Philosophy of John Austin," *UCLA Law Review,* vol. 7 (1960), 27–56.

Natural Law Forum (journal).

Olivecrona, K. *Law as Fact,* Copenhagen: 1939; reprinted, 1962.

——— "Legal Language and Reality," in Newman (ed.), *Essays in Jurisprudence in Honor of Roscoe Pound* (1962), 339–55.

Patterson, E. W. *Jurisprudence;* Brooklyn: 1953.

Pound, R. *An Introduction to the Philosophy of Law;* New Haven: 1922.

——— *Jurisprudence,* 5 vols.; St. Paul: 1959.

Rommen, H. *The Natural Law;* St. Louis: 1947.

Sayre, P. (editor). *Interpretations of Modern Legal Philosophies,* New York: 1947.

Soviet Legal Philosophy, trans. Babb; Cambridge: 1951.

Summers, R. S. "Professor H. L. A. Hart's Concept of Law," *Duke Law Journal,* vol. 1963, 629–70.

Williams, G. "The Controversy Concerning the Word 'Law,'" in P. Laslett (ed.), *Philosophy, Politics, and Society;* Oxford: 1956, 134–56.

Wollheim, R. "The Nature of Law," *Political Studies,* vol. 2 (1954), 128–44.